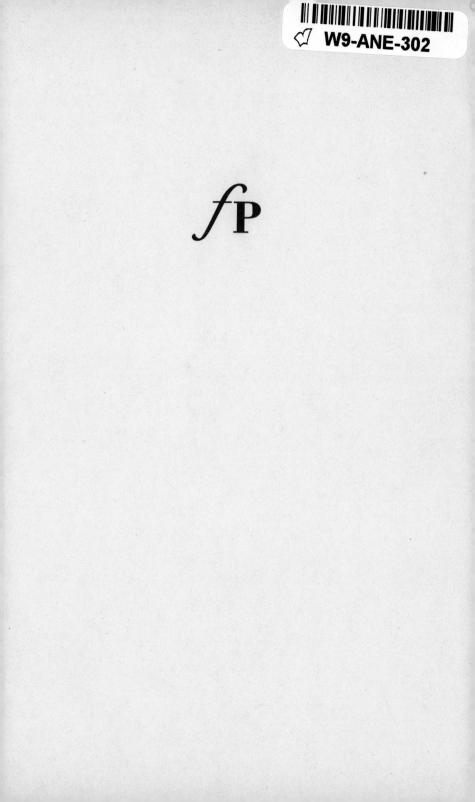

ALSO BY ELISA ALBERT

How This Night Is Different
The Book of Dahlia

FREUD'S BLIND SPOT

23 ORIGINAL ESSAYS ON CHERISHED, ESTRANGED, LOST, HURTFUL, HOPEFUL, COMPLICATED SIBLINGS

EDITED BY

Elisa Albert

FREE PRESS

New York   London   Toronto   Sydney

FREE PRESS

A Division of Simon & Schuster, Inc.
1230 Avenue of the Americas
New York, NY 10020

First Free Press trade paperback edition November 2010

FREE PRESS and colophon are trademarks of Simon & Schuster, Inc.

For information about special discounts for bulk purchases,
please contact Simon & Schuster Special Sales at 1-866-506-1949
or business@simonandschuster.com.

The Simon & Schuster Speakers Bureau can bring authors to your live event.
For more information or to book an event contact the Simon & Schuster Speakers
Bureau at 1-866-248-3049 or visit our website at www.simonspeakers.com.

Credits appear on page 271.

DESIGNED BY ERICH HOBBING

Manufactured in the United States of America

1   3   5   7   9   10   8   6   4   2

Library of Congress Cataloging-in-Publication Data
Freud's blind spot: 23 original essays on cherished, estranged, lost, hurtful,
hopeful, complicated siblings / edited by Elisa Albert.—
1st Free Press trade pbk. ed.
p. cm.
1. American essays. 2. Brothers and sisters. 3. Sibling rivalry.
4. Authors, American—Family relationships.
I. Albert, Elisa.
PS684.B76F74 2010
306.875—dc22   2010011913

ISBN 978-1-4391-5472-4
ISBN 978-1-4391-9881-0 (ebook)

For Matt,
obviously

CONTENTS

CONTENTS

FREUD'S BLIND SPOT

INTRODUCTION

I wanted to edit this anthology for the same reason anybody wants to edit an anthology: I have much to say on the subject and don't know how to say it myself. Siblings, more than parents, more than teachers and friends and lovers and pets, shape the people we are. (Well, the person *I* am, and I like to think we're all secretly sort of the same.) But in the grand tradition of anthologies and their editors, I get tongue-tied and sputter like an idiot whenever I try to talk about this stuff.

"Do you have any siblings?" someone will occasionally ask at a party or over dinner or on a train. Invariably I open my mouth to answer and can't. After a moment too long I say, "Yes." Or I say, "No." The period during which I tended to say no was brutal, but it was easier than saying yes and then having to explain: I have two brothers. Well, actually, I have one brother. Er, I'm sort of an only child. Well, see, I *used* to have two brothers, and they are the sun and moon of my earliest memories, but then one of them got sick and died and the one who's still alive has disappointed me in big and small ways over the years. For a while I could barely be in the same room with him, let alone discuss him in polite conversation, though now I'm trying to get better at both. I could say, "I'm an only child," and then move on to easier topics, or I could say, "I have one/ two brothers," and then came a haze of heartbreak, and who needs that over dinner?

Gradually I came to realize, in the grand tradition of anthol-

1

ogies and their editors, that instead of the aforementioned sputtering, the confusion and difficulty, I could simply enlist twenty-four wonderful writers to do the dirty work for me. I could ask these wonderful writers to tell me about *their* siblings—about all the ways in which their siblings are or aren't a part of their lives, histories, old families, new families. It's a neat deflection, one that garnered me precious insight and strength, of which frankly I am in dire need, then allowed me to put my name on the cover. (Total genius, this anthology racket.) Better than grappling alone, at any rate.

Siblings are the unsung heroes of our psychological development. The vertical model of psychoanalytic theory—parent-to-child—has long prevailed in our cultural imagination: you are who you are because your parents made you that way. You are the product of the people who created and/or raised you. But some scholars have lately called for a reassessment of the vertical model. *What about the horizontal model,* they ask? *What about lateral influence?*

Mind you, this is not an anthology of scholarly work. It is, rather, a collection of personal essays, anecdotal and pure. We're mostly fiction writers here, and poets; we tend to honor the raw truth of *feelings* over the detached work of research and study (though we are always glad when research and study confirm what we already know, what we already feel). We understand that our siblings are central actors in the drama of our lives: they are our earliest and deepest connections, our poles, our friends, our contemporaries, our cohorts, our first loves and resented rivals. They know strange, singular, secret routes back to fundamental truths about ourselves. We tend to define ourselves in alliance with and/or in opposition to them. They may love and support us, they may baffle and annoy us, they may let us down, fail us utterly, but there they are, forever, blood peers from whom we can't ever quite escape. Or maybe that's what I imagine, since in truth I have no fucking clue.

* * *

My birth announcement read: "David and Matthew have a sister!" And I still reflexively frame my existence that way, even though both of those beloved boys are, in one way or another—*poof*—gone. When I try to talk about them, I can get terribly upset, and fast. I'm nursing the oldest wounds I have, as fresh as the day they were inflicted, like some kind of emotional hemophiliac.

In college, I found a used copy of psychologist Jeanne Safer's book *The Normal One,* about life with a difficult or damaged sibling, and in it her reference to the influence of sibling relationships as "Freud's blind spot." That stuck with me, echoing as I lived out my little-sisterhood. I always sought out older men. Before I turned twenty-five, I had married and divorced a guy who was marginally, seductively connected to my dead brother, with a tragic brother of his own. I've tried to make of many a cool woman a sort of surrogate, wishful sister, neatly destroying many a friendship in the process. It's taken me a long time to feel even a little bit comfortable with my brothers-in-law, who are not, as counterintuitive as it can feel, a threat. I'm still tickled to socialize with people who are six or eight years older—people I can't help but identify as my brothers' age.

Commissioning and editing these twenty-three pieces has been cathartic in a nicely passive sort of way. Like other refugees from dysfunctional families, I quite simply *have no idea* how things are "supposed" to look on the inside of "real" families. What do "real" brothers act like? Is there such a thing? Are some siblings actually accountable to each other in matters of emotional importance? Are some siblings, like, *nice* to each other? What is it like to have a sister? How are other people affected by this stuff? Is it weird to have such "issues"? What's it like to have love and peace and friendship and a desire to be there for each other? I feel warped by all the hostility and stubbornness and judgment that passes for a relationship between my brother and me. I think it's been pretty awful for him too. We've hurt each other a lot.

When we were kids, our mother and father offered us a Hebrew blessing every Friday night: "May you be like Ephraim and Menashe," it says in part. Recently I learned it's because Ephraim and Menashe are the only two siblings in the Bible who get along. I should mention, I guess, that my mother has very little to do with her only brother and my father almost nothing to do with his only sister. (Other stories, those, and sad ones.) Ephraim and Menashe: ha.

I got seriously weepy in many a café while reading these essays. God, how I envy Lauren Grodstein the joy of seeing her kid brother grow into an admirable man. And what wouldn't I give to be a Soloway sister? To have that *inside* your family: a friend who is yours, irrevocably, for life. Behold Peter Orner and Eric Orner, side by side in body and spirit on a Cape Cod couch as their family flames out around them. Behold Etgar Keret, embracing his sister despite the fact that he cannot literally embrace his sister. Behold the amazing specter of both Nalini Jones and Margo Rabb, besieged but not alone—as if, Nalini writes, by simply being with their brothers and sisters, they are saved. Joanna Hershon, leaning toward acceptance and peace, opening herself entirely, at last, to the realities of her brother. Miranda Beverly-Whittemore, giving birth with her sister at her side. Ed Schwarzschild and his brothers united in their quest for a better understanding of the things that matter. Daphne Beal, working so earnestly, so lovingly, to be the best sister she can be. Robert Anthony Siegel's steadfast attempts to live alongside his brother amid the harsh realities of a not-remotely-color-blind world. Jay Baron Nicorvo and his brothers putting a roof over their mother's head. Vestal McIntyre and his big, twisted crew. Nat Bennett the singular heart of his beautiful, complex clan.

I find it fascinating that the format of questions and answers appealed to both the Soloways and to the Coopers: It's as if the dialogue itself is the relationship; how could they possibly encompass it without enacting it?

Like Angela Pneuman, I am stupidly jealous of these people. Steve Almond captures perfectly a desire for closeness in the face of distance. *That* I understand. It's the murkier dynamics represented here with which I identify most. The struggles of Victor LaValle and Mary Norris and James Cañón and Nellie Hermann: what it's like when you're asked if you have siblings and your answer is halting.

So here it is again: *Do you have any siblings?* I'll try not to flinch next time I hear the question: I have two brothers. One is no longer alive, and I miss him. The other is not who I desperately needed him to be, and I miss him, too.

Maybe we writers are a special sort of sibling: we give a shit even in the face of life's coldest refusals, and so we try and try and keep trying to untangle and articulate our feelings, our allegiances, our connections, our reactions, our wants, our hopes, our despair. Rebecca Wolff hits this squarely on the head as she passes the baton in her stunning meditation on N.

We're hard on ourselves, and we're hard on the people we love. We find it impossible to leave pain alone. Sometimes our love ferments in weird and unpredictable ways. It can't be easy to be related to us. By which I mean me.

—Elisa Albert

THE BROTHERS GRIM

Steve Almond

Meeting a Happy Sibling is like coming across an ad for one of those island resorts in a slick magazine, the kind where the people are always lounging by some impossibly blue inlet and grinning with that buttery and ferocious contentment endemic to island resort people, and while the sight of them floods me with longing and envy and rage I find relief by immediately reminding myself that these people *don't actually exist.*

The place where this analogy breaks down—if it is in fact an analogy and not just a sad and unheroic comparison—is that these people, Happy Siblings, do seem to exist.

I run into them sometimes, at brunches and softball games and potlucks. They seem especially fond of potlucks. They enjoy sharing and when they smile they mean it. If called upon to speak about their childhoods they say things like, *Yeah, I remember this one time my older brother found some lighter fluid in the park and we spent the day burning our rubber dolls.*

Like the other Unhappy Siblings unhappily listening to this, I always expect the story to go on. *Then we ran out of dolls and my brother doused my sister and me with the lighter fluid. He told us skin wasn't really flammable, but my sister had this frizzy hair. At least now, with the scalp grafts, she doesn't have to worry about blow-drying . . .*

But there is never more to the story. They just burn the dolls and hide the gunky remains in their secret fortress, the one

7

they built together under the sycamore tree out back. Happy Siblings are always doing this kind of shit: building fortresses, devising secret languages, defending each other from harm.

From time to time, I unwittingly befriend a Happy Sibling, though I'm pleased to report that the friendship rarely endures. They're too well-adjusted, and this makes me both bored and nervous. I had a girlfriend in college who used to talk with her sisters on the phone every single day. At the end of each conversation, they would say they loved each other. It was very beautiful if you're into that kind of thing. I myself am not.

Or maybe I'm so into that kind of thing, so deeply yearning, that it feels forbidden. I have no idea. I can say with complete assurance that my sibling memories are fucked-up and sad. Here are the first few that come to mind:

- At the old house on Frenchman's Hill, my older brother Dave walks up and informs me that our cat Macacheese has just had her litter of kittens and that they all came out dead because I dropped Macacheese on her head the week before. I'm maybe five at this point.

- A few years later we're out in this dirt field hitting pebbles with a baseball bat. I pick up the bat and prepare to take a cut. But I feel an ominous spongy crack on my backswing. I wheel around and see a geyser of blood where Dave's mouth used to be.

- In the midst of our weekly altercation, my twin brother, Mike, and I find ourselves face-to-face. We glare and pant and before I can even process what's happening my hand flies up from my side and smacks Mike flush on the cheek. He bursts into tears.

- I arrive home from a walk to find Mike brandishing a butcher knife. He intends to kill Dave, who's hiding in the garage. A few minutes earlier, Dave had stabbed Mike with a fork, leaving four bloody holes in his thigh. Mike's intended knife attack has, therefore, a certain domestic logic to it. Our mother, though present, is helpless, because we're all much stronger and crazier than her. Dave is a senior in high school at this point. Mike and I are sophomores.

I believe you are getting the gist.

Am I suggesting that all we did as children was injure and humiliate each other? I guess I am. That can't be right. There must have been some good times, some moments of sibling camaraderie and goodwill. I simply don't remember any.

This is how my mind works. I'm deeply invested in the narrative of my miserable childhood. It makes me feel noble and charismatically scarred, like a survivor. Writers are especially susceptible to this kind of sniveling, because it helps us justify our public acts of declamation. *You can always count on a murderer for a fancy prose style,* Humbert declared, to which I would add, *An overeager sense of victimhood doesn't hurt, either.*

Over the years, my brothers have laid the blame for our collective woe at the feet of our folks, whom they claim were too preoccupied with their work to pay us enough attention and properly diagnose our various pathologies. The problem with this theory is that our parents are psychiatrists.

To those of you now shaking your heads and saying to yourselves, a bit smugly, *Ah well, that explains everything* (meaning all of you), I can only ask that you think about why you would assume the children of psychiatrists are crazy. This is a topic for another day of course, but here's a hint: because the idea of psychiatry makes you nervous about your own loose screws.

Anyway.

I certainly agree that our parents were overextended. They met at Yale School of Medicine, got hitched, and had too many children too quickly—as the second twin, I feel sort of responsible here—all while trying to launch ambitious careers and take part in the cultural upheavals of the sixties.

I tend to see them as loving parents who tried their best

and were simply overrun by the tangled aggressions of their boys. That's my version of events. Memory isn't something we retrieve, after all. It's something we invent. It's the past as filtered through the emotional needs of our present.

My brother Dave, for instance, remembers me smashing him in the mouth with a baseball bat. But whereas I recall the event as a subconscious case of aggravated battery, he views the wound as self-inflicted. (He was told to step back repeatedly and ignored these warnings.) And Mike doesn't remember being slapped across the face; he remembers that I actually punched him and gave him a bloody nose and when I realized what I'd done I burst into tears.

Who's right about these things? I would say I am, which is typical of me. The point is that our memories are shaped to reinforce certain narratives. I look back and see my rage. Dave sees his guilt. Mike sees brutality and remorse.

What's most striking to me is that I have absolutely no recollection of the bloody nose. None. I don't doubt it happened, but my mind has been kind enough to erase the data.

Here's more from Mike:

Well, I remember a very moving incident—it just springs to mind every once in a while—when we were about ten or eleven years old. We were leaving for camp and our father was dropping us off. I should mention that Steve was closer to our father, Richard, than I was; I mostly fought with him about everything and anything. But that morning no one was fighting and as Steve and I took our seats together toward the back of the bus, we both noticed our dad standing on his tiptoes outside the bus with a big grin on his face and his hands in his pockets watching us through the window. He was beaming and it was rare. I noticed first and nodded in an "I already said bye, Daaaaad" kind of way and then Steve saw him. His response was powerful, almost like a reflex. He burst into tears and pulled this wool ski hat over his face while sinking as low as he could in the seat. One fluid movement, so fast, to try to hide his outburst. I guess it was adolescent pride, but it didn't work . . . Steve was upset because he didn't want to leave my father alone, outside the bus standing in the cold while we got to enjoy the warm seats and the trip ahead of us, one that brought us out into the world and away from the family. In short, it was the first time I recognized Steve's need to take care of others and his sensitivity and loyalty to those he loves.

This is maybe the sweetest thing that's ever been said about me and at the same time, I'm almost sure, total bullshit. Not that I didn't get all blubbery. I'm sure I did. I certainly remember those early morning trips. My stomach would knot up with dread. But I don't remember this episode as me trying to take care of my dad. I was an insecure little wreck who was scared of leaving home.

And I never saw myself as closer to our dad than Mike. Actually, I felt our dad liked Dave best, because Dave was good at science and math and most everything else and because I was too emotionally needy.

Dave and Mike and I can sort of agree on one basic thing: that we hurt each other a lot and felt insufficiently supervised by our parents. Beyond that, it all splinters.

The reason I see my folks as less culpable is because I was more openly a mess as a kid, and therefore more susceptible to their intervention. I mean by this that they carted my ass into therapy, where I've remained (more or less) for the ensuing thirty-five years. Dave and Mike had plenty of anxieties as well. But they hid them away with what seems to me now superhuman fortitude.

The most striking example: my twin brother Mike is gay. I can't begin to imagine how difficult that realization would have been to bear in a home like ours, which was, as you have guessed by now, about half-Neanderthal. He concealed this fact from the family, and perhaps from himself, until he left for college. He did such a good job that I was fairly certain he was fucking my girlfriend until he came out to me. Dave, meanwhile, suffered his own anxieties, which he concealed with remarkable efficiency from everyone but Mike.

As a kid, I envied them their stoicism. They were bigger than me, better looking, stronger in every sense of the word. I wanted to be them a lot more than I wanted to be me. And their attention and approval were far more important to me than our parents'.

Freud saw sibling rivalry as an extension of the child's Oedipal/Electra longing. Maybe he was right. He was right about a lot of stuff. But my experience was this: by the time we'd hit ten or eleven we had effectively frozen my folks out and formed our own subfamily. We'd decided that our parents were never going to give us what we needed in the way of regard and that they didn't matter anyway and should probably, most of the time, fuck off.

The problem with this arrangement, from my vantage point, was that Dave and Mike were much closer to one another than to me. This seems odd, given that Mike and I were the twins. But Dave, like a lot of canny eldest sibs, adopted a divide-and-conquer strategy. He befriended Mike and kept me at a distance. Most of the time, I was on the outside looking in. My personality (such as it is) was basically shaped in the forge of their rejection.

I don't remember getting upset when our parents left us with a babysitter for the weekend. But when Mike started spending nights over at friends' houses, I was an utter mess. I wept inconsolably. I begged Dave to let me sleep in his bed. When he refused, I curled up on the rug at the foot of his bed.

And of all the birthdays I had as a kid, and all the kind things my parents did for me, the moment that sticks is this: we're driving down California Avenue and it's my eighth or ninth birthday and Dave turns around and offers me a pack of gum as a gift. I am dumbstruck with gratitude. "Here," he says, "let me open the pack for you." He holds out the pack and I pull out a stick, or try to, and a little metal bar whacks me on the thumb. Happy birthday.

This calls to mind another memory, which Dave is not going to be happy to see regurgitated here, though I doubt he will ever mention having read it because that's how it generally goes. This took place the afternoon of my second-grade back-to-school night. I was hopelessly in love with my teacher Donna Weeks and eager to introduce her to my folks, as a first step toward marriage.

You need to know a couple of things. The first is that I still sucked my thumb. I only did it at home, but it was a reflex. The second is that we had a ristra of super-hot chili peppers hanging in our kitchen. Actually, I'm not sure I haven't told the whole story right there. But I'll carry on, for the sake of proper dramatic staging.

As I recall, I was struggling to choose an outfit based on the standard midseventies principle *How many clashing colors can I combine without actually bursting into flame?*

Dave came up to me and said, "Hey, Steve, do you want to feel something really cool?"

"Sure!" I said.

"Just put your hands behind your back," he said.

"Okay!"

This sounds incredibly naïve, bordering on perhaps a brain damage scenario. But you have to understand that Dave hardly ever spoke to me and that I wanted more than anything on earth to be spoken to by him, to be his friend, or at least to be tolerated in a manner not involving the infliction of Indian rope burns, and that this simple request therefore struck me as earth-shattering. Because Dave wasn't just speaking to me. He was involving me in a matter of some apparent enthusiasm and I felt this might signal a sea change in our relations, a sibling Glasnost if you will, and so back went my hands and Dave began massaging the pads of my thumbs with something oily and weird and plainly sinister.

"Doesn't that feel cool?" he said.

"Yeah!" I said. "That *is* cool!"

Then Dave stopped and left the room and I popped one of my thumbs in my mouth and the howling commenced.

Later on our mom got home and I tried to explain what had happened. She eventually got the basics and tried, not very successfully, to wash out Dave's mouth with soap. (I contended, to no avail, that washing his mouth out with chili peppers made more sense.) What I remember most vividly was Dave's line of defense. "But I didn't *do* anything," he observed with genuine righteousness. "He's the baby who still sucks his thumb!"

I'm sure Dave remembers this episode differently. In his version, I'm sure he was innocently mincing chilies in the hopes of preparing a delicious chicken molé for me in honor of back-to-school night, when I burst into the kitchen and demanded that he let me fondle his chilies with my thumbs.

So okay, Dave could be mean. But I'm not sure how much I blame him. He was barely two years old, just getting his footing in the world, when Mike and I came along and sucked up every available drop of attention. If I were in his spot, I doubt my little bros would have survived infancy.

As it happened, I was one of those bros. I grew up in the thrall of someone who wanted me dead. It's this sort of dilemma that puts a chip on your shoulder. I still spend far too much of my time tilting at bullies. In fact, most of my personality (by which I mean most of my personality defects) can be traced back to my brothers. My fear of being abandoned comes from feeling Mike left me behind. My intellectual insecurity and competitiveness comes from trying to keep up with Dave, who, in addition to his capacity for cruelty, happened to be a genius.

I thought flying across the country to college would allow me to become somebody new. That's what we always think. But the true neurotic doesn't evolve; he simply recasts the horror movie of his childhood every few years.

In my case, I immediately befriended a kid, turned him into my twin brother, then engineered a scenario in which he was stolen away by an older-brother figure. This was so shockingly easy to do that I repeated the pattern for the next decade and a half. I just can't get enough of that primal grief.

I would like to apologize, here and now, to the many dudes who have had to put up with my drama over the years. I won't name names, but you know who you are. And while I'm at it, I apologize to all the women I dated for being incapable of genuine emotional discourse and consumed by petty feuds with my male friends. I also apologize to my bosses and teachers, particularly the men, most of whom I made into stand-ins not for my father, but for Dave and Mike, the central love figures of my childhood.

I've gotten better over the years, less competitive and anxious and needy. This is thanks to a variety of skilled therapists, the support of my folks—who often find themselves in the unenviable role of having to suggest I seek more therapy—and a few saintly friends who have managed to outlast my shenanigans.

I wish I could report that my brothers and I have offered each other forgiveness and renewed our bonds. But like most Unhappy Siblings, we continue to communicate in a stunted, regressive manner. We fall back on old jokes and dumb movies. We rarely talk with any real candor or depth about what's happening in our lives. And we never ever talk about what we did to one another all those years ago. Nobody says, "I'm sorry! I'm sorry!" Nobody says, "I was in pain and I put that pain on you." Nobody says, "Underneath it all I love you, bro."

Instead, we've found other ways to express the love we withheld from each other. Dave is a doctor attending mostly to low-income populations. Mike does design work with a socially conscious focus. I've turned to writing. We've grown into pretty decent human beings.

Along the way, we've all done a lot of fucking up, most of it designed to keep us from a happiness we don't really believe we deserve. This is the curse of the Unhappy Sibling, this doomed loyalty to the sorrows of childhood. We want to go back and relive all the mean stuff we did to each other, all the moments when we might have chosen kindness but instead were cruel. That's when we felt most alive, I guess. Everything else is just echoes and shadow.

I live three thousand miles away from my brothers these days and I hardly ever speak to them, and when I do, as noted, it's pretty banal stuff. But everything I've ever written in my life has been for them, in the hopes of making them laugh or making them cry, making them regard me in a way they never did when we were kids.

It won't rescue us from what we did to each other. But that's no reason not to try.

ELLIOT

Lauren Grodstein

I don't know how I knew what an abortion was. It was 1983, I was not yet eight years old, and the attention I remember paying to the cultural and political landscape was appropriately minimal. Of course, I knew a few things: the president's name was Reagan (after he'd been shot, my class sent a very nice card), Michael Jackson had a song out called "Thriller" (I'd seen the video at the rink), and I was aching for a Cabbage Patch Kid. I loved McDonald's new Chicken McNuggets. I was very not allowed to see *Flashdance*.

And I did, it seems, know what an abortion was, because when my parents presented me with the news of a forthcoming sibling at the kitchen table one autumn Sunday, I suggested they procure one.

"Lauren? What did you say?"

I remember reaching out for the cat, who was sitting on the chair next to mine. I remember trying to stay calm. I remember thinking my parents would probably be relieved to find out they still had options.

"But you're going to have another sister!" my mother said, grinning timorously.

"Or a brother!" my father added, as though presenting me with all the possibilities might make me more interested in what they were selling.

"Shit," I said, and I know I said it, since I've been reminded dozens of times over the years. "Having a baby is a terrible idea."

"Shit"? To my parents!? I wasn't even allowed to say "shut up" to my sister. I was sent to my room, where I sat stiffly at my desk, clutching the patient cat.

Twenty-six years ago, and still I can remember the deep well of panic that flooded me. If I close my eyes I can almost still feel its cold reach. How was my family going to manage another child? There were two of us already, and I always had the sense that there wasn't enough time to go around; even then I felt the weight of everyone else's problems on my shoulders. And I had problems of my own. My little sister and I bickered all the time over whatever there was to bicker about: sweatshirts and Barbie dolls and my New Edition record. She followed me around the house and hung out in my bedroom when all I wanted was to be left alone by her—by all of them. At almost eight, I longed for more quiet in my life. I wanted to draw and make up stories and have friends and enjoy privacy whenever I closed my door. And now there would be another baby.

Where will it sleep? I remember thinking. We had only three bedrooms.

I often tell my writing students, when they attempt to write children, not to underestimate them—to avoid baby talk at all costs, to eschew cuteness in favor of what's difficult and real. Kids understand so much more than we think they're capable of understanding; we were all children once, but it's frighteningly easy to forget the truth about who we used to be. I don't know how I knew what an abortion was, but I did. When I consider who I really was at seven, I'm not surprised I knew. I was the oldest child of news-conscious parents. I read everything I found, including the *New York Times* they left on the kitchen table. We subscribed to *Newsweek* and I read that, too. In the basement, where my dad watched *60 Minutes* and I played with my Barbies, sometimes I stopped playing and watched alongside him. Of course I knew what abortion was. I also knew about nuclear war, and the invasion of Granada, and that the girls in third grade weren't as nice as they might seem to grown-ups.

I spent my mother's pregnancy asking her questions like, "If either me or the baby had to die, who would you want it to be?" I wouldn't stop asking until she said she'd save me. But that didn't absolve her; by the time she was visibly pregnant, I'd stopped talking to her. My dad worked a lot. I can't remember whether or not I stopped talking to him too.

Lately, inevitably, I've begun to identify with my parents in ways that surprise me. Soon enough I will be the age they were when they decided to have a third child; after all these years, I finally understand why, even if times are challenging and pressure is high, a baby feels like not just the right decision, but the only decision.

What can I add to the literature on the subject? I spent thirty-one years promising myself and anyone who would listen that I would never reproduce: I was too dedicated to my career, the world was too crappy, the usual predicament. Then my sister had her son, my surpassingly beautiful nephew. My friends started getting pregnant, eating ice cream, furnishing nurseries. I wanted a baby right away, right this second, *yesterday*. I told Ben, my husband, and he agreed that maybe it was something to consider. Consider! Four weeks later I was peeing on a pregnancy test, thinking, *Could anything this extraordinary really happen to me?*

The very thought of babies can make a certain type of person, at a certain point in her life, ridiculous. What was I thinking? We were living in a Brooklyn tenement; my job required a two-hour commute, my musician husband was about to leave for a several-week tour, and I had no idea how we were going to pay for child care, much less a better apartment. And it was still true that I was too dedicated to my career and still true that the world was crappy. The morning I peed on the stick, for instance, a cyclone was wiping out a good chunk of Bangladesh.

No matter; the baby—the very *idea* of the baby—seemed like a miracle worthy of the Old Testament. I peed on the stick, the test came up positive, and even though I'm an atheist I whispered a thank-you to God.

Which is why I know my parents weren't thinking about a new second car and a new set of school clothes, another college tuition to save for. It's not that they were naïve—they saw we needed more space and they knew sometimes tensions ran high. But first steps and Halloween costumes and graduations and summers smashing crabs in Rehoboth always outweigh cramped shared bedrooms and spats over sweatshirts. Explosive moments of joy will surprise you again and again amid the hours of tension or anxiety that are intractable parts of raising children. My parents had been through it twice already. They knew the happiness of a crowded house.

Elliot was born on a Monday night in the late spring. I got to see him the next morning. He was red and screaming and looked like a particularly sorry chicken. This is probably no surprise: I took one look at him and, for the first time in my life, fell swiftly and entirely in love.

These days, to talk about Elliot is to use too many superlatives. My brother is at the top of his class at Columbia medical school; in his free time he jets across the country to harvest organs for organ transplants, and in his other free time he volunteers for an ambulance corps. He is wickedly funny, cheerful, handsome, and best of all, he's kind. One of the memories that makes me happiest is from the year he spent studying in Hong Kong; we agreed to meet one April evening at a hotel in Kyoto, and after twenty-four hours of mind-numbing travel, I found him right where he'd said he'd be, in the lobby, waiting with a newspaper. While the bellman took up my luggage Elliot and I had a martini in the hotel bar. He ordered for me; he'd already learned a handful of phrases in Japanese.

From a distance of twenty-six years I am grateful to my parents for both my siblings, who have turned out to be not just my closest friends but also two of the people I am proudest of in the world. Jessie, my sister, is a corporate lawyer who completed the New York marathon five months after my nephew was born. She's hiked the Rockies, defended Fortune 500 companies, and changed two diapers at once on a cross-country flight. Elliot is—well, you've already heard about Elliot. I rely on nobody the way I rely on them. And nobody knows me like they do.

My reaction to the news of Elliot has become family lore, a story laughingly recounted at family reunions: *To think she didn't even want you! And now she flies all the way to Kyoto just to see your face!* I've laughed too at how silly it seems, or how adorably precocious. An abortion! What a gas.

I'm thinking about it now, however, in a serious way for the first time since who knows when, and I know it wasn't silly. At almost eight, I was wrestling with more than my parents could have possibly realized, for nobody but an almost-eight-year-old can understand exactly what an almost-eight-year-old wrestles with. I should have forgotten it, too. But because of my brother, and my outsized response to him, I am reminded of who I was, what I knew, what I feared. And I am reminded of everything my son will one day know and fear.

But fortunately, he's still only one; he knows little and fears absolutely nothing. For instance, a few months ago, Elliot showed up at our house and scooped up Nathaniel and said, "Let's go to Coney Island." It was a Tuesday, he had the day off, the sun was shining. Coney Island. We got in the car—I let Elliot drive—hit the Jersey Turnpike, sang our favorite songs together, including a particularly screechy rendition of Talib Kweli's "Get By" that left Nathaniel, in the backseat, screaming and covering his ears.

"Hungry?" Elliot said as we looked for parking near the water. "I know a place."

21

We ate dumplings in a Russian restaurant, fed Nathaniel cold borscht. The baby got borscht all over him, and sour cream, and pumpernickel crumbs. The waitress said something to him in Russian, and Nathaniel answered back in babble that sounded sort of like Czech. The waitress nodded and smiled. We presumed she understood.

We took the stroller, strolled the boardwalk, found the amusement park, and maneuvered the baby past the barkers and the Wonder Wheel and the Spook-O-Rama, then back to the kiddie rides. "We should totally take him on something," Elliot said. "That one, the carousel."

"He's too little."

"He's not too little. Look at him."

And it was true that Nathaniel was leaning out of his stroller with his tongue almost wagging and a desperate look on his face. "That!" he said. "That!" Which was the one word he spoke that didn't sound like Czech.

"What if he doesn't like it?" I said, clutching the stroller. "What if he gets scared and we can't take him off?"

"He's not scared," Elliot said. "Don't be scared for him."

My little brother is a doctor in training, a Jersey Turnpike hero, a guy who knows the go-to restaurant in Coney Island. I trust him.

"You'll hold him up?"

"Always," Elliot said.

And so the brother I never wanted and the baby I vowed never to have strolled off together toward the carousel. I was happy that they were together. I was happier still they both belonged to me.

ANY DAY NOW

Joanna Hershon

Three years ago, when I was newly pregnant with twins, my "high-risk" OB asked all the requisite questions about my family history. I had spent more than a year doing battle with infertility and now that my husband and I were actually *expecting,* I was doing my best to tamp down my fears. I told my doctor how my brother was developmentally disabled and it was because he was premature, or something had happened during the birth, or maybe my mother was sick during her pregnancy, but it wasn't anything hereditary. As I heard myself speak, I was thinking about how this story, which I'd been stiffly repeating my whole life, sounded pretty vague. My doctor wasn't entirely comfortable with the information either. In fact, those were the words she used: "I'm not entirely comfortable."

No, I think I said, *me neither.*

When I think of my family together, I often think of us traveling. I think of what we saw, but more often I think of how the world saw us. Or, more accurately, I think of how I was always acutely aware of how we were perceived, and how, when I was with my family, my desire to meet other people was barbed because there was always that moment of waiting for their reactions. If people were rude to my brother I was sad and angry, and if people were friendly I was still sad because I could see them assessing the situation, going out of their way to be patient. When I think of us I think of water. The Old Testament commands that a man teach his son to swim—it's no less than a moral obligation—and I remember my father with my brother, putting in the time. My father was raised in a beach town. He grew up bodysurfing on ironing boards, watching his mother swim the canals, his father power through waves. And it was at my grandparents' house where I remember feeling safe, lulled by hours on their front porch surrounded by only those who knew us well. We rocked back and forth on a glider swing, facing out to sea.

When my grandparents and their house are long gone and I stand with my father on a different beach one August afternoon, I think: *Here is where I know and love my father best: by the water.* I ask him if he's read the most recent story I've written. It's been published in an esteemed journal and I've given it to my parents, hopeful they'll be proud. "I read it," he says; he nods, watching the tide come in.

My mother taught me to say "severe learning disabilities" but I figured out fairly quickly that this didn't begin to approach a realistic description. My brother Jordan is uncannily sweet, intellectually stunted, and has a very good ear. He loves music and would scream and cry as a child whenever an alarm sounded. He once heard a Hebrew service at a Long Island synagogue and told my parents the rabbi was from Mexico, to which my parents smiled, only to meet the rabbi after the service and find out that he was born in Guadalajara. He has great difficulty knowing where to stand in proximity to other people. Aside from staring at people for far too long, he has excellent manners. He wears Velcro sneakers and loafers because he has never learned to tie his shoes. He makes heartfelt speeches on special occasions. He'll never be able to drive. He is a natural athlete who will never learn to sustain a game or keep score. He looks great on a ski slope. He loves watching television and though places without a TV confuse my brother and make him anxious, he is usually too polite to mention it. He is so nice. As a child he was nice and hyper but as an adult he is nice and quiet. Too quiet. Sometimes he stares at strangers and I can see how this unsettles people and I want to tell them: *You have no idea how nice this person is. He is staring because he is curious about you. He is staring because he doesn't know how not to.* Often when I've thought people were unsettled by or judging my brother, I've allowed that maybe I'm paranoid, or that I'm simply reverting to being a self-conscious teenager, but recently, while traveling once again with my family, my brother and I were spacing out in a hotel swimming pool together and a man sidled up to me in the water before asking if I was okay. He said it under his breath and I had no idea what he was talking about. Then he said, "Is that guy bothering you?" and I realized he was referring to Jordan. Was it was painful that someone would think my brother was just some creepy guy in a hotel pool? Yes. But more than that, was I giving off a signal that he wasn't with me? What was I doing or not doing to give this man the impression that Jordan was there alone?

When I told my parents that my new OB sent me to a genetic counselor and the genetic counselor wanted to test Jordan's DNA, they were wholly cooperative. Then, soon after my request, during a visit with them on Long Island, my mother is driving and I am in the front seat and we are going to pick up some chicken salad at Kitchen Kabaret and my mother— after thirty years of insisting that there was never a diagnosis for what my brother has—says something extraordinary. She mentions, as if she's just thought of it, that she has basically always known what it was.

"*What do you mean you basically know?*" I've always been someone who asks questions. And I'm not proud of it but I am hard on my parents; I don't let things go. It wasn't as if I hadn't asked. And asked. Also, my parents weren't the types to pretend everything was normal. They've done an exemplary job of raising us differently—taking my brother to physical therapy and taking me to ballet, having separate sets of appropriate expectations. He is three years younger than me and as early as I can remember I was told about how my brother was different. Jordan always went to special schools but still, at those schools, no one had seemed like him. Over the years I'd asked repeatedly about his disability—why wasn't there any concrete explanation? Inherent in those questions was, of course, anxiety: about how it had happened and why it had happened and if it might happen again if my parents tried for another child or if one day I had a child of my own. Their answers had always been inconclusive. *It's just the way it is,* they'd say. *It's nothing you need to worry about.*

She says: "Grandpa thought it was Williams Syndrome."

I have never heard of Williams Syndrome. If my mother's father, who was a pediatrician, came up with a diagnosis over thirty years ago, why hadn't it ever been repeated, or, more saliently, why hadn't a specialist affirmed or denied it?

And there was someone else who knew. My mother admits that when my brother graduated from his equivalent of high school (a lovely place on Cape Cod, near cranberry bogs and staffed by the most devoted and energetic of teachers) a woman approached my mother and introduced herself. There had been a graduation dance and her daughter had danced with my brother. "I think your son has what my daughter has. Williams Syndrome?" My mother admits that this well-meaning question, this search for common ground, sent her into a depression and she'd ignored the woman; she'd been rude.

"You were depressed?" I can't recall a time that my mother has ever used this expression in any kind of serious way. "Why do you think it made you depressed?"

"I even went to a therapist." This is shocking. I am unreasonably thrilled and proud of her.

"You did? How was it?"

"I only went once." She shrugged. "What does giving it a name do? What could be done about it?"

"You could have had . . . I don't know . . . a community of support?"

She nodded. "We didn't want that."

"I would have wanted it."

"I understand that," she said. "But that's you."

We get back to the house and I head into my brother's room, where the computer is kept. Surrounded by his things—his bigfoot and Yankees memorabilia, his photos of motorcycles and a framed piece of paper on which I wrote as a five-year-old *Dear Jordan, Good luck at your new skool*—I Google, and there are the sites. Hundreds of websites about a syndrome of which I'd never heard. There are heart-wrenching photos of smiling children who look so much like Jordan as a child. Big eyes, big ears, adorable and strange. And there are lists of symptoms: "Elfin appearance . . . a unique personality that combines over-friendliness and high levels of empathy with anxiety . . . more interested in adults than their peers . . . sensitive hearing . . . a love for music . . ." Each website states the symptoms a little bit differently but they all say there is no cure. Here are quali-ties I'd known to be only my brother's qualities, and it turns out they are shared. Here is a rare, genetic, nonhereditary dis-order in which certain genes are missing. Here are theories that people with Williams Syndrome are the basis for age-old stories about elves.

Later I'll ask my mother whether she feels any relief know-ing that it wasn't because she was sick or that anyone made any mistakes during her pregnancy, and that it wasn't because of either of their genes, and I'll be able to tell she feels nothing close to relief. My mother is usually so literal, so logical; she easily places her faith in doctors, so it is particularly striking when I realize that, for her, the new scientific evidence means exactly nothing. "You don't *believe* it's a random genetic fluke, do you?"

"No," she says.

"Even with the DNA, even with the years of research that has gone into this diagnosis."

"No," she says, almost laughing. "I think they'll figure out there's a link."

"To the mother not feeling well during the pregnancy?"

"It's just what I think."

And yet she was so lighthearted when I was pregnant and anxious; she was so sure everything would be fine. She is also the first to suggest I have more children. When I tell her that I am just so scared, so frightened of the unknown, she asks: "Why?"

The genetic counselor was, coincidentally, the same doctor who had seen my parents in those early dark days of my brother's infancy. She's famous—among the first women in her field. And she remembered my brother and my parents. She tells me that she suspected Williams Syndrome and that she'd told them. But it has been possible only in recent years to determine the syndrome positively through DNA, and now that my brother has cheerfully come into the city to have his blood drawn, now that he has gone to the doctor under the impression that he is having a simple checkup, I am imagining with a new intensity how scared my mother must have been when she spoke with this imperious doctor and how powerless my big strong father must have felt, how furious and confused. When the results come in days later, it turns out that both my late grandfather and this doctor were right. My brother has Williams Syndrome. It had nothing to do with my mother not feeling well during her pregnancy. Should they have gone on to have more children, as I asked them to throughout my childhood, that child would likely have been fine. The statistic is one in twelve thousand for everyone. A fluke.

While what differentiates my brother from "normal" is obvious, putting a name on the differences still somehow—

at least for my parents—yields greater pain. They might argue that this isn't true and that there simply isn't any reason to talk about it. While I don't feel that way, and in fact believe there is much to celebrate about having Williams Syndrome, I do understand this feeling. Investing too much in a diagnosis or letting the diagnosis define a child's identity can certainly be its own challenge. And my heart starts speeding each time I read the descriptions. It's like I'm finding out over and over again how my brother—and perhaps, by extension, my family— might always inspire at least a tinge of pity. I bristle every single time someone uses the term "retarded" as a way to describe something or someone slow or annoying. I'm shocked on a daily basis that this is part of the common lexicon. I'm sure this would come as a surprise to most of my closest friends. It would surprise my friends because—honest and open as I pride myself on being—I can't bring myself to tell people I feel this way. What a hypocrite. If I imagine mentioning how insensitive and frankly kind of cruel I find that word in off-hand contexts, I feel so far away, like I've been sentenced to do some kind of language-police work for the rest of my days.

Maybe, for my mother, hearing the name of the syndrome (even that it's called a *syndrome*) brings that small flinching sadness a bit closer. And my father? That day on the beach when he finally responded about having read my story, he said only this: "You need to get off of this brother thing." He shook his head. "It's enough already." He seemed angry. He seemed angry with me. I didn't expect this reaction. Not only was all of my previous writing decidedly not autobiographical but I also never realized that my father had made a personal connection to siblings as a theme in my work. But my father is sensitive (if sometimes not easily able to convey his sensitivity) and he is, of course, not wrong that my brother influenced the story, has probably influenced everything I've ever written. The little boy in my story is overly friendly and intellectually slow, and much of the story's pathos stems from him.

And my father believes in getting on with things. Oft-used expressions are: *What can you do? That's the way the cookie crumbles. That's the way it goes.* I tease him about these expressions, which tend to be frustrating conversation stoppers, but I also can't help but admire his approach. My parents do get on with it. They have taken my adult brother all over the world—on safari in Africa, climbing on the Sydney Bridge, white-water rafting in New Zealand—and they are able to laugh and laugh at various awkward (and likewise touching) interactions with strangers spanning many continents. My father is also a former football star, a handsome man beset with the requisite jock injuries, and it's always his physicality I think of first. Even as I recall the moment he answered me on the beach, when he told me to stop writing about "this brother thing," as I remember the slate-blue Atlantic and red clay from the cliffs and my competing feelings of disappointment and embarrassment, it's his physical presence that overpowers the memory—big and strong and a little bit in pain.

We have fraternal twin boys now. They are three years old, bright and inquisitive, and they love to say "my brother." As in: "You can't have that truck; that's my brother's truck," or "My brother made three poops," or "I love my brother." They are at each other's sides—at least for now—almost every moment of every day. They idly hold hands while watching movies.

Though Jordan's diagnosis was supposed to offer me peace of mind (and it did, when I learned it wasn't a mystery and it wasn't hereditary) not a day goes by that I don't feel like I have seriously gotten away with something. With this relief comes too not a small sense of sadness, for doesn't this relief implicitly mean that I don't want my sons to be like my brother, who is nothing but loving and good?

But: "Hey, boys," he says when we all convene at my parents' house. My parents have been married for almost forty years. My most familiar childhood sight was seeing them hold one another's bare feet. "You being good boys?" He is a loyal and taxpaying employee at Walmart who loves a schedule, a task, his sports teams, and his bands. I recently read that people with Williams Syndrome hear music differently, more intensely than the rest of us, and that if they listen to happy music they are affected positively long after the music has played. I wonder what it means that my brother's taste in music runs to Pink Floyd and 1970s classic rock. He has seen *The Wall* countless times. When we were teenagers and I asked him what he thought it was about he replied: "It's about a man who is going to the dark side." And yet, he has always been a notably joyful person.

Right before an autumn dusk, while sitting with his nephews and me, my brother sang the Bob Dylan song *I Shall Be Released*. He half crooned, half croaked those sad sad lyrics about a framed man in a prison.

At first I couldn't help but think that my brother chose this song because he identifies with it and that he wants a certain release that he can't identify or describe.

When I tried to figure out what the lyrics really meant— *from the west down to the east*—I realized for the first time that the light was moving backward. Most explanations of this phenomenon involve the apocalypse and the expected trajectory of the sun on doomsday, but I prefer this offering: a man lies on his back in his cell taking notice of the light's subtle route overhead, on his ceiling. Apparently that is what he'd see. West to east. I want to be released from this small sadness I have felt and continue to feel in the space that lies between my brother and me and in the vulnerability I can rarely shake off while moving through the world at his side. I want to be released from the shame that accompanies this vulnerability. I can see it all, the sun and the shadow, the confines of an increasingly irrelevant room. Because it isn't my brother who needs the release. I realize he's already there. West to east: what an image. What odd, specific light.

ISLANDERS

BY ERIC ORNER

OUR PARENTS WERE AT THE BACK DOOR OF THE HOUSE WE'D RENTED FOR THE SUMMER, CALLING FOR US TO COME INSIDE. IT WAS WEIRD SEEING THEM STANDING THERE LIKE THAT. LATELY, EXCEPT FOR ARGUING DURING MEALS AND GOING OFF EACH MORNING TO PLAY TENNIS, THEY MOSTLY IGNORED EACH OTHER, WHICH LEFT US — MY BROTHER AND ME — WARY AT THE SIGHT OF THEM SIDE BY SIDE, CALLING US FROM THE SAME DOORFRAME.

33

"YOU THINK THEY'RE WISE TO US?" ASKED MY YOUNGER BROTHER. HE WAS TALKING A LITTLE LIKE STARSKY AND HUTCH THAT SUMMER.

WE'RE FIVE YEARS APART, WHICH IS JUST FAR ENOUGH FROM EACH OTHER IN AGE FOR US NOT TO HAVE HAD MUCH TO DO WITH EACH OTHER UNDER NORMAL CIRCUMSTANCES.

WHICH FAMILY VACATIONS WEREN'T.

ONCE OR TWICE A YEAR, THROWN TOGETHER IN THE SMALLER SPACE OF A RENTED HOUSE OR A HOTEL ROOM, WE SUDDENLY SHARED A COMMON AGENDA:

WHADYA HEAR?

Shhhhh.

INCOMING!

POK POK POK

STEERING CLEAR OF DAD.

BOYS? YOU IN THERE?

BOYS! OPEN THIS DOOR!

YEARS LATER I FEEL GUILTY ABOUT THIS, SEEING NOW THAT IN HIS OWN PECULIAR WAY OUR DAD WAS TRYING TO BE A GOOD FATHER. HE WASN'T AN ALCOHOLIC OR PHYSICALLY ABUSIVE. HE DIDN'T GAMBLE. HE TOOK US ON TRIPS. BUT EVEN SO, THERE WAS SOMETHING ABOUT HIM, THIS WEIRD COMBINATION OF CONTROL-FREAKINESS & HYPER-FUSSINESS THAT MADE HIM SCARY TO BE AROUND. IMAGINE MUSSOLINI CROSSED WITH FELIX UNGER AND YOU'LL HAVE THE PICTURE.

34

ANYWAY, HE AND MOM WERE ARGUING ALL THE TIME ABOUT HIS OBSESSIONS: SMUDGES AROUND THE KNOBS OF THE KITCHEN CABINETS, OR RINGS ON THE COFFEE TABLE BECAUSE SOMEONE DIDN'T USE A COASTER. HE WOULD NITPICK UNTIL SHE COULDN'T STAND IT ANYMORE.

HAPPILY, THAT SUMMER THE OCEAN WAS ONLY 100 YARDS FROM OUR FRONT DOOR, BECKONING US WITH REFUGE, DIVERSION, AND

THE PROMISE THAT THE ROAR OF THE SURF WOULD DROWN OUT THEIR FIGHTING.

SOMEWHERE ALONG THE LINE WE GOT THE IDEA TO DIVE FOR TREASURE.

AND THE SECOND OR THIRD OF THESE DIVES, PETER CAME BACK TO THE SURFACE WITH SOMETHING WE'D NEVER SEEN BEFORE:

A CHANNELED WHELK.

MAYBE BECAUSE WE WERE NORTH SHORE CHICAGO BOYS ACCUSTOMED ONLY TO SWIMMING IN OUR VAST EMPTY-BOTTOMED LAKE, WE THOUGHT THIS SEASHELL WAS THE AWESOMEST THING WE'D EVER SEEN.

WE'D SHOWER OFF CAREFULLY OUTSIDE. (HE'D HAVE A COW IF WE TRACKED SAND INTO THE HOUSE.)

THEN WE'D PULL DOWN THE LARGEST OF A FAMILY OF FANCY COPPER POTS THAT DAD HAD BOUGHT AT AN ANTIQUES STORE IN EDGARTOWN.

A FEW MINUTES LATER, IT WOULD BEGIN TO HISS AND POP AND FOAM UP SMELLY RIBBONS OF WHELK SCUM.

I CAN HEAR THEM SCREAMING!

NO YOU CAN'T.

MEANWHILE, OUT BEYOND THE WALLS OF OUR QUICKLY-GETTING-STUNK-UP KITCHEN, OVER THE HEDGE, DOWN THE MAIN STREET, AND SOMEWHERE ACROSS A NEIGHBORING VILLAGE LINE, PREPPY COUPLES WERE PAYING CALLS AT EACH OTHER'S COTTAGES.

FAMOUS SINGER-SONGWRITERS WERE THINKING THAT SCONES ARE MORE RELIABLY PLEASURABLE THAN BOYFRIENDS.

AND CERTAIN EX-FIRST LADIES WERE ON THE PHONE WITH CERTAIN EX-FIRST SONS, WORRYING ABOUT HOW TO GET THEM INTO BROWN IF THEY FLUNKED MAKEUP SUMMER SCHOOL ALGEBRA, SPANISH, AND CHEMISTRY.

NO SWEAT MA.

INEXPERIENCED COOKERS, WE FIGURED WE NEEDED TO BOIL UNTIL THE WATER WAS ALL GONE. THEN WE'D OPEN UP THE WINDOWS TO AIR THE PLACE OUT.

AND CHUCK THE BOILED-UP WHELK MEAT INTO THE BACKYARD.

THERE WASN'T MUCH TIME TO ADMIRE THE FINISHED PRODUCT—THE TRANSLUCENT LINENY PERFECTNESS OF THE OUTER SHELL AND THE PEACHES-AND-CREAM SILKINESS OF ITS INSIDES.

BECAUSE WE USUALLY HAD ONLY A FEW MINUTES TO CLEAN UP THE WHOLE MESS BEFORE THEY GOT HOME.

TWENTY MINUTES LATER, MOM'D BE GRILLING CHEESE SANDWICHES RIGHT WHERE, A HALF HOUR EARLIER, WE'D HAVE BEEN IN THE THICK OF OUR OPERATION.

HOW WAS YOUR MORNING, BOYS?

AND DAD WOULD BE STANDING IN HIS TENNIS CLOTHES, NOSE TWITCHING LIKE A YORKIE'S, ASKING MOM IF SHE DIDN'T SMELL SOMETHING OCEANY.

FOR GODSAKES, RONNIE, WE'RE ON A BEACH!

39

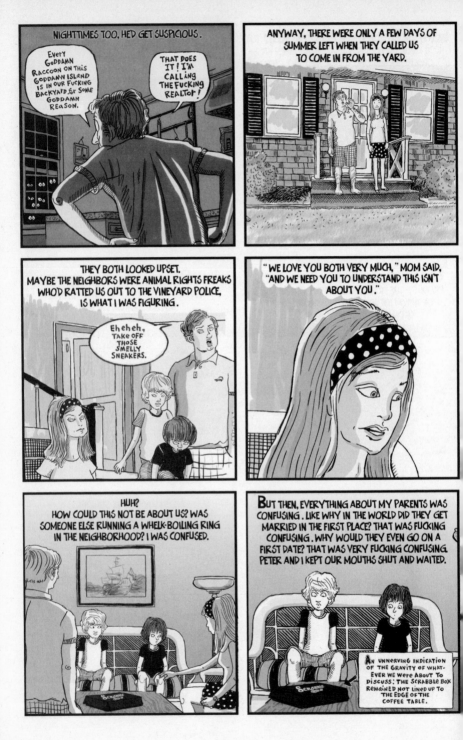

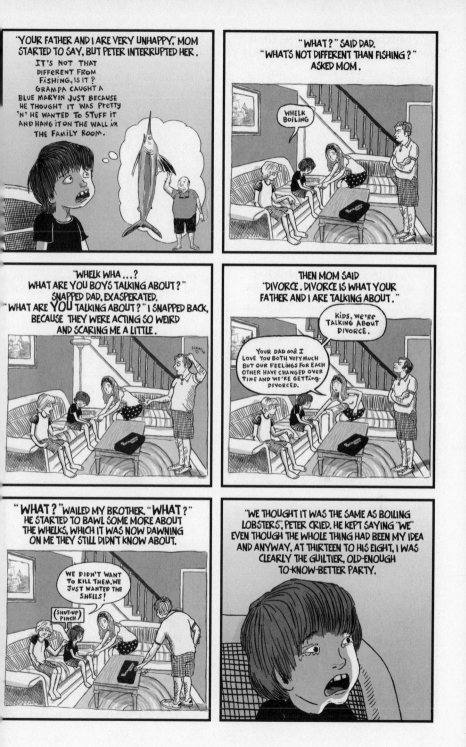

41

DYKE BRIDGE

Peter Orner

CHAPPAQUIDDICK, MASSACHUSETTS, 1976

My brother and I in the knee-deep water, standing in the tidal current, under Dyke Bridge. We are hunting whelks. Yes, it is the water Mary Jo Kopechne drowned in. I know all about it. About Teddy drunk and how the story of what happened was less covered up than simply muddled. My brother tells me all about it. How Teddy was still grieving his brothers, both his shot-to-death brothers, and that maybe he drank too much. Not that this excuses what happened, my brother says. *But wouldn't you drink if somebody shot me in the head? And then your other brother? If you had another brother? Wouldn't you drink a whole hell of a lot and probably crash a car?*

We are on vacation with our parents on Martha's Vineyard. We are from Illinois. It is classy if you are from Illinois to take a vacation on Martha's Vineyard. And Kennedyesque. My parents are still married (to each other), although my brother and I would prefer this not to be the case. We have ridden our bikes out to this bridge to see this very spot, to muck around in this famous water. My brother is wearing a T-shirt with the face of Sam Ervin, the hero of Watergate, on it.

I want to remember that we were alone, that it was only the two of us, but somewhere, in some stack of pictures, in some cabinet in my father's house, there are pictures of the two of us standing under Dyke Bridge, so it must be that at least one of our parents was with us and recorded it, and since my mother rarely took pictures it had to have been my father, but let's leave him out of this. Just my brother and I in the knee-deep water and my brother telling me that Teddy was heading back to the island that night, back from the even smaller island where they'd been at a party. That he was driving a black Chevrolet, because the Kennedys may be richer than God but they aren't ostentatious. When you're that rich you don't drive a Mercedes. And that Mary Jo Kopechne wasn't even very beautiful. She wasn't Teddy's wife either, he says, but that goes with this territory.

What territory?

The territory of being richer than God, my brother says. The landscape of sex and whisperings and innuendo.

I would rather fish up a whelk than listen to this, a live whelk with the black body inside, a Jell-O-ish squirmy thing that we will take back to our rented house and boil alive on the stove.

Even so, I ask, how much not very beautiful was she?

And my brother says, not particularly unbeautiful. Just not that beautiful for a Kennedy. She wasn't Jackie, is what I'm trying to say. But anyway nobody was Jackie. But still, Teddy may have even loved her even though he hardly knew her. Especially after she suffocated to death.

What do you mean?

My brother stares at me for a while. He and I have the same eyes, which is sometimes creepy. You don't know yourself coming and going, as my grandmother used to say. Then he squats in the water and takes up a couple of handfuls of ocean water and raises his hands to his nose as if to smell the water as it flows through his fingers. Don't we kind of love what we kill? my brother says. What about the whelks?

Our bikes are on the bridge, leaning against a broken piling. Dyke Bridge is a tiny bridge, a minature bridge. It is not much bigger than the width of a Chevy and nearly the same length. Driving off it is the bathroom equivalent of falling out of the bathtub.

I send an e-mail to my brother and ask him if he remembers all this. He writes back and says he doesn't remember it that way. And he is still very sensitive when it comes to the Kennedys. Like my mother, he remains a staunch believer in the notion that the New England wisdom embodied by the Kennedys will save this doomed country yet. My brother works for a congressman in Washington.

The bridge is bigger than a bathtub. Why do you have to exaggerate? Isn't the truth bad enough? You think Teddy Kennedy doesn't curse his soul every day for that night? Leave the man alone, even in your lying memories. I remember. We were out there with Dad. He took pictures. He thought it was funny. He kept saying be careful not to step on Mary Jo's face. You were annoyed because he kept saying you had to hold still for the picture.

And furthermore, my brother says, I should not, even over private electronic communication (*remember, don't use my .gov account for things like this*), provide aid and succor to the haters who still love to dredge this story up out of the muck. Remember Chappaquiddick! Besides, he says, why don't you ever just pick up the phone and call me? Why do you e-mail your brother? It gives the illusion of distance, I tell him. Pretend I'm in Shanghai or somewhere.

He replies: *Anyway, isn't anything driveoffable if you put your mind to it? Or even when you don't, especially when you don't? You're gonna pass judgment? Look at your own life.*

My brother is right. He is right. Even when is he not right he is right. Look at my own life. And nothing he has ever told me have I forgotten.

It is only that something happened there, under that bridge, where my brother and I once swam. As things do, as they always have, so many more things (strange things, impossible things) than we can even imagine. Dream it up and chances are it already happened. One minute you're drunk and laughing and your hand is on her bare thigh and the next the hood of the car is in the sand and water's flowing in through the cracks in the windows and the car's like a big fat grounded fish and there's this woman—what is her name?—flailing her arms in the darkness and shouting and you wonder for a moment if you love her. What was her name again? I'm confused. This is all so much black confusion. Shouldn't I be swimmingly noble? Don't I know the cross-chest carry? Aren't I a Kennedy? Aren't I the brother of the hero of PT-109? Isn't now the time?

No. Now is not the time. Now is the time to save yourself. Doesn't matter who you are (or your brothers are), Senator, save yourself—and then run. Everybody runs. My brother once said (though he doesn't remember): don't we sort of love what we kill? Maybe it's even true. But before that you got to run like hell. This I've learned on my own. There'll always be time for nobility, honor, sorrow, remorse, yes, maybe even love—in the morning.

The shadow from that little bridge over our heads. Us in the dark water, my brother and I, in the gummy sand, July 1976.

SEAN

Robert Anthony Siegel

The first time I saw Sean, I had no idea that we would become brothers. I watched him wander through my parents' living room, with its endless supply of child-lethal bric-a-brac, then gathered my courage and picked him up, just to be on the safe side. I was twenty-four and had no experience with toddlers. "See this?" I said, holding up a little brass Buddha. "This is a wise man with some kind of sharp pointy crown on, so be careful."

"Yes," said Sean, taking it in his hands. He wasn't timid or shy, just limited to a small pool of words. For the most part he was silent.

"And this is Hanuman, king of the monkeys."

"Yes," he said again, taking that statue too.

Twenty-three years later, I recognize how fragile was the chain of circumstances that brought us together, how one slight alteration would have left us strangers. My mother worked for Child Welfare as an attorney prosecuting abuse and neglect cases; some months earlier, she had been assigned a case involving one of Sean's brothers, who had gone to the hospital with a broken arm of the kind that usually comes from parental yanking, and who had then gone back later with a third-degree burn from an iron. The four boys had been farmed out to different homes, and for the older three, those homes had become permanent. Only Sean was left. He suffered from persistent nightmares that forced him awake, screaming; a series of well-intentioned but sleep-deprived people had ultimately declined to take him on permanently. The one immediately before us had reached the end of her endurance and decided she needed a break—right away. Sean was with us, I was told, for just a few days, on an emergency basis.

To be honest, I can't remember how deeply his story penetrated my postadolescent self-absorption. My big obsession back then was trying to figure out how to write a novel in the interstices of the kind of absurd part-time jobs (door-to-door furniture salesman, tour guide) that only the hapless recent college grad can stumble into. I had no particular sensitivity toward little kids and no desire for a new sibling. I already had two: my brother David and sister, Perrin, both of whom were away at college. We were exceptionally close, members of an exclusive club devoted to deciphering our eccentric parents and complex family history. We tended to be inward looking, wary of the outside world.

While Sean watched some cartoons on TV, I sat with my parents at the dining room table. "So you've got him for the weekend?" I asked, looking at the diaper bag, that strange, padded piece of luggage.

"The week, probably," said my mother.

"Could stretch longer," said my father.

A nervous silence. My parents looked exhausted already: two people in their middle fifties who had lived hard lives and were not in the best physical or emotional condition. My father reached for his bottle of antidepressants and swallowed one thoughtfully, as if in preparation for the challenges ahead. But beneath the air of quiet terror there was some other feeling, something steely and certain. They looked like gamblers who had stumbled on a not completely certain but nevertheless highly probable thing, the jackpot that might very well make their lives good again.

I was alarmed. My parents were decidedly high-maintenance. Now that David and Perrin were away, I got all the calls for help: my mother needed a lift somewhere, needed me to wait in the apartment so a repairman could get in, needed me to convince my father not to do something disastrous (usually involving money). For his part, my father needed me to help him to the doctor when his back went out, or to file papers for him at court so he didn't miss a deadline—he was, like my mother, a lawyer—or just needed company when the melancholy of daily life became too much. Both of them wanted me to listen and untangle their many complicated and vociferous disputes with each other, involving spending, housecleaning, mistakes, and slights sometimes a quarter-century old.

The last few years had been especially hard on my father. He'd once been a prominent criminal defense attorney, the sort you would see interviewed on the local news about some big case or other, but in recent years he had been reduced to taking whatever floated his way. He now worked out of a tiny home office off the living room, with a desk covered in dirty laundry and fancy Italian shoes—he loved shoes—and a phone he never answered; he met with his clients in the McDonald's across the street.

All of this worked in Sean's favor. Common sense, caution, a respect for order, solid finances, and a full night's sleep—all the things that had stopped previous families from adopting— were not my parents' concerns. What they wanted was love, the kind of love that would propel them through their midlife confusion. Sean came that weekend and never went back; my parents filed for adoption. They lasted through a year of his nightmares and frustration tantrums, until the sheer constancy of their attention quieted the fear inside him. They took meticulous care of his asthma, and it, too, began to improve; there were fewer and fewer late-night trips to the emergency room. He started to talk more, and then it became a flood. The silent little boy was now a nonstop commentator on the world around him, smart, observant and relentlessly opinionated. I started to notice phrases reminiscent of my parents: "Who knew?" he would say, an all-purpose exclamation of surprise and satisfaction whenever an unexpected treat came his way. "Who knew?"

My mother and father seemed to relish this second chance at parenthood. Always tottering on the edge of exhaustion, overloaded with plastic grocery bags, they nevertheless looked grounded, certain of their place in the world. I remember my father pushing Sean around the neighborhood in a stroller as if he were chauffeuring a celebrity. I remember my mother at home in her nightgown cradling Sean in her arms and cooing with deep satisfaction.

Of course, they couldn't stop being feckless, either—and, to be fair, their schedules were now so complex that even the most organized people would have been overwhelmed. I still got the emergency calls, but instead of having to take care of my parents, I now had to take care of the little boy my parents were supposed to be taking care of. I complained, of course, sputtering over the phone about how important my writing time was, blaming them for preventing me from becoming a writer, but I never actually hung up on them. The truth was that the hours I spent with Sean were actually among the most genuine, human moments in a life that had become confusing and a little bit lonely. When I first took up fiction, I was under the impression that you composed a novel by pulling out a piece of paper and writing down whatever occurred to you, just as it popped into your head. But it didn't seem to actually work that way. After a couple of years of trying, the silence of the empty page had become frightening.

Taking care of Sean was something of a mystery too, but at least it felt alive. I had no idea how to entertain him at first, and my parents gave me no pointers. I took him to the park and experienced the strange slowdown of kid time, something I would relearn many years later after my own children were born: those long, lyrical moments in which you do somersaults on the grass or play excruciatingly cute games of peekaboo, only to check your watch and find that exactly two minutes have gone by, and the rest of the afternoon still stretches ahead.

Once, I cheated and took him to the movies, a grown-up movie, no less, as there were no kids' films playing nearby. It was safe enough—a romantic comedy with Tom Selleck, no violence, no sex—but looking back, I marvel at how I could have rationalized that move. Desperation, of course. I sank into the padded seat with utter relief, and the movie, at which I would normally have sneered, was bliss, simply because it did not involve pouring wet playground sand into a broken dump truck. I followed its every plot turn with such deep gratitude that I remember it all to this day. Sean was quiet enough for me to pretend that he might be content, though when I finally looked over I found him standing in his seat, facing the back of the theater, as if the show were supposed to materialize there. I realized then that he had never been to the movies before. "No, you watch the screen," I said, pointing. "The screen, over there."

"Why?" he asked.

"So you can see the movie." I watched him turn to dutifully stare at the giant image of Tom Selleck, and I saw the sad folly of what I was doing. "Come on," I said. "Let's get some candy. We'll go to the park."

Even as a rather callow twenty-four-year-old, still hanging on to a long list of adolescent grievances, I started to gain some grudging appreciation for my parents: if nothing else, they had staying power.

Have I mentioned that out in the larger world, Sean is considered black and the rest of us white? That we are brothers stuck on opposite sides of that strange classification system known as race?

When Sean was four, he seemed to realize for the first time that his skin was a different color from ours. I remember a confusing episode in a Chinese restaurant over the holidays, when Perrin and David were both back from school. It's possible that the sudden expansion of the family had left him feeling a little lost; in all probability, he wasn't getting much attention at dinner that night, until he blurted out, "Everyone has white skin except me!"

The conversation around the table stopped. "What did you say?" asked my mother.

"Everyone has white skin except me!"

The woman I was dating at the time was Japanese. "I don't have white skin," she said, holding out her arm. "See?"

"You're not *brown*," said Sean, sounding disgusted at this quibble.

"What's wrong with brown?" asked Perrin.

"I hate brown!" He didn't seem sad so much as frustrated and angry. His face quivered on the edge of tears.

We all began talking in a nervous rush, not so much to console him, I think, as to drown him out with our reassurances— reassurances meant for ourselves as well. "Brown is beautiful," said my mother. "Like chocolate."

"I wish *I* were brown," said my father.

"Brown is my favorite color," said David.

No one knew the magical words that would make this problem disappear, but then a moment later it was simply gone, as mysteriously as it came: Perrin took Sean on her lap and gave him a pile of sugar packets to play with; more food arrived for the adults; conversation resumed. But the nervousness remained, just below the surface.

Sean brought up his skin color a number of times that year. He wanted to look like everyone else in the family, wanted physical, visual proof that he belonged and could never be left out—a powerful hunger for a little boy who had already lost one family. All any of us could do was explain, over and over again, that looks don't make a family, knowing that time would prove it.

And I think it has. If Sean and I don't look alike, we certainly sound alike, much like our father, who grew up on the Lower East Side during the Great Depression and had a bit of borscht belt to him. Sean and I share the same love of dumb jokes, the same penchant for grandiose plan making, whether it's about kayaking the Atlantic or biking the continent. I was at his adoption hearing, at his big tap dance performance, at all his school graduations. My wife and I signed him up for his first photography class, a small gift that bore extravagant fruit: photography became his college major and then his profession. He paid us back by taking the pictures at my first book party. He was at our wedding, at the hospital when our oldest child, Jonah, was born, at the bris. Seven years ago, we stood with Perrin and David beside our father's coffin; now, when I come to town, we all drive out to the cemetery together to visit Dad's grave and walk among the headstones, telling jokes and laughing just as our father would have.

My worry in even mentioning race is that I might end up misrepresenting our experience by focusing on something that is irrelevant to the fabric of our daily lives as siblings. The problem, however, is that silence would be equally distorting. For if race is a purely social construct, a figment of the collective imagination, a thing out *there,* on the street, not in *here,* within the family, it can bounce around in highly unpredictable ways and have oddly distorting effects.

Soon after Sean arrived, I took him with me to spend the day with a bunch of people at a house in Fire Island. We made a splash. He was completely outgoing, interested in everyone, full of laughter. People passed him around from arm to arm, cooing over him. Someone said to me, "This is just the most wonderful thing you're doing. You've rescued a child and given him a home. A little black boy."

That felt odd. I hated the way it flattened out the interactions between complicated individuals and turned the whole thing into an act of charity. There was no recognizing us in that. We were basically instinctual people, neither political nor principled, and more than a little selfish. "Oh no, really, it's the other way around," I said, though the more calculating part of me already realized that this too would be taken as an expression of modesty and simply get me more kudos—which is why I said it, of course.

Indeed, as these encounters multiplied over the next few years, I got over my unease and started accepting the praise, then basking in it, then expecting it, even courting it, feeling miffed when it didn't come my way. I started borrowing Sean from my parents whenever I had a social occasion where I wouldn't know many people. He was perfect for backyard barbecues in Brooklyn, picnics in Central Park. With him in my arms I stood out: I was the guy with the cute little brown brother. I would carry him around the party, introducing him to all the women, and thus introducing myself in the most flattering, if contrived, light: Mr. Sensitivity, the urban saint, but also hip, because Sean was a hip little kid with his incredible smile and wonderful ringlets.

Of course, that wasn't the only type of dynamic we had. Soon after the trip to Fire Island, we were riding downtown on a city bus when I noticed a middle-aged white woman across the aisle, watching us very closely. Sean's asthma was acting up and he was coughing, a wet, ugly chest cough that always made me upset—I hated that he had to struggle for breath. "That's a nasty cough," said the woman.

"He's got asthma," I said, feeling obscurely accused of something, some sort of negligence—or maybe it was illegitimacy.

"He should see a doctor."

"We have medicine for it."

"Mmm," she said, looking skeptical.

From that point on, I started noticing a pattern wherever we went: older white women peering to see if Sean's coat was properly zipped, if I held his hand when we crossed the street, if I let him drink from the sippy cup he'd just dropped on the sidewalk. It took me a while to realize that they didn't see the hip older brother, Mr. Sensitivity, urban rescue hero. They assumed I was the *father*. And though I was twenty-five by then, I was the sort of baby-faced twenty-five that looked eighteen, and not particularly prosperous, either, in my repertoire of old jeans and T-shirts. Sean was still in the thrift shop clothes my parents had inherited with him, which contained an alarming number of Michael Jackson tank tops. Stuff from the bottom of the box at Goodwill. I can only imagine how these women filled in the blanks: teen parents, black and white, poor, hapless. A sort of interracial *La Bohème,* with a coughing, wheezing child.

The somewhat pathetic truth is that I was secretly flattered and did nothing to dispel the impression. I guess I felt a little possessive of Sean by that point, but there was more to it: fatherhood was grown-up, and nothing else about my life felt that way. I was working part-time, living with a roommate, and writing nothing worth keeping or showing, but I walked a little straighter when I had him with me.

Later that first year, I got a call from my mother, who told me that an organization of African-American social workers had weighed in on Sean's adoption. Its interest wasn't Sean's case specifically, but the broader issue of adoption policy; it believed that African-American kids should go to African-American families, and it asked some cogent questions: How would black children raised in white homes understand their African-American heritage? How would they learn how to navigate the difficulties of race in America without African-American role models?

I could see that they had a point; I just wanted them to make it using someone else's adoption. My parents got worried. They were receiving regularly scheduled home visits from social workers as the adoption process continued. What if policy changed and the agency started recommending against transracial adoptions? "He's half-white," said my father. "Why isn't he considered white? I mean, why choose one half rather than the other?"

"Look at his skin," my mother said.

"He looks like he got a tan at the beach." That was pretty much true. Sean's biological father was African-American, but his biological mother was Caucasian. His biological half brothers all had Caucasian fathers and looked positively Nordic, with blond hair and blue eyes.

"You're not being practical," said my mother.

But my father was stuck on his point. "He's not black or white. He's a harlequin, black *and* white."

"That's idiotic."

My parents, never people much into preparation, made an effort to forestall any possible criticism. They started dressing Sean in a dashiki for big occasions, such as Passover and Yom Kippur. We all made a halfhearted effort to celebrate Kwanzaa, right after Hanukkah, getting instructions from a book.

The adoption started to get a little messy for other reasons. Sean's mother had abandoned the boys in the middle of their brother's abuse case; she'd run away to Puerto Rico with a janitor from the homeless shelter they lived in, and my parents were worried that she would return to contest his adoption. If she did, there wouldn't be a chance of winning; he would have to go back to her. My parents discussed this possibility at night, when Sean was asleep, during long, circular discussions. "She let the other three go," said my father.

"She's unpredictable," said my mother.

"She won't come back."

"She might."

She didn't; what actually happened is that my mother's agency realized that Sean had been tangentially connected to the abuse case my mother had prosecuted a couple of years back, involving his brother with the broken arm. The agency brought up the possibility of what it called "the appearance of impropriety." What they were worried about was a tabloid headline, something like CITY LAWYER STEALS KID FROM MOM, LEGALLY! My mother was called in to talk to her boss, and then to her boss's boss. She was passed over for a promotion that had once looked like a sure thing and then transferred out of the courts altogether, to a job doing paperwork. The inspector general's office brought her up on a battery of charges, some of which were pretty far-flung—an effort to find something that would stick.

This new twist was especially frightening for my parents: now that my father was in what was delicately called "semi-retirement," my mother's job was their primary support. But what really concerned them was the potential impact on the adoption. My father would get worked up into long, dramatic rants. "I'll never hand him over," he told me. "I'll take him and go on the lam."

"Does anyone even say *lam* anymore?" I asked, trying to lighten the mood.

"I'll change my name and drive out west. They'll never find us."

"Isn't that called kidnapping?"

"Who cares what it's called."

I couldn't help feeling that my father had been looking for reasons to go on the lam for years before Sean arrived, anyway. He often fantasized about radical personal transformation: living on a sailboat, opening a bookstore in Vermont. And yet I also understood his sense of crisis. Sean had taken root inside our hearts; whatever the law said, there was no disentangling him now.

The charges against my mother were eventually dropped; the adoption went through. Yet a sense of insecurity stayed with us for years afterward. Would Sean have been better off in an African-American family? A younger family with more energetic parents and siblings closer in age? Part of this was a reaction to the bumpiness of the adoption process, part of it just a by-product of who we are: overly ruminative, insecure people. But there was something more, too: a sense of the willfulness of choosing a little boy still too young to choose you back. Sure, he seemed to love us, all right, but given the opportunity, would he have *chosen* us? This question, fundamentally unanswerable, was more an expression of anxiety than anything else. No one frets over the fact that biological children don't choose their families. But irrational or not, it lingered.

Five or six years after the adoption went through, the entire family was in my parents' little Japanese station wagon, making a slow arc around the concrete island at the center of Times Square. Traffic was snarled and we crept along, only slowly becoming aware of a commotion on the center island. Someone was shouting through an old PA system, and though it was hard to make out every word, we could all understand enough to know that he was very, very angry. *Jew* was one of the few words that cut through the distortion.

An African-American man stood on a portable stage, a microphone in his hand. He was dressed like the genie in *Aladdin,* in a turban, a sash, and the trademark puffy pants, and behind him stretched a line of other African-American men dressed in the same style, looking determined and scary despite the harem pants. A banner read THE TWELVE TRIBES OF ISRAEL. "The Jews have stolen everything from us," said the man with the microphone. "Not just our freedom but our identity. *We* are the true Israelites. Not them. Us!" He had a lot to say about Jewish bloodsuckers, slave masters, bankers, and pawnbrokers, but what got me was not the anti-Semitic rhetoric so much as the look on Sean's face as he listened next to me: confused, guarded, bruised.

The smart thing would have been to respond with something right away, something about how crazy these people were, how they didn't matter, how families can be black and white, Jewish and not-Jewish, how they can be anything they want to be as long as the people in them love each other.

Instead, we all sat very still, trying to act as if nothing were happening while we willed the light to turn so we could escape.

It was Sean who finally spoke: "They're not talking to me."

I think of the time on the subway not so long ago when an African-American man came through the car handing out flyers. It took a moment for me to realize that he was giving them only to African-Americans. Some glanced, others spent a little more time, but nobody seemed surprised by what they had been handed. I took one from the seat beside me and read: *The White Man Is A Demon Without A Soul.*

If I'd been with Sean, the man with the leaflets would have had no idea that the paunchy middle-aged Jewish guy and the big brown kid in hip-hop gear sitting next to each other were in fact brothers. He would have handed Sean a leaflet; he would have skipped me.

It works the other way too, of course. The 2008 presidential election was fairly contentious in the small Southern city where we now live. It pained me when I passed houses hanging Confederate flags and when a woman at the playground told me that black gangs would be unleashed downtown if Obama won. It pained me not in some abstract, principled way, but with a stab to the gut. It was as if they were trying to push me and Sean apart.

I have two children of my own now, a boy and a girl, and like most every parent I eat it up when people tell me, "He looks just like his dad," or "She has her father's face." Phrases like that trigger a primitive sense of ownership in me, a surge of connection that is sweetly intoxicating. But I know from my brother Sean that family is not defined by blood. It is not defined by race. It is not even defined by a shared voice or way of telling a story. Family is who you choose to love. The unfathomable complexity of those two terms, *choose* and *love,* starts to feel simple after a while, when you live them day by day.

Our oldest child, Jonah, was born in 1999, while we were living in an apartment in Tribeca, right beside the Hudson River. Sean was fifteen then, a big, burly teenager, already a head taller than anyone else in the family, but he held the baby with a natural, unself-conscious gentleness that I had never seen in a young man. And he was genuinely interested, too: as Jonah grew, Sean would come over and play with him for hours. Eventually we hired him to do a little babysitting in the apartment, so my wife and I could get some work done or just get some rest. He learned to feed, change, bathe, and burp, learned how to take away a breakable thing with one hand while offering a toy with the other, and in the process became such an important part of Jonah's life that the mere sight of his uncle in the doorway would make our son start to laugh and clap.

In time, we got up our courage and sent them outside together: Jonah's first foray into the world beyond the apartment without his parents. It felt momentous. I secured him in the snuggly that Sean wore on his front (have you ever seen a teenage boy comfortably wearing a snuggly?), double-checked the bottle, and then watched them disappear out the door. I remember the long wait at the window till they appeared on the street, ten stories below. I remember my wife leaning against me, watching too. I remember them crossing the West Side Highway to the river and continuing onto the newly renovated pier, with its hot dog stand and benches. The pier was surprisingly narrow from the height of our apartment, surrounded on three sides by the muscular, glistening river, and on our side by the cityscape, with its tall buildings, its rushing cars. They were tiny figures out there, but I could see Sean's arms wrapped around Jonah in the snuggly. My brother, carrying my son.

JACKIE

Margo Rabb

When I was twelve, I fell in love with a TV show called *Double Trouble*. The show was about two fifteen-year-old twin sisters, Kate and Allison, who had identical glossy brown bangs, dimples, and almost unbearably perfect teeth. They slept in twin beds an arm's length apart, wore bright-colored sweater vests and freshly laundered nightgowns, and performed dance routines with matching leotards, pantyhose, leg warmers, and spotless white sneakers. The show's theme song—performed by the sisters themselves—went: "Uh oh! We make a great team! Life gets so much better whenever we're together!"

I dreamed of having a *Double Trouble*–like sister. I wanted someone to talk to after the lights went out, to unburden my heart to; this fantasy sister and I would wake up together every morning, brush our teeth side by side, share wholesome egg and toast breakfasts, and travel together to school, all to the tune of the eighties-pop *Double Trouble* theme song.

My real-life sister and I barely grunted to each other on school mornings. We argued so often about which subway station was closest to our house that we huffed off to the Forty-sixth Street and Fifty-second Street stations separately. In the car with our parents, she'd sit in the front seat to talk to my father; I'd fall asleep with my head on my mother's lap in the back. She was three years older, and when she got her period—

a box of Kotex mysteriously appeared in our bathroom—I was eager to share in the delights of her budding womanhood. "What's it feel like?" I asked her, shocked and elated, expectant and jealous.

"Shut the fuck up," she said.

Physically, we looked so different that at one summer job, a boy we worked with said, "Seems like you know each other kinda well. How did you two meet?" And we continually heard the refrain "I can't believe you two are sisters!"

We had our *Double Trouble* moments, though. We didn't share a room, but after we received walkie-talkies one year, we whispered into them after we were in bed, which we called "Night Magic." We shared a devotion to *Little House on the Prairie* books, Sherlock Holmes mysteries, and semi-obscure old movies like Claudette Colbert's *It's a Wonderful World* and Audrey Hepburn's *How to Steal a Million*. On hot summer nights I'd sleep in a cot in her room, which had the only air conditioner. We didn't have heart-to-hearts about boys or periods, but I loved those nights. When she left for college, I felt a surprising sense of loneliness and emptiness; I took the train to Philadelphia several times to sleep on the floor of her dorm room. Yet what I most wanted—the epitome of my sisterhood fantasy—was to talk. To confess our feelings and dreams and desires, to have the kind of deep friendship I thought the word "sisters" should embody: best friends sharing our closest emotions and secrets.

This sisters fantasy always seemed to hang over us, accompanied by the strange knowledge that if we weren't related, we wouldn't naturally seek each other out to be friends. She continued to be frustrated with me because I loved fashion and makeup and the city, and was the type of person who'd love a show like *Double Trouble* in the first place; I was frustrated by her temper and sports love and complete disinterest in girl bonding.

I went to college in another part of the country, and we

started our separate lives. Then, when I was eighteen and my sister was twenty-one, our mother developed severe pains in her stomach; the doctors thought it was hepatitis and she went into the hospital for tests. A few weeks later she was diagnosed with malignant melanoma that had metastasized to her liver. She died ten days later.

There was no TV-movie-type bonding between my sister and me as our mother was dying: we didn't talk directly about her or how it felt to lose her. I called friends to cry and talk. What my sister and I did was laugh at the absurdity of everything—the disturbingly cheery funeral director who bounced on his heels as he showed us the coffin choices; the rabbi (we called him Rabbi Don Johnson) who wore Ray-Bans and a gold necklace swinging over his hairy chest. And then we went back to college and rarely talked about our mother at all. I found friends who'd lost their mothers also, and I grew closer to them during that time.

One afternoon, a family friend took me out to lunch and asked me how we were coping. I told her I was frustrated with my father and sister's reticence. "They're not coping well. They won't speak about my mom or talk about losing her."

"How do you know you're coping any better?" she asked me.

I was offended by her question; I thought that of course my method of grieving—talking about the loss, writing poetry about it, writing in my journal—was the healthiest way to cope with losing someone. And I felt jealous that my sister still had our father, to whom I believed she was closer—usually, he and I had only spoken on the phone for a minute before he passed the receiver to my mother.

Over the years our family knit itself back together in a lopsided and complicated way, and my father and I did grow closer, but I'm not sure that losing our mother bonded my sister and me to each other more deeply. We finished college, found jobs, and bickered as we always had.

Then, seven years after our mother died, on an August afternoon, our father died suddenly of a heart attack.

My sister was in Hawaii at the time; I was with our father in New York. In the hospital they wheeled his body into a separate room, and the nurses let me use a phone to call my sister and tell her he had died.

I stared at the white phone in the busy nurse's station.

It was the worst phone call I ever had to make. All I could think was that if I was in my sister's shoes, I wouldn't be able to handle it. I wouldn't be physically able to book three last-minute flights and board them and travel across an ocean and a country. I wouldn't be able to make that trip. I'd drown myself in the ocean. I'd do something drastic.

And yet she made it. I met her at the airport and we hugged and cried, and she told me the flights weren't so bad after all: she'd befriended a man beside her and he'd told her he'd lost a parent as well; he understood.

That phone call, and those flights, were the beginning of something, a sea change. It reminded me of the time my father had taken me to the airport to go back to college after my mother died. In the past, he'd always dropped me off at the curb, not wanting to pay for parking. After her death he parked, he waited with me through the check-in and security lines, and he even asked the security person if he could come through to the gate—we'd just lost my mother, he explained. She refused, and so he waited by the window, watching until my plane took off. He'd become a different person.

Our father's death fiercely changed the relationship between my sister and me. I wasn't prepared for how it would feel to have no parents, to be a family of only siblings, to be a family of two. All our grandparents were dead; my mother had no siblings, and our father had one brother to whom he wasn't close. Neither of us were married or had boyfriends. It was just the two of us, alone.

Overnight, we went from carefree twentysomethings to

homeowners and landlords—our father had been in the process of renovating a part of the house into a studio apartment, which he'd rented out to a young woman. "He said I reminded him of his daughters," she told us. Our parents' house had gone downhill in the years since our mother died, with squirrels in the ceiling, random leaks, a decaying sewer problem, and abandoned rooms our father filled with furniture and belongings he hadn't been able to part with.

At night, my sister and I slept in our parents' huge bed.

We decided to sell the house, but that left us with the enormous task of repairing it and cleaning it out. We hired a parade of contractors and workmen, including a plumber who showed us his green *S* tattoo and said, "They call me Sewer Man because I know my shit," and a squirrel remover who doggedly set up his Hav-A-Heart traps to relocate our ceiling-dwelling squirrels to Long Island.

We began to sort. And pack. And sort. On top of the things our parents had hoarded during the thirty years they'd owned the house, the basement was filled with mountains of our dead grandparents' possessions.

In some ways selling the house and sorting through their belongings was worse than the deaths themselves. Day after day we had to confront a thousand memories, to physically cast them out into a yard sale pile, onto a thrift store truck, or into the garbage. My sister was better at this process than I was; she attacked the sorting more methodically and practically than I did. I'd find something my parents had saved—old letters and photos, or the corsage from my eighth-grade graduation—and I'd have to take a break to go brood under the covers. After a while I couldn't stand to sort through any more things and packed a tower of boxes to put into storage. When we held our massive yard sale (we made over $3,000, selling most items for under five dollars), I hated to watch strangers root through our parents' things, and I had to go hide in the house and cry for a while. But my sister plugged through.

And yet, overall, that time in the house with my sister seems strangely charmed in my memory. On Halloween we had to run to the corner store three times to buy enough candy to keep up with the steady stream of trick-or-treaters; their tiny bodies clustered at our door reminded us of Halloweens from our childhood. Our neighborhood in Queens was steps away from Manhattan, yet it still had this strange small-town feel, which was oddly comforting. Friends from the city and from out of town were constantly visiting and seemed to relax in our parent-free home.

My sister and I got along better then than we ever had. We didn't fight over any of our parents' possessions. We barely fought over anything. Even the idea of fighting over their belongings seemed ridiculous. We had a mock argument over a contraption our father loved called a Gilhoolie; it was a small gadget that opened bottle tops.

"I want that Gilhoolie, and I'm willing to sue you to get it," my sister said over lunch one day.

"See if you can get past my lawyers!" I told her.

"Oh, I will. I will sue, and I will win."

(Eventually I agreed to let her have the Gilhoolie, though she later bought me my own on eBay.)

Our last night in the house, we knew we were going to have to stay up until three A.M. to finish packing, so we went out for sushi and ordered the largest platter they had. It was called the Boat—a portion for two people so huge that it arrived on a special wooden ark. We ran into my sister's best friend from childhood and her husband at the restaurant, and they joined us for dinner and admired our Boat-tackling stamina. We didn't talk about it being our last night in our parents' house. Instead we talked and laughed about Sewer Man and squirrel removers and Gilhoolies. You would think that the last night in your childhood home after your parents had died would be unbearably depressing, but somehow, with my sister, it wasn't. We shared a resilience that I didn't quite know was in me until I saw it in her first.

It was this resilience that stunned me. Maybe the sister connection I'd been dreaming of for so many years had always been there, just not in the way I'd imagined—not in my long-held sister fantasy, but in a strength we both had within us, which I'd never known existed. I learned from her that coping isn't always about talking it through. Coping can be just doing what you have to do and forgetting about it. There's a power in *not* talking about it, and in moving on.

Of course, we never said these kinds of things to each other. I never said aloud to her that I couldn't have survived it without her. There isn't a Hallmark card imprinted with *Our parents are dead, but I'm so glad I have you! Uh-oh! We make a great team!*

While writing this essay I looked up *Double Trouble* online and read that in real life, the series' twin actresses had lost both their parents by the time they were twenty-one. I wonder: Did they feel anything like what we felt? Was that the real strength underlying the connection between them?

The television-family fantasy hovers over not just siblings, but all aspects of family life. There is the ideal of a gathered-round-the-turkey family that everyone falls short of, and yet the fantasy persists; it's always there in the back of the mind. I'm still frequently undone by grief—weeping inconsolably before my wedding and while pregnant with my children—and I'm somehow still shocked, even though ten years have passed since we lost our father, and almost twenty years since our mother died, that they're gone.

Whether we speak of it or not, my sister is the only person who understands this. We share genes, a history, and the only bits of our parents that we have left. And she's the only person who understands how we can sit beside our parents' graves on a sunny afternoon, and then go out for sushi and stuff ourselves and still laugh, even now, until we nearly burst.

GENDER STUDIES

Mary Norris

For a while after Dennis announced that he was transsexual, I
was relieved, because I thought he wouldn't get AIDS. He had
given me the Jan Morris book *Conundrum* and explained that
before he could do anything drastic—that is, undergo what
is delicately referred to as "gender-reassignment surgery"—
he had to have permission from a psychiatrist and live as a
woman for a year. I let myself hope that Dennis would be content to stay semi-in-the-closet so he could keep his job teaching music at a Catholic school in the Bronx, that he might be
content to feel subversive playing the organ in the choir loft
while wearing ladies' underpants. I should have known better: Dennis had always been capable of achieving with surprising speed things that seemed impossible, like saving up from
his paper route to buy a pool table while he was still in grade
school. Within days of deciding he was transsexual, he was
taking hormones. "Someday you'll get to take these," he said,
meaning when I hit menopause. The hormones stopped hair
from growing on Dennis's hands and arms, encouraged breasts
to grow (but not enough to please him), and discouraged male
hormones, causing, eventually, chemical castration.

He was also making subtle adjustments to his clothing. I
could not believe anyone could derive so much pleasure from
buttoning a shirt from right to left, but Dennis was obsessed

with such details. In the spring, he talked about a girl at school who threaded her ponytail through the opening at the back of her baseball cap. "It's so cute!" he said. A few months later, he came out of his apartment wearing a baseball cap with his hair in a bushy ponytail threaded through the back.

Dennis had tried to explain to me the difference between sex and gender. There were primary sexual characteristics (womb, gonads) and secondary sexual characteristics (breasts, Adam's apple). A man could achieve breasts and even a vagina, but not a womb. ("I'll never menstruate," he moaned. I laughed in his face.) Gender referred to some metaphysical orientation that made women more receptive and men more aggressive (extrapolating from their sexual characteristics). Dennis kept trying to convince me that it was not that big a deal for him to change gender, and I kept thinking, *Well, if it's not that big a deal, why do you have to do it?*

Whereas, in a crisis, Dennis took up a new instrument—he had contacted his former harp teacher and bought a concert harp—I took up a new language. A friend and I found an Italian teacher. Another friend told me of a sublet in Venice, available for August, and I grabbed it. Of course, in language, there is a gender issue. I'd studied French and German and Spanish and Greek but had never had a gift for divining the gender of nouns. If the nouns referred to people—*man, woman, wife, husband, brother, sister, aunt, uncle*—I had no problem. But what made, say, a table (*tavola*) feminine? Or a glass (*bicchiere*) masculine? Does a glass have an Adam's apple? If you turn a table upside down, will you expose its genitals? I could not get it through my head that a noun's gender was not about the physical characteristics of the thing, that it was arbitrary.

I set about memorizing the gender of Italian nouns one at a time, using free association. Some words fell neatly into place. *Voce*, voice, is feminine. My voice is a soprano and I am female (but not particularly feminine); I have my mother's voice (often my father could not distinguish between us on the phone); my mother was always talking or singing, prating and blowing, always using her voice—she never shut up. So *voce* is triply feminine. *Chiave,* key, is feminine, though I'd have made it masculine, because of St. Peter and his keys, and because of Freud (doesn't the man have the key that fits the woman's lock?). I drew keys in various positions, the working end pointing up and to the right, down in a cross, like the symbols Dr. Zorba drew on the blackboard at the beginning of *Ben Casey:* "Man, woman, birth, death, infinity." I printed the word in all capitals—CHIAVE—and isolated the "I" and circled the "AVE," as in *Ave Maria.* Eureka: Maria was feminine. And to certain people, being feminine was the key to everything.

It kept coming back to my brother. One of the first sentences I formed in our Italian class, because I was sad and preoccupied, and the teacher was trying to draw me out, was *"Mio fratello vuole essere mia sorella"*: "My brother wants to be my sister."

Among the guidebooks I took with me to Italy was Jan Morris's *Venice,* a classic of travel literature. But I resisted reading it. I was mad at Jan Morris. *Conundrum,* her book about her journey across the sexes, infuriated me. I recognized in it many of the ideas my brother had picked up, like her descriptions of the effects of female hormones: how masculinity was like a carapace that he shed, becoming more responsive to the world, more compassionate. Much of what she describes as feminine seemed ludicrously romanticized or frivolous to me: sunbathing, not being able to drive in reverse. ("Women cannot drive in reverse," my father had said when he was teaching me to drive, and I was determined to prove him wrong.)

My family had nothing in common with Jan Morris's. First of all, there was the enchanted childhood in Wales. James Morris was the youngest of three boys. His mother painted and swanned about the house in fine clothing. He was educated at a choir school in Oxford, with its robes and incense and mysticism. All of this contrasted rather harshly with life on the Cuyahoga. Our mother and grandmother had calluses, our father was bent on getting us the cheapest education possible, and the music at St. Thomas More Roman Catholic Church, in a suburb of Cleveland, was provided by a warbling old organist, the wife of the school crossing guard.

James Morris had always felt the tug of the feminine, but he entered the service and married his soul mate and had children and became a well-respected journalist who broke the story of Sir Edmund Hillary's ascent of Mount Everest. He experimented with female hormones but stopped and sired another child, and then started hormones again and consulted the best doctors. When the time came, he went along to a clinic in Casablanca and had the surgery, almost as an afterthought. Every step of the way, he had the love and support of his wife and family. I couldn't believe it had been quite so easy. I didn't think it would be so easy for Dennis, and I knew that it wouldn't be so easy for me. Suppose Jan Morris had had a sister? What might we have heard from her?

But I had to admit that the book on Venice was wonderful. It begins at the Campanile, which I climbed at the first opportunity. The author counts the lions in La Serenissima and hires a boat to venture out into the lagoon with the children, to the islands where the Venetians grow their vegetables. I was slightly outraged that a woman's name—Jan Morris— was on the title page, when the book had been written some forty years earlier by a man, James Morris. I would not have been able to rent a boat and go off by myself in it. Women are supposed to be helpless around boats. I thought it was somehow disingenuous of Jan Morris to put her name to things that James Morris had done.

One night the phone rang at two A.M.: Dennis. I am never happy to be woken up by the phone, and it was a foggy conversation. He was just calling to say hello. He missed me. All was well with Mom and Dad. I both resented and admired his obliviousness to the time difference between New York and Venice.

Before going home, I went to a fancy drugstore and bought a basic makeup kit—a compact, mascara, lipstick, Issey Miyake perfume in a tall conical bottle, and a nail brush—in anticipation of having to compete with a transsexual sibling.

In a weird way, my brother's reincarnation corresponded with my father's decline. That Christmas, Dennis and I went home together. It was a little chilly in the house, and my father was wearing two shirts. I gave him a tape player, and my feelings were hurt when he put it aside. Later I saw that he couldn't retain how it worked and was embarrassed to admit it or ask for help. He started a conversation with "Seen any good movies lately?" He had become a master of all-purpose responses, like "I wouldn't be at all surprised."

At some point, Dennis and I snuck off to the cemetery to find Patrick's grave. It had been one of the rituals of our childhood: going to the cemetery, usually at Easter. It was a long drive, out Denison to Harvard to Broadway. The landmark we had always watched for was a stone pony in front of a restaurant. Then came the gates of Calvary. Patrick was buried in the children's section. I remembered the sign that read OUR BABIES and a statue of an angel soaring up out of a mound of shrubbery; our older brother Miles used to catch grasshoppers there in summer. My job was to fill a jar with water from a tap in one of the pipes sticking up along the cemetery roads, for flowers my mother had brought. Patrick's grave was a tiny rectangular polished stone, flush with the earth. My mother would busy herself brushing the grass back from around the edges.

Now Dennis and I stopped at the administration building to get a map and directions. We found the stone, brushed it off, read the inscription: PATRICK JOSEPH NORRIS, BELOVED SON, 1950–1953. Neither of us said anything for a while. I don't know what I was expecting to feel. I had gone through life in a miasma of guilt, certain from the way my mother told the story of how Patrick, just shy of three years old, had choked on a piece of bacon at the kitchen table that if it weren't for me—if it weren't for the very fact of my existence that morning at the table and in the world—Patrick would not have died. Guilt was my element—I breathed it.

It was an odd thing: as Dennis and I got older, instead of getting over it, we became more and more obsessed. I never married or had children—I had always put obstacles in the way of that. I had seen what my mother went through when she lost Patrick, and deep down I just knew that it was too much of a risk. At the same time, I had the biological imperative to pursue men, but always men who, for one reason or another (they were gay, I was fat), had no interest in me.

Finally, Dennis broke the silence in the graveyard. "This is where it all began," he said. Dennis grew up in the full knowledge that he was conceived to replace Patrick. If he had been born a girl, he might not have been so freighted with that. Meanwhile, if, as it seemed to me, Mom and Dad had needed another boy, clearly being a girl was not good enough. Mom favored Dennis, Dad had a soft spot for me, and Dennis and I were each convinced that the other was better off.

On the way home, we stopped at the place with the stone pony out front. The White Horse Tavern was a totally ordinary neighborhood bar and restaurant, but for us it was the fulfillment of a lifelong dream. We did not tell our parents we had been to the stone pony or to Calvary—we said we'd just been driving around. Later, we were looking at family albums—my mother and Dennis and I—and came across a rare picture of Patrick. I tensed up, but all my mother said was "There's poor little Patrick." At some point, Mom had put away the picture of Patrick that she kept on her dresser, and we'd stopped going to the cemetery. She and my father had mourned and let go. Miles and his wife had named their firstborn son Patrick, as if to heal the wounds of the past. Only Dennis and I still felt governed by it.

* * *

That summer, Dennis was working as a lifeguard at the McBurney YMCA, in Chelsea, and by the fall he had gotten permission from his supervisor to "present" at work as a woman. He had a ladies' red tank suit, he told me. He did not use the women's locker room, or the men's, but had his own space to change in. I ran into him on Seventh Avenue one day when he was on his way downtown after work. He was wearing a blouse and a plaid pleated skirt. "As you see, today I'm in Catholic-school drag," he said. He was excited because that day a vendor had been filling the soda machine at the Y just as Dennis came to get something to drink, and a maintenance man said to the vendor, "Give the lady a Coke."

I'd passed up an earlier opportunity to see Dennis in drag. He'd made a dinner date with my friend Barrett Mandel. Barrett, my first college English professor, was an example of someone I introduced Dennis to and then watched, not without a fleck of self-pity, as an independent relationship developed. Barrett invited me along to dinner, and I was tempted to go, but Dennis called to warn me that he was going to use the occasion to wear a skirt in public for the first time. I was not ready for this and declined. Barrett later reported that he and Dennis had stopped to shop for earrings, and that although my brother was wearing a skirt, he did not seem noticeably feminine in manner.

Another friend, Ed Stringham, my former boss at *The New Yorker*, died that summer. Ed was an old Beat—he knew Jack Kerouac when Kerouac was walking around at Columbia with the manuscript of his first novel, *The Town and the City*, and he had enough history with Allen Ginsberg that when he saw Ginsberg coming, in his saffron robe, he'd cross the street. Ed had systematically read, listened to, and looked at all the literature, music, and art in the world, and retained it. He and Dennis had become friends, having long conversations in the office at night, lending each other books and music. A memorial was organized at a bar near Ed's old apartment. There would be many people attending who knew Dennis, and I was afraid he would use the opportunity as a kind of coming-out party and distract everybody from eulogizing Ed. "This is not about you," I told him sternly. "Okay," he said witheringly. He wore an embroidered vest and had his hair pulled back; I noticed that his face was fuller. People told stories about Ed or read aloud from a work that, if not for Ed, they would never have encountered. Dennis read a passage from *Simplicissimus,* by H. J. C. von Grimmelshausen, about a man who does penance by walking long distances with peas in his shoes. A woman who knew Dennis pointed him out to me and asked, "Who is that lady?"

"That's no lady," I said. "That's my brother."

Dennis suggested that I join a support group for friends and family of people with transgender issues. It was called the GID Project, and it met one night every two weeks at the gay-and-lesbian center on West Thirteenth Street. The leader was a woman with a thick brown braid and a kind face, who was so practical and down-to-earth that she made this freakish business seem normal. One of my laments was that I felt saddled with Dennis. A husband and wife can get divorced; a parent can disown a child (though I knew that my parents would not disown Dennis). But a sibling is forever. Of course, I knew that siblings were sometimes estranged: my own parents were estranged from their siblings. But I loved Dennis, and I didn't want to go through life without him.

On my way out of that first GID session, I had to pass through a meeting room where a small crowd had gathered. A man draped in a sheet was standing at the front of the room, and another man was on the brink of a demonstration of the proper use of the cock ring.

Another night I had a breakthrough. When I said that I felt I could not cut my brother out of my life forever, the kind woman with the braid asked, "Why not?" She said that often a person who has a sibling change gender experiences it as a death. Oddly, this was a relief to me. I hadn't put it to myself that way, but it did feel as if my brother had died and this demon was capering in front of me, trying to take his place. It would be perfectly understandable, the woman said, if, rather than be miserable, I bowed out of his life. Really? Just to hear someone say that this was possible gave me permission, and once I had permission I no longer needed to do it. I told Dennis, almost gleefully, that I experienced his gender change as a death: my brother was dead. What to me was a consolation was to Dennis deeply disturbing. "It's not very nice to be told you're dead," he said.

Mom was not in the habit of making long-distance calls—it was as if she didn't know how—but she had called me earlier in the fall to ask what was wrong with Dennis. They had talked, she said, and "he sounded so sad." I'd told her that Dennis would have to tell her himself and tried to reassure her that he was okay, that he wasn't sick. Then I wrote to Dennis. We had not seen much of each other recently. Going anywhere with Dennis left me puzzled and off guard. If we went to a bar, instead of him elbowing his way through the crowd to the bar to get us each a drink, we both just stood there, and I would suddenly realize that I was not with my brother. What were we doing there together? He was completely involved with mastering gender behaviors. I was like a sidekick—a little dowdy, a little crabby—a satellite in unstable orbit around a highly combustible planet.

Once, after leaving a bar, we were crossing a street in the Village, I in my drab blend-in-at-all-costs raiment and Dee in some spangly getup, when a taxi grazed me, and Dennis blew his top, pounding on the hood of the cab and cursing the driver.

But when I was worried about my parents, Dennis was the one person in the world I wanted to be with. Whatever he called himself, he was still of my blood, we still had these parents in common, and it was blood that was calling. So we got together to talk about Mom and Dad. Sitting in a booth in a quiet bar on the Upper West Side, I caught a glimpse, for the first time, in this new person Dee, of my brother. It was there in his eyes, like a dock I could tie up to and give in to my own sadness, which was a relief and a comfort.

Mom had had to put Dad in a nursing home, and Miles had invited her to Oregon to spend Christmas with his family. I made the pilgrimage to Cleveland to watch out for Dad while she was away, and Dennis came, too, taking the train, as soon as his duties at the church were over on Christmas Day. We met at the doughnut shop where we used to go instead of church on Sundays: St. Sno-White Donuts. He was wearing his embroidered vest and hot-pink sweatpants. He'd had a seat all to himself on the train. "No one wanted to sit with me," he said, cackling.

"What'd I do wrong?" Dennis said when he came down the stairs the next day.

"Too much makeup for nine o'clock in the morning," I said. He was made up like a hooker to go to the nursing home and help keep Dad calm during an MRI. I rubbed off some of the blush and tried to blend it in. Lynn, a woman from a home-help agency who was helping to nurse Dad, said she thought the old man had given him a funny look. Dad had always had a comment on Dennis's hair. In high school, he wore it in an Afro, which drove Dad crazy. Dee wanted to do some shopping while we were in Cleveland and had told me that shoes are particularly hard for a transsexual, because men tend to have big feet (and hands). I remembered a shoe store for big and tall girls in the arcade downtown and found it in the phone book: Mar-Lou Tall Girls Shoe Shop.

The saleslady seemed to think I was Dee's mother. He went in with a bag of cashews in his hand, and I had to cue him to put away the nuts. "He wants some ladies' shoes," I said, aware that I had already stuck my foot in my mouth. Dee picked out masculine-looking shoes, which surprised me. He liked a pair of low black leather bootlike shoes with buckles. The slip-ons looked surprisingly nice on him; he was excited about having shoes that he could kick off. And he picked out a pair of brown oxfords with thick tread. Size 11½ wide. He said he needed at least one pair that would work both ways. He kept the brown shoes on and bought two other pairs, and carried them proudly in his Mar-Lou Tall Girls Shoe Shop bag.

We went to find a favorite old bar called Otto Moser's, an ancient place that used to have pictures from the vaudeville circuit on the walls and served beer in fishbowls (thick goblets), like the ones at Baron's, my father's favorite bar, before it burned down. Otto Moser's had moved and been slicked up, but they still had fishbowls hidden away for nostalgic beer drinkers.

After a while, Dennis went to the restroom and it was only when he was coming back to the bar that I realized he had used the ladies' room. "I always use the ladies' room," he said smugly. Then he directed my attention to the shoes that made his feet look smaller and said, "Wouldn't these look perfectly natural if you saw them under the stall in a ladies' room?" There was something about his pleasure in these things that struck me as sick, as if he were getting away with something.

Living together in my mother's house had never been so hard. Over the fall, I had felt as if I were getting used to Dee a little. But waiting to use the bathroom while your brother is in there putting on makeup, and running into him in the upstairs hallway with his hair down—an alarming sight—and having him come downstairs in the morning wearing a sweater that emphasizes his new little boobs, and watching him get up from the kitchen table to freshen his lipstick, and then finding lipstick stains on the cups and glasses . . . This project of his was in my face all the time. He seemed to be building an image of himself as a beautiful woman and trying to foist that illusion on me.

Whenever the phone rang he would answer it in a new sing-song way that he imagined was feminine: *Hel-LOW-ow!* His friend from high school, Fran, came over to deliver some plates that he had commissioned for my mother. (Fran was a potter. Eventually she became a plumber and joined the pipe-fitters' union.) She had had a brush with uterine cancer, and just that morning she had found out that her cancerous cells were back and she had to have a hysterectomy. "Hey, Dee, do you want my uterus?" she said. "I don't need it anymore. You can have it." This was the kind of friend Dee needed, I could see.

They went shopping together at a thrift store. I went to a movie by myself in Westlake, driving out I-90 through the Cleveland suburbs, bleak and flat. I visited my friend Patti, the older sister of a friend from high school, and unburdened myself to her. Dee was up that night when I got home, pleased with the piles of clothing he'd found at the thrift shops. His bed was heaped. There were sweaters with eccentric sleeves and necklines, lots of scarves, some of which looked like things I owned. He said that one pair of pants was too big in the butt—"maybe they'd fit you." He'd have liked it if I'd done the sisterly thing and let him model his new wardrobe piece by piece, but I was crabby. Still, I saw a lot of the items over the course of the week, because Dee changed clothes several times a day. At night he marched upstairs and came down defiantly in his "nightie" (a word, like "panties," that I have always hated). It felt like he was appropriating my territory. I was the one who got to sit around in her nightgown.

The next morning he was off to the thrift shops again. He said he was going to see if he could find some feather boas. I went to visit another friend, Mary, the older sister of my friend Susan, whom I'd known since kindergarten. I had always been drawn to girls with older sisters. Mary had two grown daughters, and she said it seemed sort of natural to her that Dee would go overboard at first, like a teenage girl.

And that is exactly what he was like—a deranged fourteen-year-old girl. It was as if his entire adolescence was compressed into one glorious-miserable week in Cleveland.

The next day I felt kinder toward him, but he was mad at me. Finally, we sat down and talked. I was making him feel so bad that he was thinking of flying home. This was his vacation: It was his big chance to come out of the closet, to experiment, and it was important for him to wear makeup in order to let people know that *he* at least thought he was a woman. And I was so mean. At one point, in the car, when he had gotten out a little pot of lip gloss and a brush to apply a fresh coat while I was backing out of the driveway, I slammed on the brakes. I thought it was funny.

That night our mother was coming home. "It'll be the first time I see Mom," Dee said earnestly. Actually, it was the first time Mom would be seeing Dee, but I didn't correct him. I wasn't looking forward to it. Once again, Dennis would be getting all the attention, eclipsing me. I was aware of the irony that what Dennis was going through was not an enviable experience, yet I felt envy.

We got through the day. We visited Dad (Dee did not see any problem with Dad, which I thought was so strange that I couldn't even begin to process it; I thought my father's inability to grasp what was going on with Dee was the silver lining to his dementia). We went to a movie together at Parmatown, the ur–shopping mall of our youth, and it was just like old times: sitting there in the dark, chomping popcorn and swilling beer. We looked in the stores afterward. He tried on ladies' coats, "just for size" (16). Then we set out to have dinner at the Great Lakes Brewing Company. It was crowded, and we had to stand in the bar area until there was a table available. Every once in a while I'd be aware that although I thought I was with a man, he thought he was a woman. I tried seeing him as a woman: tall, deep-set eyes, narrow face. He needed some help with his eyebrows. Quiet. Terrible teeth, but he could take care of that. A delicate face with a fine complexion. My complexion. Our mother's complexion.

Finally we got a table and ordered, and I was chattering

away about something when the waiter arrived with our order. "Cheeseburger?" he said.

"That's his," I said, and picked up my fork and the thread of our conversation. But something was wrong. Was it something I said? Or was it that they had neglected to give him a slice of raw onion?

"I'm so depressed," he said. "It feels so hopeless. You say 'That's his' and don't even know you've said it."

Abruptly, I lost my appetite. I shoved the plate away. I had thought we were having a good time. "You are such a fucking pill," I said, and got up and walked away. I went only as far as the ladies' room and soon exhausted the possibilities in there. I could take my coat and go home. Dee had the keys to the car. He could pick Mom up at the airport. I could leave for New York before they got home.

At the table, Dee was counting out money. He'd asked the waiter if he could have the food to go. He said he was sorry and thanked me for coming back. I was relieved that he didn't expect me to apologize for using a pronoun that I had used for him without a second thought since I could speak. I told him he had to get some new friends, people who would know him only in his new gender. How was I supposed to know that his fondest wish was not to have the cheeseburger but to have the waiter think he was giving the cheeseburger to a girl? I had ruined it.

Dee paid for our meal and we went to the airport for Mom. She seemed a little dazed. She kept calling him Dennis or Den, and although I wanted to join her, I cued her relentlessly with "Dee." There was a moment in the living room when Mom picked up Dee's new shoes—a time-honored gesture in the house of Mom. We were always leaving our shoes lying around, and she was always squaring them away, in the closet or under a chair. She did a double take when she saw how big they were: *These aren't Mary's shoes.* Maybe she wouldn't let the thought go any further than that—just ladies' shoes that were larger than any she'd seen in the house before. It was a small domestic gesture, freighted with meaning.

Mom was very sweet to Dee. In the morning, while Dee was taking her time in the bathroom (our drive home through Pennsylvania would call for full evening makeup), I went out for doughnuts. "You look nice," Mom said to Dee when she came downstairs. They talked clothes a little, which thrilled Dee to no end—Dee was just dying to talk girl talk with some female member of the family. Mom said, "I wish I could see all your new things"—Dee's thrift-store buys were packed in two huge Hefty bags—but I was all for hustling us out the door. It was New Year's Eve, and I was going to have to drive Dee through Manhattan traffic, all the way to her door. Mom even admired the shoes—"And they make your feet look smaller"—which was just what Dee wanted to hear.

"He looks kind of cute, doesn't he?" she said to me on the way out the door. I said I'd seen quite enough of him that week and that I didn't like the competition. "Oh, you don't have anything to worry about," she said. But I did. I had to get us all the way through Pennsylvania without ramming the car into a ditch and killing us both.

THE GOSPEL ACCORDING TO P—

Victor LaValle

My brother P— plans to be America's first Filipino hip-hop star. No, the guy from the Black Eyed Peas doesn't count. P— wants to be the first, though really he'll only be the first *half*-Filipino hip-hop star because our dad is white. P— has schemed and dreamed for at least a decade now and after all this time one thing seems certain: his dream will never come true.

I didn't even know P— existed until I was ten years old. His was a name I'd heard floating around, but I never actually attached it to a human being. Like I know Napoleon was real, but when I imagine him I'm really only conjuring his portraits. My mother asked me if I'd like to spend Christmas with my dad that year, 1982. This was meant as a kind of present, I guess, but felt more like a punch in the beans. I'd never met my father. He and my mom divorced before my first birthday. And now, ten years later, we were suddenly going to spend Christmas with him?

No, I had it wrong.

Not *we*.

A real nut punch.

But I said okay, of course. I felt curious. I just wanted to see the man, you know? I'd peeked at pictures, but what do pictures ever really expose?

So my mother bought me a Greyhound ticket and packed my Snoopy suitcase with comics, snacks, and a few clothes. As I got on the bus at the Port Authority I felt scared and bold. Me, all alone, on the five-hour trip to the city of S—, my father's hometown.

As the door closed my mother gaped up at me, so nervous she clasped her hands frantically. She didn't even seem to realize she'd made the gesture. Like her body was saying a prayer her mind refused to entertain. I smiled down at her, waving, amazed to discover my tough mother could ever feel such fear.

And then the bus pulled out. I read a bunch of comics, ate my snacks.

My mother worked as a legal secretary and we lived just fine in Flushing. My dad apparently sent a little money each month (and I do mean a little). But my mom never talked bad about him for this and that saved me from having to carry her resentments with me.

If you've never been to the Greyhound bus station in downtown S—, let me invite you to keep it that way. But if you really want to approximate the experience maybe there's an open sewer line closer to your home that you could visit. Stand outside the pipe and inhale. Pretty much the same thing. It's not that the station literally stinks, but there's a whiff of deep rot all the same.

My bus arrived in the evening, exactly on time. But not my dad.

I climbed off the bus, Snoopy suitcase weighing me down enough to give me a limp, and this guy was nowhere. But I felt no panic yet. I had a bunch of coins in my pocket and this station had those plastic chairs with televisions attached, a whole row of them in the waiting room. I can't remember if the screens showed black and white or color. Who cared? As long as I had quarters I had a babysitter. But, frustratingly, all I could find were commercials! I'd flip to one channel, get impatient, turn the dial, and find another ad for some crap. Switch from that and get another. That lasted about twenty minutes and then all my damn quarters were gone.

I figured I'd call his home number. My mother had written it, and my father's address, on a white sheet of paper that she'd taped to the inside of my suitcase. I still had plenty of dimes and nickels. I wandered to a bank of pay phones. My father's new wife picked up the line.

I said, "This is Victor."

"That's Victor there?!" she shouted. "Well, Victor, how are you?!"

The lady bellowed every word even though the line was static free. Her English pronunciation wasn't the best, so she shouted to compensate. Louder being the equivalent of clearer, I guess. I told her that my dad hadn't shown up.

"He is not there? My Lord and my God! How did this happen to him?"

To him? I thought, but then I realized what she'd meant.

"You will talk to me," she said. "Until your father shows up. My Lord and my God, I will be too scared to let you hang up!"

So that's what I did, using up all my coins. Then I read her the number on the phone and she called me back. She and I probably gabbed for another twenty minutes. I answered all my stepmother's questions and she answered mine, no matter how dumb. (For instance, "What kind of name is H—?" "It's mine!")

And sometimes H— pulled away from the phone, speaking with someone else. I heard a high-pitched voice behind hers, like a yipping dog. But dogs don't generally ask questions like "Who's that?" And "Where's the Pepsi?"

When I finally asked who it was, hesitating longer than I would've expected, H— answered quietly. "That is your brother, yes? That is my little P—."

She wasn't whispering; she cooed each word.

But this didn't bother me. A loving mother? I had one of those.

Then I saw my father shuffle into the bus station and without explanation, or hesitation, I hung right up on H—.

My dad. He wore glasses that made his eyes look tiny and flat. His hair was cut short, quasi-military style, and he had a round, soft face. He looked kind of like an owl wearing glasses, though in cartoons such creatures are made to seem haughty and professorial. My dad didn't come off that way. He just looked kind of surprised. As impossible as a real owl wearing human glasses. I wore glasses too. Mine were in those giant plastic Medicare frames; his were thin wire.

After I hung up the phone I stumbled over to him and said hello. He huffed a greeting and shook my hand. His hand probably could've wrapped around my bicep as easily as it did my fingers. That's how it seemed to me. Then he took my suitcase.

"Too much traffic," my father said. I took this as explanation and apology though it really wasn't either.

Who gave a shit? Here stood my father! Walking me back to his car in the largely empty parking lot. He swung my Snoopy suitcase faintly as he walked. Its weight didn't affect his stride. I did some speed walking to keep up. He owned a nice new car, though I don't remember the model or make at all, just that it was the newest latest. He told me this with pride.

"Every year I trade in and get that year's model."

I could see this made him giddy and I didn't begrudge him.

He and I must've spoken in the car, though I don't remember most of the early stuff. Instead I remember his tone of voice. He spoke with a curled lip, half sneer and half smile. He kept his teeth gritted even as he completed whole sentences. The words strained from between his lips like a child rejecting soft food. He seemed kind of frightening and remote.

"How's your *mother*?" he asked at one point. "She still like to eat whole loaves of white bread with butter and marmalade?"

What the hell was this guy talking about?

"It's *true*," he said. "She used to eat a whole loaf in one sitting and if I brought home a pie or something she'd go *crazy*."

He sneered so hard I saw his gums. Now I felt like choking this dude.

"Said I was trying to make her *fat*. Well, I think a whole jar of marmalade will do that for you, *sweetie*."

He would return to this loaf of bread/butter/marmalade story about ten times in my three-day visit. And pretty soon one thing became clear: he still loved my mother. I mean, I'd been living with her for ten years and I couldn't remember what she'd eaten last night, forget about a decade back. Hard to fathom that he might've been there in upstate New York all these years, cradling his wounded heart, while down in Queens my mother—I don't want to be cruel—down in Queens my mother wasn't.

But before I might've asked more we arrived at his house. A fine three-bedroom home in a tarnished neighborhood. The kind of place where front lawns suffer from extreme baldness. I never knew white people could go broke like this. My own neighborhood in Queens was largely colored. We were the children of recent immigrants from the brown and black and yellow parts of the world. Most of our families were just as insolvent as the people in my father's neighborhood, probably even more so, but it was taken for granted that many of us in Flushing were on the way up. Here you could see they were falling. The white men and white women, and even the white children, walked in their yards or down the sidewalks, all moving with shoulders hunched, heads down, as if preparing for the final crash.

Seven or eight inches of snow had fallen in the past few days, a hardened layer that looked like icing on the roofs of most homes.

My father pulled into his short driveway and I watched the door of his garage rise with a button touched inside his car.

Color me impressed! But before he could pull inside, this little figure in a blue ski mask shot out of the garage and ran right up to the headlights, waving. My father braked and rolled down the window with another button.

"P—!" he shouted. "I could've killed you!"

The figure came to the lowered window. The tiniest bandit in town. Only his eyes showed: large and black and glassy, like a doll's. His lips moved under the mask.

"Don't kill me, Dad!"

My father shook his head. "Well, I don't *want* to kill you, but running in front of a moving car can have that effect."

"Not if I'm fast," the little bandit said.

My father (ours?) pointed at the dashboard. "This is an au-to-*mobile*, P—. You can't go faster than that."

Now the bandit was silent; his large eyes just blinked and blinked.

My dad sighed and pointed to me. "This is your brother."

Now the bandit looked at me. "I know."

Then our father said, "See you inside." And rolled up the power window as he took his foot off the gas pedal and coasted into the garage, until the nose pressed against the back wall.

The garage door rolled down, clanking like the Tin Man falling down the stairs. But P— didn't step under in time. He stayed out. My father opened his door, grabbed my suitcase from the backseat, and said, "Well, come on then."

But I didn't go inside with him. Instead I followed P— outside. It had started snowing. It was as if the weather was on a switch and somebody, maybe my new brother, had just flicked it. The flakes fell heavily now, landing on my glasses and clogging up my portholes. I had to pull them off and blow on them until the flakes melted. I tried wiping them dry but that didn't work, so when I put my glasses back on the whole world seemed to be melting.

Meanwhile my brother had gone down on his knees in the

snow on their small lawn. If his legs were wet or cold, he didn't seem to notice. I was ten and he seemed to be about seven. At that age enthusiasm produces a constant internal heat. He could've been running around barefoot and I bet he would've just whooped with pleasure. A snowstorm in December, that's practically number one on many a kid's wish list.

P— looked back at me and even though he had the mask on I could tell the kid was grinning. His eyes crinkled, became brighter. He was there on his knees, in front of two small snowmen. They were poorly made, meaning lopsided and lumpy, but impressive nonetheless. I don't think I'd ever had the proper snow to pull off such a feat down in Queens. You can't build Frosty the Snowman out of slush.

I walked over to my little brother—even the phrase seemed impossible, let alone the person—and he reached up with one gloved hand and grabbed mine. The cotton of his mittens had soaked through long ago, so when he squeezed my fingers it made them itch. He didn't actually pull me down, just held my hand. I finally realized what he wanted so I hunkered down reluctantly. Now I noticed that the kid wore snow pants while all I had on was a pair of jeans. He hummed to himself, a tune I didn't recognize. It wasn't hip-hop—he was too young to have made its acquaintance—but he already had music on his mind.

Once I got down next to him he let go of me and put both hands to work. He patted at the snowmen. Their deformities differed: abnormally huge head for one—Frosty the Hydroce-phalic Snowman? The second suffered from scoliosis, apparently. But otherwise they were pretty similar. Same general height, same snowy complexion.

"That one's me," P— said, shouting over the winds blow-ing up the corridor of the street. Then he pointed at the other. "That one is you. I made them both."

My brother had even fashioned arms out of twigs for the snowmen siblings. The outer arms of both were raised high, like the snowmen were cheering. But the inner branches were lowered, reaching out across the few inches' distance. They were touching.

My little brother looked up at me.

"See?" he said. "They're holding hands."

My first thought, after he said this, consisted of only three words:

What. A. Pussy.

And that moment pretty much sums up my entire time with my brother. For the next three days he attacked, a campaign for closeness, and I consistently beat him back. They had a third bedroom in this house, one used for aunts and uncles visiting from the Philippines. A spare little place with a thin mattress and a window you couldn't actually open. A guest room. I hid myself in there when I didn't want to yap with P——.

On the big morning my dad gave me a Hess truck toy. One of those gifts you buy at a Hess gas station when you've run out to grab some milk at the last minute and then remembered you've left someone off the gift list.

We went to church as a family. P—— and I sat beside each other at the end of the pew, probably even traded a few jokes, punches, and all that. But I kept looking past him, past my stepmother, to my father. Was he a religious guy? Did he enjoy the church service? I really couldn't tell. My father wore the same impassive expression any time he wasn't speaking. He could sneer or he could stare; that seemed to be about it. My brother kept trying to interest me, but I wasn't studying him.

Then the three days were over and my dad brought me back to the bus station. We made it early so he took me inside and we sat at two of those plastic chairs and watched television side by side. We hadn't spoken about much; chitchat about my interests always led back to my mother and that loaf of bread. Even at breakfast, as my stepmother served us toast, I noticed that she only kept jelly—no marmalade—in her fridge.

And by evening I'd returned to the Port Authority, met my mother when the bus let me off, and told her as much as I could remember. I didn't mention my father's story about her. At our apartment, my grandmother had a welcome-home dinner prepared and we all ate together in front of the television. Then the phone rang in the kitchen and my mother went to get it. When she returned to the living room she wore a big smile and said, "Someone wants to talk to you."

To my surprise I actually ran to the wall where the phone hung adjacent to the fridge. I picked up the receiver and said, "Hello?!"

"Hi, Victor!" my brother said.

If you'd been there I swear you would've seen my legs deflate. "Hi, P—," I said.

"How was the bus trip?" he asked. But before I could even answer he said, "I cried when Dad took you to the station."

I flopped backward into a seat by the kitchen table and then my little brother went on and on and on. The kid could talk! Even more so than when I'd been with him. Except for little burps of agreement I didn't actually have to say much.

"After Dad came back he took Ma and me to the Wegmans. We got a lot of Pepsi 'cause me and Dad like Pepsi.

"Then the whole drive back Dad was playing that music. Big band! Big band! He always yells that at me when I tell him to change the channel.

"He let me hold the steering wheel when he pulled into the driveway. I was sitting on his legs."

By then I noticed this hot feeling in my neck. I felt it in the hand that held the phone.

Envy.

That's what it was, though I didn't understand it at the time. Shared taste in beverages; familiarity with musical preferences; and shared rides in daddy's lap. Weren't they just the dynamic fucking duo! My heart slowly closed to P— and I didn't try to stop it. I sat there in the kitchen and imagined my face becoming as unreadable, unreachable, as my dad's. To pass the time on the phone I grabbed some sheets of paper and a pen and scribbled little images of monsters or cubes or stick figures. And then a half hour passed and I told my brother I had to go. He asked when he could speak to me again. I said to try me in a week.

Two nights later he called again.

And this went on, honestly, for almost *two decades*.

A polite relationship, even friendly. I can sort of excuse the childishness at first because, well, I was a child. But what about when I turned sixteen or seventeen? How about when I hit twenty-five? Still nothing changed, I must admit. He and I might talk for hours—about his burgeoning love for underground hip-hop, for instance—but I really never returned the affection. Each time we hung up the phone it was like he stopped existing. He even stopped being a name and just became an area code I dreaded seeing on my caller ID.

Twenty years after my brother's first call I was thirty years old, living as a writer in New York; it was 2002. I got a call coming from the familiar area code. I let it go to the machine, my pattern for years by now, expecting my brother's voice leaving a three-minute message where he rambles on about plans to get his touring ideas to 50 Cent when 50 comes to town, but it's my father on the machine instead. So, yeah, I picked it up.

"Dad?"

"This is your father," he said quickly, no real inflection to any of it. "Having a little trouble with your brother."

And even then, a grown man, I felt myself recoil. This was about P—? God*damn*. What's a motherfucker got to do to get a little attention?

I didn't say this.

"Police were over here yesterday. They had to sub*due* P—."

"Subdue him for what?"

I heard my dad shift in his lounge chair, he and the furniture groaning with age.

"Well, this may surprise you, but not all has been well with P— for a very long time."

"I didn't know," I said.

"He's been preaching. The Gospel according to a nudnik. He's been indulging this nonsense at the *mall* and on *street corners,* but most of all here at home. Aren't we lucky?"

"For how long?" I asked him.

"I'd say about six months. P— comes into the house and you know he's quite big by now. Much bigger than your stepmother or myself. Much bigger than *you,* I'd guess. He comes into the home and he pushes us around. I finally had enough so I called the cops."

Of course he'd grown. Two decades' worth of sprouting. And yet all I could imagine was that seven-year-old face hidden by a blue ski mask, smacking my father and stepmother around.

My father said, "Two officers came over at first, but they couldn't handle him. Even when they used their *tasers.* It was quite a show. His mother was crying the whole time, of course. Praying to *God* and hurting my ears. Finally two more officers arrived and the four of them got him down. Handcuffed him and took him to the hospital, straightaway. Just thought you should know."

I've only spoken to my brother once since then. A quick phone call after he'd been released the second time, but before he went back in for a third.

He was actually pretty calm and lucid when we spoke. He hardly mentioned the cops and the tasers and the hospital. Instead he was back to his dreams of hip-hop stardom. He'd come up with a few stage names and he listed them for me: Deciduous Trees and the Filipine Fanatic.

He liked the first one because deciduous trees lose their leaves, but next year they bloom again. They always come back. I smiled when he explained this to me because I realized one thing we had in common: sometimes our ideas are too damn complicated.

As for the second name, Filipine Fanatic, that was *not* meant ironically.

He mentioned that the worst part of the incident with the cops was that he'd missed the G-Unit tour that month so he'd never been able to reach out to 50 Cent. I'd grown up in Queens and he wondered if I might have some way I could get the tape to Curtis Jackson. We spent about an hour on just this issue but eventually he accepted I did not know the dude at all.

Finally, I just broached the subject of his . . . episode? Snap? Freak-out? What would he call it?

He was reluctant to answer. In his silence I thought back on how many times I'd ever made the first move and called P—. The number of fingers on one hand; in twenty years, it was hardly more than that. I didn't flatter myself that I might've saved him from his condition. Instead, I just marveled that keeping distance from my brother all this time hadn't brought me any closer to my dad. And now P— was hidden away behind a barrier I don't think I'll ever be able to scale.

He said, "When I'm telling people the Gospel it's not me. When those cops jumped me, it wasn't me. It looked like me, but it was God inside. When I get like that I'm just a vessel. God wears me like clothes."

He hadn't sounded so happy, so loved, in years.

WHO WILL SAVE US NOW?

Nalini Jones

In the winter of 2003, my whole family traveled to Bombay to see my maternal grandparents for Christmas, a pleasant season of bright days and cool nights. My father, who has visited India regularly since marrying my mother, relished the chance for sun and rest. His job, producing music festivals, required long stressful days, and though in his late sixties, Dad refused to delegate many of the demanding physical tasks that most other producers would never touch. He enjoyed working with the crew—crawling under dressing room trailers to rig plumbing hookups or dangling over the windy edge of a three-story stone fort roof to hang banners. At the end of the summer season he was exhausted, and he had spent the autumn pursued by colds and flu bugs. No one imagined anything out of the ordinary when we saw Dad, asleep in his chair on the sunny terrace of my grandparents' home, enjoying the blast of Indian heat in December.

After New Year's I was to remain for another month, working on a book. The night I saw my family off at the airport, my father was running a slight temperature—a mild reaction, he was sure, to the bone-chilling air-conditioning of the "deluxe" overnight bus that had conveyed us to Mangalore the week before. His fever lingered even after my parents reached the States, but he spoke to me merrily on the phone, wondering about the cricket match and the state of the leftover pork my grandmother had already served for several days running. On January 6, feeling increasingly weak, he was taken for blood tests to see if he had contracted dengue fever. By the next morning, still waiting for the test results, he was unable to stand. My mother wrote in an e-mail that his legs "just buckled" beneath him; he decided to go to the hospital. Sometime on the eighth, the numbness in his arms and legs reached his chest. He "crashed," my husband told me when he called to say Dad was in intensive care, on a respirator. I asked if Dad was dying and he told me firmly to come home.

Planes to the West depart only at night. I spent the day making fruitless rounds to various airline offices, whose flights had all been oversold in the busy holiday season. By evening my bags were packed and I had taken up my position in the airport, begging to travel standby. The mosquitoes had settled into a drowsy cloud in a corner and light throbbed in the sky when I finally slid onto an Air India flight. We took off during the early morning rush hour and I remember spinning up and away from gridlocked roads, panic and triumph both surging in me. I was too anxious to sleep. Dancing girls wobbled like slow tops on the video screen, making me ill. The airline's iconic maharajah, painted on the curved wall of the cabin, bowed so deeply that I imagined him tumbling over and breaking the sharp tips of his mustache. Again and again I asked the flight attendants: *Where are we, exactly?* I wondered whether I would miss seeing my father by a matter of hours.

We stopped in London for fuel but New York–bound passengers were not permitted to disembark. I could not call my sister to find out if Dad was still alive. The cleaning crew tidied the uppermost layer of rubbish from the cabin and I was left staring out through the smeared oval glass at a gray sky. I unfolded and reread the letter our family doctor had faxed to the airline, confirming that I must reach home as soon as possible. "Her father is very acutely ill with a loss of ability to breathe."

I will never forget how Dad looked the first time I saw him, trapped inside a thicket of cords and monitors. His eyes already seemed wider—with shock, perhaps, but also with the effort of taking everything in. For months he would communicate only with his eyes.

That memory of Dad—powerless, beseeching—still breaks over me like a terrible wave. But alongside it is another: my brother Chris looking up hopefully when I stepped off the elevator, and my sister Radhika jumping up to greet me. "You made it!" she said, without a hint of reproach for all the hours they had waited alone. "You're a hero!" As if anything had changed by my coming. As if simply by being together, we were saved.

Growing up, rescue opportunities were thin on the ground. I occasionally spoke for my sister, eighteen months younger and inclined to watchful silence as a child, but that was more in the spirit of service. I sometimes felt a throb of concern for Chris, five years younger, which inspired such safety measures as refusing to let him climb onto the porch roof with me, ordering him to step back before I struck a stolen match and lit a mound of kindling in the middle of the woods, and insisting he hold on tightly as we were lifted high out of the water on the nose of a speedboat bumping over Atlantic swells. Once he toddled into the deep end of a pool and I grabbed the cloud of his hair until my cousin hauled him up, shocked and spluttering. At best, a rescue assist.

No daring exploits, no epic adventures. On the superhero spectrum, we made a disappointing showing: a trio of gangly, asthmatic kids, too bookish for their own good.

Recently Radhika sent me a passage from Zadie Smith's novel *On Beauty*. Kiki is the mother. She is black, her husband is white.

"Kiki was vulnerable to compliments concerning her children, but she was also familiar with them. Three brown children of a certain height will attract attention wherever they go."

I understood Radhika's delight at once. Our mother is from India and our father is white, making us three brown children of a certain height. Did we attract attention? Of a sort, I suppose. We spent a decade of our childhood in a predominantly white suburb of Cincinnati where we must have stood out—though perhaps not as much as I felt at the time. I was all legs and glasses and self-conscious retreat, so painfully attuned to difference that I quivered like a tuning fork in the locker room when the "American" girls began to shave their legs before I did. I rode the wave of that awkward stage straight through the eighties; if there were compliments, they didn't penetrate.

But the cultural dissonance between my household, with its echoes of India, and my classmates' homes—well-stocked with Atari, fried chicken, and the inestimable advantage of experienced older sisters—was not actually at the center of my childhood. My attention was usually turned inward, to the small world I created with Radhika and Chris. We had games and codes so meticulously developed, so peculiarly refined, that even our adult selves cannot always elbow their way back in. I remember scraps: elaborate schemes to hoist Chris onto a large brown goat; a pact to dispatch pesky neighbor children; long negotiations to name dogs and horses we would never own; and a bizarre practice in which we dumped out all our Halloween candy on a bed and divided it, piece by piece, so that each child had an even store. The candy ethic sometimes carried over to the equitable distribution of babysitting money, too, and protracted trading sessions between Radhika and me for dolls in international costume (Spain was valued most highly for her red-tiered flamenco dress, touched with black lace, and Little Dutch Boy was ranked low because one of his wooden shoes was always clattering off).

I was the eldest; I must have been the architect of these rituals, which prized, above all, staying even with each other. But my purpose in orchestrating them is no longer clear. Of course I was caught in the usual web of sibling rivalry. Radhika—I had been told by one of the nuns of our school—had an IQ a few points higher than mine, making her a genius and me a lucky girl. Chris was the youngest and a boy; early in his life, Radhika and I took to calling him "small but mighty one" for the power he exerted over the household, which was all the more maddening because he hardly seemed to notice it. But I was also acutely aware of the moments when I excelled and they did not, moments that might satisfy some small competitive hunger but that ultimately left me wishing that we could all win every race, every game, every contest. I couldn't entirely enjoy scoring a goal if Radhika was having an off day on the soccer field. I made sure Chris reeled in at least one fish on summer expeditions; I could take more pride in my own catch once I knew he hadn't been left out. I was unusually reluctant to see any one of us overtake the other in any realm, even when age or talent or luck might naturally have divided us. I did not want to feel divided.

However our internal dynamics may have shifted, to the outside world we were a united front: three brown children in a mostly white landscape. When the landscape turned brown, our connection grew even stronger. Our Indian family is Catholic, with everyone named for saints, and my grandmother was a professor of British literature with a decidedly Western sensibility. Set down among other Indian families, we three shrank into a single confused postcolonial unit, moving set-faced into groups of laughing children and then drifting back to our dad, who didn't care how ignorant we were about Divali. Our own cultural bewilderment found expression in his perennial wonder about how late dinner would be served. In Bombay, we were suddenly three fair children, speaking American English with accents that made our family laugh, listening to the Hindi our uncles and aunt and mother tossed over our heads in a linguistic game of keep-away. We did not need to explain to one another our pleasure in sleeping beneath mosquito nets, our fascination with autorickshaws, or the deep, sonorous tones of our boredom during televised cricket matches. We asked inconvenient questions during encounters with beggar children, emptying our uncles' pockets. We wrote dutiful descriptions of our days in travel diaries and we did not talk about the nights of our departures: everybody crying in the parking lot, everybody giving one last tight hug.

Still, we argued, we whined, we tattled. I knew how to tease Chris until he ran to the kitchen, howling for justice, and Radhika knew how to madden me with silence and a smirk. But as I grew older, I felt a new reluctance to fight with them. The childhood we'd shared was happy but difficult to explain to kids who spent their summers at the pool. When we weren't set down in Bombay, we were set loose backstage at one of Dad's festivals, rolling empty instrument cases around, stacking towels in dressing rooms, and digging through ice for the best sodas. No one at school knew what we meant when we puffed our cheeks out like Dizzy Gillespie. Nobody cared about the drumsticks that sweating musicians sometimes presented to us on the way to the dressing room. When we spoke of drivers named Big Dave and Bigger Dave, we spoke only to each other.

As adults, even when that sort of understanding about each others' lives eludes us, we find it difficult—and distasteful—to break the habit of alliance. And so, despite our differences in temperament and situation, we don't really argue. Instead we deal in tactful withdrawals. One of us slips out of range, distant and polite, until everyone comes curving back toward each other as though by elliptical orbit.

We have never failed to return to each other, never spun away entirely. But I am particularly vulnerable to these periods of estrangement. I find them profoundly unsettling, as though some crucial tether has been cut and I am in danger of drifting. My sister and brother were once my daily companions; now they have become a kind of gravity, a steadying that nothing else provides.

* * *

Even after Dad was stabilized, the doctors seemed uncertain. Our recent visit to India had exposed him to polio and malaria, and he was kept in isolation until the infectious-disease team had conducted their examination. Finally he was diagnosed with Guillain-Barré, a syndrome usually triggered by a common virus that lingers in the body long enough to provoke the body's immune system to attack itself—specifically, to destroy the nerve cells that connect to muscles. The result is paralysis. Dad stopped breathing because he could no longer move his diaphragm.

"Guillain-Barré is a lightning strike," a doctor told us. "It's just bad luck." The syndrome runs its course in two or three weeks, but nerve cells grow back very slowly, by which time muscles have atrophied. The damage takes years to repair. Dad would have to relearn every muscle movement, we were told, from breathing and swallowing to the complicated motions required to take a single step.

For almost two years, Radhika, Chris, and I tried to manage whatever the crisis tossed up: Dad's care, our mother, the house, his job, the bills. Here is the way I want to write about that: one of us could not bear to be in the hospital for more than a few minutes at a time, another could not bear to leave. One could comfort my mother, another seemed to agitate her. One updated a vast network of friends about his condition, another tried to sort out insurance claims. I want to write sentences that balance what was unbalanced—sentences that smooth over the frustration, fill the silences on the phone, soften the demands we made on each other. I want to protect us all.

So what I remember best is a summer night when Radhika, Chris, and I found ourselves a trio again, without friends or aunts or cousins, without my husband or Radhika's fiancé, without our mother. We collapsed in my house, trying to reply to that day's crop of encouraging messages, but we could not summon the requisite grace. We could not be optimistic or courageous. We were alone and so we allowed ourselves to say what seemed weak or ungrateful in the face of people's attempts to cheer us: Things were bad. Very bad. Only bad. Unending in their badness. Eventually the word *bad* began to sound funny—which reminded us of the day Dad had tried to blink a message to Chris. Since he could not speak or make gestures, he had learned to communicate with his gaze. We held up alphabet boards and watched carefully as his eyes moved from one letter to another, spelling out words. S. O. B. E? R. E?

"Sober, Dad? This is sobering? Yes, it is."

Dad blinked furiously, no, and tried again, losing his place in the spelling again and again, until finally he closed his eyes and half smiled—his head, always on its pillow, seeming at rest. At last Chris had understood: SO BORED.

By then the three of us could not stop laughing. We laughed at the lunacy of depending on Dad's spelling. We laughed at the hideous watches the family of the junk jeweler in the bed next to Dad's had given us. We laughed at the postponement of Radhika's wedding and at the shocking understatement a girl had used to break up with Chris: he was not, she said, sighing, in a very good place. We laughed at the way I had abandoned my half-written book just weeks after the contract with the publisher was signed. We laughed at the absurdity of knowing how to suction our father's chest, and at the amount we paid for parking at Mount Sinai, and at the story Dad used to tell us about his first day of army training. His company had been divided into religious groups to determine their holidays. At the end, one kid stood alone, announcing he was a druid. A few weeks later, the kid claimed a druid feast day had arrived and took a religious exemption on the day they tested the gas masks.

I want to write about how badly Radhika, Chris, and I needed a druid holiday too, how long it would be before we'd have one. On that night, laughing together was the best we could do.

I was the one who couldn't leave Dad's hospital room. I don't think there's any virtue in that kind of vigil; I experienced it as an incapacity. I could not stand to think about all the hours he had to spend alone, able to feel his limbs but unable to move them. He was utterly trapped in his body, and I chose to be trapped in the hospital. I flung myself into the ward and stayed there, thin and sallow, five or six days a week.

Radhika came and went gracefully. She kept Dad company when she could and did not seem shattered when she couldn't. But Chris, who lived a few hours away, stayed away for two or three weeks at a time. When he darted into town, his visits were usually brief.

At first I didn't notice his absences, and then, for a long time, I wasn't bothered by them. We had all come together in a new and terrible way, a different kind of family, forged in the waiting rooms and corridors of hospitals.

A few months later I was with Dad the first time a specialist took him off the respirator and encouraged him to practice breathing on his own. The test lasted only a minute, but Dad's eyes widened as though he were drowning. I held his hand and kept my promise to the specialist, urged Dad to keep trying. But I wanted to grab the tube myself and reconnect him to the machine. On the way home I kept thinking of the other half of the druid story, the part Dad never told us: when all but the druid kid were shut up in a room and the gas came pouring in. I pulled over on the highway, my car rocked by the motion of other cars speeding past me while I took deep mouthfuls of air.

My panic soon gave way to exhaustion. The doctor had explained that Dad would learn to breathe again in increments, first one ragged minute, then two, four, ten, fifteen, thirty. I thought of Dad's terror and thirty minutes seemed impossible. I lost the power to imagine him breathing again, every day and every night, and breathing was only the beginning. Next would come swallowing; after swallowing, an endless struggle to move arms, legs, chest, back, hands, and feet. I was furious this had happened to Dad, furious I could do nothing to help, furious that the doctors could offer no better remedy. My fury at the insurance company might have blotted out the sun. And in a slow, bitter turning, I began to resent my brother for all the days he had stayed away.

I don't know what I hoped to accomplish when I called Chris. Was I trying to keep score, weighing my visits against his? Did I imagine we could lay out all the hours in the hospital between us—all the pain and loss and struggle—and divide them as though we were children again? What would have been even, what would have been fair? Did I lash out because I wanted to save Dad and could not? Did I believe my brother could? Maybe I just wanted someone to save me.

No matter, since I didn't bother to explain. I felt we were beyond such banalities by then; of course I was lost, of course I was exhausted, of course nothing was fair. Of course Dad wanted to see Chris, of course I did too. But with all that I left unsaid gathering in my throat, the words burst out of me, blunt as bullets. *You need to visit more. You need to take more days in the hospital.*

I can't, Chris said, his voice stiff as something scarred over. He made no excuses. But in that moment I remembered the way he had looked as a child—his round open face, his shock when I teased him—and I knew he was telling me the truth. I thought of the way he always hesitated before ducking his head and pushing himself into Dad's room, and I was instantly overcome by the simple wish to spare him. I hated to see Chris suffer and of course he was suffering. Of course we all were.

This is not the story I want to write. I'd prefer a story in which we rescue each other, though I suppose we didn't need full-scale heroics. We were not torn apart, like so many families in crisis. We did not openly argue. But Chris must have heard the strain in my voice, the accusation, as surely as I heard the coldness in his answer. We know the ways in which we quietly failed each other.

We've never spoken about it, just as we never spoke about the great distances that loomed before us every time we left India. But I think these silences are rooted in understanding. I quickly realized that I was condemning my brother for what we all felt: it was unbearable to see Dad diminished or in pain. Of course I see aspects of myself mirrored in my brother and sister; when I am angry with them, I am angry with myself too.

We could not save each other; we could not save our parents. But we had Dad's example to follow: not just his determination to be well, but the surprising grace with which he accepted his illness. What strikes me now is that Chris gave me the room to save myself. I don't want to be the person who called my brother that night, resentful and demanding, and because he has never cast that shameful moment up to me, I believe he sees that. He has given me the chance to be someone better, someone more generous. In the story I would like to write, I've given him new chances too.

The state of emergency has lifted. Dad has learned to breathe again; to swallow, eat, and speak; to sit up; to walk. My daughter has learned alongside him. She does not know he used to fingerpick guitar, so she will not miss hearing him play. They are both careful on stairs.

My husband, one of two brothers, was comfortable with the idea of a single child. We were happy, he pointed out soon after her birth, and busy in our careers, and getting older. At first I was able to speak calmly about my reasons for wanting a second baby, but soon I heard my voice rise in panic. *What happens when we get sick? Who will be with our girl?* The night when Radhika, Chris, and I holed up in my house came back to me, and I could not imagine raising a child who would not have that moment of grace: laughing, besieged but not alone.

Our second daughter is six months old, and already I see the small ways the girls rely on each other. I know they cannot keep each other safe or happy. But in the moments when I feel wounded or lost, the moments when I feel beyond rescue, I think of Radhika and Chris. They don't always make me feel better, but I am most powerfully myself when I remember that I am their sister, that the earliest connections I've known still hold.

I still think of the kid who called himself a druid; I'd like to write his story too. Imagine him: a smart-alecky kid, made to stand before a lisping sergeant who had never heard of a druid. Imagine the other soldiers, all those boys lined up at Fort Dix in the winter of 1960; imagine what was coming, all the ways they would need to be saved. Imagine my father among them, young and thin and watchful, his face so much like my brother's. He will refuse to bear arms; he'll be assigned every miserable duty the sergeant can contrive; he'll collapse with pneumonia—a pale shade of what's to come forty years later during the long cold months on the respirator.

But on that day at Fort Dix, he was grinning when the druid was ordered to fall in with the Protestants. Nobody guessed that the kid had just saved himself from the gas. The whole company shouted with laughter and everyone thought that was the end of it.

THIRTY-EIGHT QUESTIONS
I'VE ALWAYS WANTED TO ASK
MY BROTHER STEVE BUT
NEVER HAVE UNTIL NOW

T Cooper

From: T Cooper
Sent: Sunday, August 30, 2009
To: Steve Cooper
Subject: Hello & Questions Finally

Hey Steve,

How you doing? I hope you had a really good weekend. I did; I got a new (street-legal) dirt bike last week, so I've been riding it on trails and doing errands with it and stuff. It's a really fun bike, a 2001 Yamaha XT225, so a little bigger than my last one, which was a 1999 Suzuki DR200. I think you rode that one once when you came to the city years ago, right? Zippy.

Did Mom and Dad tell you I'm living on a farm in upstate New York now? It's only about two hours from the city, so we'll be back and forth to the apartment, too. It's the best of both worlds. I was actually wondering what you thought about sending me a gun for up here. I gave you back that .38 hammerless handgun years ago, because I always felt uncomfortable having it. But I'm thinking it's so isolated here, it might be smart to have one for, I don't know, rabid, patchy coyotes attacking the dogs, or even crazy country dudes who might come on our property and hassle us or the kids. What do you think, might you have something to lend me that you're not using right now? (Don't mention to Mom and Dad, I don't feel like dealing with all the anxiety.) I can't imagine actually going out and buying a handgun. I would never do that, and the last time I drove cross-country alone, I remember you were trying to foist some gun on me to put under my seat for the trip.

Also, I'm finally sending those questions I told you about. They're attached to this e-mail as an MS Word doc, and you can just go ahead and answer the questions you feel like answering in the spaces between the questions. It's not light stuff. I mean, I've never asked you about some of these things before. I hope it's not too much.

Let me know how things are. Talk to you soon.

Love,

T

From: Steve Cooper
Sent: Monday, August 31, 2009
To: T Cooper
Subject: RE: Hello & Questions Finally

T,

I'm doing okay. I have been working a lot of overtime and the heat out here is making things very uncomfortable to work in. The new dirt bike sounds like a lot of fun and I hope you enjoy it. Just don't get hurt. I didn't know you got rid of the handgun. Dad must have it or maybe it's in my gun safe somewhere. If I can find it do you want it back again? If you do I will send it up to you. I will look for it later and let you know if I have it or not. If I can't find it, I have another one for you. It's a .357 pistol Dad gave me to hold on to, four-inch barrel and stainless, not aluminum, so it's a little heavier and can also shoot the lighter .38 cal, or you can load it up to .357 Mag. I think that would be perfect for you to have in the house. Either way I wouldn't tell parents about anything.

I briefly looked at the questions you sent me and found some of them kinda interesting. I have no problem answering them but want to spend some time on each one, so it will take me a week or so to finish it and send it back.

So what is going on with the wedding? Are you two going to do it or not? In any case take care and I will talk to ya soon.

Love,
Steve

From: T Cooper
Sent: Friday, September 18, 2009
To: Steve Cooper
Subject: Update?

Dude, any progress on those questions? I have a deadline coming up, and I'd love to make it if I can. Hope you're good—

Thanks,
T

From: Steve Cooper
Sent: Tuesday, October 13, 2009
To: T Cooper
Subject: Questions Reply

Hey T,

Sorry it took me so long. Better late than never, right? Anyway. I hope it's what you needed. I also attached a couple pics from a

SWAT competition I did with some of the guys. We competed against a bunch of full-time SWAT teams from all over California. I was the sniper, that's why I have a different rifle. Only had to fire four shots. They gave me a description of the suspects before our run, and I had to pick and identify the targets by memory through my scope. They had the targets set up with photos of the heads on the targets. I only could shoot at the head from 100 yards. Easily done from the prone position. We placed eighth or something I think. Also a pic my partner took of me on the horse at the beach.

Love you,
Steve

From: T Cooper
Sent: Wednesday, October 14, 2009
To: Steve Cooper
Subject: RE: Questions Reply

Thank you! I'm eager to look at them, and I will as soon as I can find some quiet time. Thanks also for the photos . . . I actually have one of them already, the one of you patrolling the beach on the horse, it's up on the "family and friends" wall here at the farm. That competition sounds cool.

I know it was a pain, all these questions, but I do appreciate it.

Love,
T

From: Steve Cooper
Sent: Wednesday, October 14, 2009
To: T Cooper
Subject: RE: RE: Questions Reply

Didn't have a chance to call today because of work, but I'm glad you got the e-mail because I was having problems sending it to you. Anyway, let me know if you need anything else. Also, I will call you in the next few days to talk about the gun thing.

Steve

THIRTY-EIGHT QUESTIONS, THIRTY-SIX AND A HALF ANSWERS

1) What do I do? What's my profession, would you say?
A "writer" of course.

2) If you weren't a police officer, what else would you be doing, do you think?
I would probably still be teaching SCUBA diving, since that's the only thing that I really knew how to make money at before I became a cop. I might've even become desperate enough to get back into music, but I don't know if I could have supported myself with that.

3) Here's one of my strongest memories from when we were kids: You were spear-fishing and I was tagging along. As I recall, I was on the beach, and you were out in the water, and then you came in and there was blood all over your foot and ankle. You had been tracking a fish while floating on the surface and when it swam under you and you released the spear toward it, your foot got in the way and the spear went through your heel, like in between your Achilles tendon and the bone. Did this really happen, or I should say, do you remember this incident? And if it did happen, or something like it, is my memory of it somewhat close to yours? I think my memory of it must be exaggerated. Tell me what happened, from your perspective or memory.
Well, you're correct about where the spear went through my foot, but this is how it happened. I was spear-fishing off the big rock with a spear I had made from a wooden broomstick

or dowel, can't remember exactly which. I had attached a steel three-prong frog sticker tip I had gotten from the hardware store for $3, and a rubber sling on the other end. I was using the old yellow longboard that Dad got for me at a garage sale on the road when I was around ten, I think. Anyway, when I was paddling in and got to shore into about knee-deep water, I put the surfboard under my right arm and the sling part of the spear around my right wrist and started to walk out of the water. I was hit by a large wave and knocked down on my right side. One of the prongs with a barb on it stuck me on the inside of my heel where you remembered correctly, but the spear was lying on the sand with the surfboard trapped between me and the spear. Every time I tried to get up I couldn't because the spear was holding me down with the board on top of it. That's all I remember. I don't really know how I got out of that mess with the waves hitting me and all but I do remember that I had to really work that barb around for a while before I could get it out. It hurt like hell.

4) What's one of your strongest memories of me? I'm going to guess it's the story of when I was about two and tried to stab you with a diving knife. Or was it an abalone knife? And did I really try to stab you? Did you really kick me across the room? And why was I holding an unsheathed knife in the first place?

Yes! That is it. I don't know why that is such a strong memory but it is. The way I remember it is we were fighting over something, I can't remember what, and there was an abalone iron of mine that you picked up. I remember you were crazy, really mad, and I could see you were way out of control, even for me, and you came at me with it over your head when I was lying on the floor or on a bed, so I just push-kicked you. I think I nailed you on your chest and you went flying into the closet door. I also remember a time when you stabbed me with a pencil in my thigh but I don't think I did anything that time.

I think we both just stood there looking at the pencil sticking out of me. I was surprised that a pencil was sticking out of me and I think you were surprised that you did it.

5) Do you really—in complete honesty—think I was trying to kill you?

Thinking back, no. I think I just saw something in your eyes that told me you didn't know what you were doing. You used to get so mad sometimes.

6) Do you think about being adopted often? How often? Every day? Once a week? When does it come up, if ever? Did you think about it more when you were younger?

I don't think about it at all now, but I remember when I was about sixteen I had a long talk about it with Mom and Dad. I don't really remember what my issue was, but I remember I was having issues. I also had a talk with them about eight years ago about my biological parents because I needed to know about any inherited medical issues. At the time I was having heart problems and had some plaque in my heart and the doctors wanted to know if I had a history of that in the family.

7) Do you think the fact that you were adopted and older and I was biological and younger has made a difference over the years as far as how we were raised, how Mom and Dad treated us?

No. At least I don't think it was an issue with me. I think you always felt that they liked me over you, but I think you were wrong.

8) Do you know how I found out you were adopted? Our cousins were in town visiting, playing with me on my bed, and one of them, I think it was L—, was like, "Steve's so cute, I want to marry him," and I was like, "You can't marry him, he's your cousin," and she was like, "No he's not. He's

not even your *real* brother." I was really upset and cried. Mom and Dad said they told me that you were adopted a lot before, but I guess things sink in when they sink in with kids. **Do you remember when you realized you were adopted? Did Mom and Dad tell you, and what do you remember of that? What did you say? How did it make you feel?**

No. I never knew that happened to you. L— was such a bitch. She still is, I think. As far as what I remember or when they told me, I have no specific memory of it. It's like I just always remembered that I knew it. I think they started telling me about it very, very young. The story they tell now is that when they told me I said to them, "You mean that you stole someone else's baby?" I don't remember saying that, but I was too young to remember.

9) Did you want to find your birth parents ever? Is that important to you, or was it? What do you know about them? I know next to nothing. Mom told me one thing about the time she almost met your birth mother at a hotel in down-town L.A. or something. She didn't end up talking to her face-to-face, maybe just Aunt Ricki and Dad did. Do you know this story, have you heard it?

Wow! I never knew that. They never said anything to me about it. As far as me ever wanting to find my birth parents, the only time I did was so I could know any medical history. Other than that, it doesn't really matter to me.

10) How do you think your being adopted affects how you feel about your daughter not getting to know that you're her birth father? Do you think she'll ever learn that you're her biological father?

That one I think a lot about. I mean at least five times a day. I think it's a very different thing to be adopted as opposed to [my daughter] M—'s situation. M— will learn one day soon that I am her real father and that I was lied to about her existence. I don't want her to think that I was part of any of the deception she had to endure. I want her to know I loved her from the day I saw her for the first time, and I never gave up trying to be in her life.

11) Do you think you'll have more kids?

I would like to, but at the rate I'm going and considering the issues I have with trust, I really don't know if I ever will. I think about it every day.

Okay, I was almost finished and then I had to come back to this and add a couple things. I think part of the reason I haven't found someone else and had kids is because of my learned lack of trust in people, and the other is that I still love [M—'s mother] N—, and think I always will. Part of the reason I can't fall in love with anyone else is because I feel somehow I owe it to M— for some weird reason I don't understand. I hate N— for what she has done, but I still love her. One day I will try to fully explain if and when I ever understand myself.

12) Now that I have two (step)children, I'm seeing first-hand what it's like to raise kids who aren't related to you biologically. I'm not sure I could feel more for them or that I could be more influential in their lives if I were actually related to them biologically. But then again, I don't have my own biological kids, so I have nothing to compare to. I think maybe you can't know unless you have both adopted and biological children, like Mom and Dad—or Brad and Angelina. Have you ever asked them (Mom and Dad, not Brad and Angelina) if they felt a difference in their feelings toward you and me? I don't think I'd ever ask them that, but do you ever wonder? Have you ever asked them, or wanted to?

Actually, T, I did have a talk with them about you and me. I don't remember when, but I did. It was when we were kids and always fighting; I think I wasn't even nine years old. I had issues because I needed more attention I guess . . . LOL. They sat me down and told me that they loved us both the same and that I couldn't have all the attention and I needed to try to understand. I doubt I understood but it was something that I would have figured out eventually with a little age.

Also, I have seen some research on how stepchildren and biological children are loved by parents. Basically it said that men who marry into a family with children who are not their own biological children are much less likely to develop the kind of bond or love like they would if they were their own biological children. It also said that women are different in that they can and do develop a bond with children who are not their own.

13) We used to call you "King Jesus." Well, we still do sometimes. Do you think that title was earned at all?

I suppose it was, but I really can't pinpoint it.

14) Do you think we would've been closer growing up if we had been less than seven and a half years apart in age?

That's a good question. I think because we had different interests and different friends that we never could be as close as we could have been if we were just a few years apart.

15) Would you say you were a happy kid?

Yeah, I think so. Although I definitely would change a few of the choices I made.

16) Would you say I was?

I think you were. I'm probably wrong though, since you are asking the question.

17) Are there ways in which you think you are more like our parents than I am? What ways?

Hmmm . . . I will have to think about this more.

18) Are there ways in which you think I am more like our parents than you are? What ways?

See above.

19) Do you think we're similar in any way? When friends of mine have met you, they have said that it seems like you and I are very different from one another, in fact couldn't be any more different. Have you had a similar experience?

I'm a Republican, so of course we are different, LOL! Seriously though, I don't really know. We live across the U.S., and I very rarely see you, and when I do see you, you usually do your own thing. I mean it seems you don't really want to do anything with me and don't seem like you want to spend time with me; I'm a little afraid to upset you and I don't ask why. I suppose I am to blame as well and just accept the status quo. Actually I have become quite good at accepting things I don't like and feel that I really can't change anything. If that makes sense.

20) Did you ever walk in on Mom and Dad having sex? I don't think I ever did.

Thank God I never have either.

21) Do you think you'll ever end up shooting somebody and killing them in the line of duty? Do you think about that prospect, and if it ends up happening, how do you think you'll deal with it? How will you feel?

I never really talk about that with you, do I? Yes, I probably will, given the line of work I [am in] and that I [am] in L.A. As far as thinking about it? Yes, I think about it, but probably not in the way you do. Every time I get out of the car or off the horse when I stop someone, every time I go through the door on a search warrant, and every time I go to a call (when I used to work patrol), the last thing I say to myself is, "Front sight, trigger press, follow through."

Those are the three most important things in a gun fight out of the seven elements of marksmanship that an old SWAT dog, Scotty Reits, taught me in the training we do twice a month. In fairness to your question though, I have almost shot at least six or seven people, and at the last second they either fell down after being shot by another officer, or they dropped the gun before I pulled the trigger. Or I didn't have the angle to see the gun in their hand and another officer in a different position did see it and shot.

As far as dealing with it? I have no problem shooting someone who is trying to kill me or another innocent person. I don't believe in the death penalty either. Defending yourself or someone else by shooting and possibly killing the bad guy, in my mind, is way different and I wouldn't think twice about what happens to them. They are shit heads who deserve what they get.

22) Would you say I've "been there" for you over the years?

Yes and no. I never really come to you with any of my problems, so how could you be there for me? On the other hand, when I did come to you with an issue, then I would say definitely yes. What comes to mind is the M— thing. You were the first person I went to and you were there for me. I never said thank you. So, thank you.

23) Would you say you've "been there" for me?

Probably not. Partly because I don't think you ever needed or came to me with anything, but I would be there if you did. By the way, the few times you have confided in me, I've always honored your wishes and never told Mom or Dad.

24) How many times have you actually thought about killing yourself? I was scared you were going to do that when I was younger. Was that an empty concern of mine?

I don't think I was ever really serious. Just a silly young boy. I view killing oneself as cowardice.

25) Did Moon Zappa really ask for your autograph when you were in your punk rock band? Did you sleep with her?

Yes she did. It was my first and only sincere request for an autograph, and I told her that. It was after I left Symbol Six though. I was playing at the Country Club in Reseda when I was in Rapid Fire and we were opening up for Poison. The Steve Vai band opened up for us. Steve Vai was Frank Zappa's guitarist and was trying to have his own band and Moon went to see him, so she was hanging out backstage with us. Also Dweezil Zappa came onstage and played a song with Steve Vai.

26) Did you get a lot of tail when you were in that band? I remember going to a few shows at the Whisky and Troubadour and stuff, but I was really young. It seemed like there were a lot of girls around. Did you do a lot of drugs, or just pot and lighter stuff like that? I had a tiny crush on your guitarist Gary, the one with the limp. Or am I imagining the limp?

That's funny. I never took to the girls around those places and never hooked up with any. I didn't do anything but pot then and I didn't even like it, but I was young and stupid and thought I needed to fit in sometimes. Gary did have a limp. He had something when he was younger that gave him that permanent limp. I don't think it was polio but it was something like that. Actually I had a beer with Phil, our drummer, a month ago. They got the old band back together to do some shows because I guess there is a following for the eighties punk bands still. I haven't talked to him since then but will probably go to see them play.

27) Why did you quit the whole music thing? You were really good.

Thanks, but I never thought of myself as being good at much. Sort of a jack of all trades but master of none. I quit mainly because of Dad. He would always harp on me about getting a job and I needed to do something. I tried to do both for a while when I had the Marina del Rey Divers store, but I guess I finally succumbed to Dad's pressure and it was difficult to do both. And also, my band, Rapid Fire, told me I had to make a choice. I think that was the moment I chose. It's all or nothing with me and I almost never pick up the guitar anymore because I'm afraid I won't remember how to play. I want to remember how I used to be able to play.

28) Why didn't you come to my high school or college graduation?

I was there at the [high school one], you idiot. Billy Crystal spoke at the ceremony.

29) I remember going to your graduation from SaMo High, and I remember Mom and Dad saying they didn't think you were going to graduate for some reason. What was that reason, or were they joking? That always stuck in my head because it seemed like you were always getting into trouble. Did you get into something really bad that jeopardized your graduation? I feel like your diploma holder thing was empty when you received it, but you walked in the ceremony anyway . . . Was that true?

I did graduate, but because I didn't have a tie on, the asshole almost didn't let me get my diploma that day.

30) Remember when you picked me up from middle school one day? I think it was when Gammy was dying and in the hospital. I think you were with [your girlfriend] Lisa at the time, so she was in the car, too. I think you took me to Westwood or something . . . Do you remember that day at all? If so, tell me what happened, because I just have an image of me leaning between the two front seats and us waiting on Wilshire to turn left onto Veteran. I don't remember much else—except that you never picked me up from school, so it was a different day for some reason.

I honestly don't remember any of that. I do remember sitting next to Gammy in the hospital and holding her hand. The next day she died, but we were not there. That's all I remember.

31) Do you remember when I almost cut my two fingers off while carving pumpkins? Where were you when it happened? I was about seven, so you were around fourteen or fifteen. Mom and Dad rushed me to the hospital in downtown L.A., but I don't remember where you were. What was your memory of that whole thing? I don't think I came back home for a couple days after surgery. Who stayed with you?

I think I remember you doing it but I don't remember if I was there when you did it. I can't remember what happened after that.

32) Have you ever read any of my books? If so, what have you thought of them? I can't remember your saying anything either way.

I got through about half of *Lipshitz Six*. But I couldn't really get into it so I put it down with the intention of finishing it later. I still plan to. I really liked *The Beaufort Diaries*. I still can't understand how you came up with the whole bear thing. It was a metaphor for something; I just haven't figured that out yet. I view books kinda like music. It doesn't matter what other people think of it because you made it how you wanted it to be and it was for you. If other people like it and it makes money, great. If they don't like it, fuck 'em, because you didn't write it for them anyway.

33) Where did you pick up the whole squeegeeing-the-shower-doors thing after you shower? Do you always do it? When did it start?

That's a funny one. I can't believe you remember that. I got that from Lisa years ago. I don't do it anymore because I have shower curtains now. But if I did have glass, I don't think I would do it anymore. Back then I was crazy clean with the house because Lisa got on me all the time for that, but she didn't clean anything herself. I became a clean freak I think because I hated spending hours once a week cleaning, so I would just clean everything right after I made a mess so I wouldn't have to do it once a week. Now I'm a mess. Mom had to convince me to let a maid come last week because there was a thick layer of dust all over because I never clean anymore. Outside of work I'm actually lazy now, if you can believe it.

34) When did you start reading *Soldier of Fortune* and being interested in guns?

I think I was around thirteen and it was a kid thing. I haven't read one of those things since. I think part of the gun thing was because I liked to take things apart and put them back together again, and guns did that for me. For the past fifteen years guns have been part of my everyday life because of work. Believe it or not, I hate cleaning guns now, and every time I have to clean after a training day, I get mad. We have to shoot all three kinds of guns that I have to shoot, rifle, shotgun, and pistol, and then I have to go home and clean them all that night.

35) I wanted to be like you very much when we were younger. Did you know that?

Really? I didn't know that. I didn't think you liked the same stuff that I did.

36) Why do you think we don't talk a lot now? Do you think that if we lived in the same city we'd see each other more than we talk now?

I don't know exactly why, but I would like to see and talk to you more. I just get the feeling you don't want to and have other things to do. Maybe I'm guilty of that too. I think if we lived closer we would make time, but ultimately I have no good excuse. Actually I'm a bit of a recluse and don't talk to anyone much. It's not just you.

37) What's the most fucked-up thing you remember from childhood? I always think about your friend Shane who died when he snorted that rat poison, thinking it was cocaine. What did you think when that was happening, when he was dying in front of you? And when he initially offered you the powder to snort, too, why didn't you do it? (I've never, not once, tried any drug that you snort because of that incident.) Do you ever think about him and that moment when you guys found the stuff?

I don't know what I was thinking when that happened. All I remember is that I was scared, scared for Shane, myself, and I didn't fully understand what was happening. I don't know why I didn't do it. I didn't really know much about cocaine, but if I didn't really like pot I think I knew I would hate cocaine, I guess. I used to think about him a lot for about ten years after that, but I don't really think about it much now. Mostly I would think what his life would've been like if he hadn't died, and if he would've had a family. I never really thought about what would have happened if I'd tried it because I know what would've happened—I would've died, like him. So I didn't try it and I didn't die. That's about the extent of it. I'm really glad you never tried that shit. No one needs any more monkeys on [his] back than life already gives us.

38) How was it for you answering these questions? I feel a little exposed asking them.

I think it was kinda weird. Partly because some of the questions were things I thought you already knew and was surprised to find out that you didn't, and partly because some of the things I never knew. I wonder what you, Mom, or Dad would say to some questions I could come up with. I don't have any in my mind right now, but I bet I could think of something.

I read these questions when you first sent them to me, thinking I would gather my thoughts before I wrote anything. Then I let time get away from me until you reminded me. Then I was a little afraid of my memories. I wasn't sure I wanted to think about some things I haven't thought about since they happened. It makes me sad to think that one day we will be gone and no one will know who we were, what we were, and how we lived. I would like M— to know about me one day and remember who I was. Oh well.

By the way if you haven't figured it out by now, you should understand that I never lie, except to criminals to get them to talk, and even then I don't like doing it; I just haven't figured out how to get what I need from them sometimes without lying. I'm not very good at expressing myself in writing, so most of my answers are matter-of-fact or maybe even cold sounding, but it's all the truth.

It's hard for me to get close with anyone these days because I'm a scaredy-cat of losing them. That's why I don't have pets anymore, and that's probably why I don't stay in relationships for very long. I feel best now when I help victims of crime. Or get a child away from parents who have their children hold drugs for them. Or better yet, put a person who preys on the weak away for at least a day in jail until a sympathetic jury feels sorry for him and sets him free to start the process all over again.

Anyway, I love you very much and would like to talk to you more.

Steve

From: Steve Cooper
Sent: Friday, October 16, 2009
To: T Cooper
Subject: RE: RE: Questions Reply

Happy birthday, T. I hope you have a good one.

So did you read my answers, and were they what you needed?

Love,
Steve

From: T Cooper
Sent: Monday, October 19, 2009
To: Steve Cooper
Subject: Thank You

Hey Steve,

Sorry it's taken me a bit to get back to you. Thank you so much for taking the time to answer all of those questions. They will indeed work perfectly for the story, which is turning into a sort of Q&A interview/discussion between siblings. I think it is revealing and touching in a lot of ways.

Your answers were interesting to me, and yes, in some cases surprising. It's hard to think about some of that stuff, especially when you look back at the years (I just turned thirty-seven, if you can believe it) and think about time lost, not necessarily wasted, but definitely gone.

I've been thinking a lot about what you wrote about our not seeing each other much—I've always thought it was *you* who didn't want much to do with *me*. Sometimes you say mean (or meanish), provocative things when we're together, so I just assume you're annoyed at having to do family stuff, or see me, whatever it is. I think we do have some things in common, even though we're different in a lot of fundamental ways, but I guess I thought you didn't like me very much. So that's where I assume you don't want to hang out beyond the obligatory. I know I'm to blame, too, because I do sort of just do my own thing. But I think you're that way, too—and definitely growing more reclusive over the years. Anyway, I do hope we get to spend more time together.

I *did* have a pretty happy childhood! I was just wondering how you'd answer those questions. We were so fortunate in so many ways, but there are of course some ways that were challenging. Probably nothing you don't already know. Anyway, I do trust you and always have, and I hope you know you can trust me, too.

That said, thanks also for the birthday wishes. Also, since you asked, we *are* planning to have the wedding next summer, probably in late July, up here at the farm. So I hope you can come. I'll let you know the date far in advance, so it'll be more likely that you can arrange to make it.

Oh: the heater situation. I found out you have to get a hand-gun permit to own a pistol here in New York State. So I guess I have to settle for a rifle; what do you suggest, just a .22?

Okay, gotta go get some work done. I love you, and I'm really glad that you were amenable to doing this. I guess I feel closer, even through just those few questions, and even though it was over the Internet.

I'm also curious, since you brought it up, what you are planning to do with the M— situation? Are you seeing N— at all, is she letting you see your daughter? I know her birthday's coming up next week; how old is she going to be now, and do you think you'll get to celebrate with her?

Talk to you soon.

Love,
T

TRUE BROTHERS

James Cañón

> I don't believe the accident of birth makes people sisters or brothers. It makes them siblings. Gives them mutuality of parentage. Sisterhood and brotherhood is a condition people have to work at.
>
> —Maya Angelou

The morning of October 27, 2002, our father summoned my four brothers to a "very important" meeting. It wasn't the first (allegedly important) meeting he had called, but it will go down as the one in which our family's size doubled. I didn't attend. I was excused because I was living in New York, 2,500 miles away from home.

According to Hernán, the five of them met at an inconspicuous cafeteria in Ibagué, the small Colombian city where my siblings and I were born and where my parents still live. We children all migrated to larger cities in search of work and to better our lives, or just start new ones. They sat together in a circle, and over cups of hot, strong coffee, Father, a newly converted Christian, began with a confession: "I've had many extramarital affairs over the years." He paused and gazed around the table, waiting for my brothers' reactions. Nobody blinked an eye. We had known all along about his misadventures. Most of them had involved his employees (he favored personal secretaries and finance managers), but there were also a few restaurant waitresses, a neighbor, and even a hospital nurse who cared for him after his tonsillectomy.

Father went on, first with a justification—"We're humans, and humans make mistakes"—and then with another confession: "I'm afraid that some of those affairs resulted in babies." Another pause. A new gaze around the table. The same lack of reaction from my brothers.

Years before, on separate occasions, two of Father's all-time favorite employees had suddenly "resigned" from their jobs soon after they started showing pregnancies. Both times, Mother and we confronted him about it, and each time he denied the accusations, naming them completely false, defamations with no foundation whatsoever.

But that was Father then. Now he was a saintly white-haired man, a newborn Christian, someone who had repented his sins and asked Christ to come into his life. If he had any celestial aspirations whatsoever, he had no choice but to own up to each and every one of his mistakes. Those mistakes (his own choice of word) were full-grown people, two of whom had been named after him: José Miguel and José William. The final count, however, was larger than any of us had anticipated.

"Six," Father said without warning, while Hernán poured some milk into his coffee and Carlos reached out for the sugar bowl. "Six," while Oscar tapped his index finger on the table, while Pepe shook his right leg. He said, "Six," and suddenly we, the Cañón Five, became Eleven.

A heavy silence fell around the table.

"Six, huh?" Oscar, the eldest, managed to say at last, addressing his own lap. He was visibly affected by the news and could barely look my father in the eye. Father assented, then he went into detail about our new half siblings. Each was by a different mother; all but two had been given his surname; there was only one girl in the bunch; one of them was dead: a communist guerrilla killed in a battle with the national army. A bus driver in Bogotá, a college student in Medellín, a singer in Barcelona . . . As my father went on, my brothers considered, privately, whether they would like to meet their half siblings. I, for one, would agree only to meet with my half sister. I had always wanted a sister to bring a little balance to our family.

"So we know all the truth," Oscar said, interrupting Father's speech. "Now, what do you expect us to do?"

"All I want," Father replied, adopting a martyred attitude, "is for my children, all of them, to meet and love one another."

"I won't do that," Oscar retorted. "I appreciate your coming clean after all these years. I really do. But at my age I have neither the desire nor the intention to meet *any more* half siblings, much less to start building family ties with them."

Twenty-nine years earlier, during a "very important" meeting called by our father, a teenage Oscar had heard a different number. "Four," father had said while Oscar tapped his index finger on the table. He'd said, "Four," and suddenly Oscar, the only son, had become one of five.

I met Oscar on Christmas Eve of 1973. He had just returned from New York, where he had lived for two years. I was five years old and until then had known only three siblings: Hernán, born in 1964; Pepe, born in 1967; and Carlos, born in February of 1973. Oscar was introduced to us simply as our "new" brother. New as in recently created, as if he were a newborn, although he was older than Hernán by nine years. I was never told that my father had been married before meeting my mother and that Oscar was the result of that union, so I assumed he was my full-blooded brother. I learned the "half" part by osmosis, the same way I later learned that before going to New York Oscar had been jailed for being a communist, or that my parents weren't married because Father's marriage to Oscar's mother was indissoluble, or that my brothers and I were bastards.

Oscar was eighteen at the time, a handsome, long-limbed young man who could swear in more than one language. He was different from most people I knew. He dressed carelessly, wore tan leather sandals on bare feet and uncombed hair down to his shoulders. Sometimes he wore round glasses high on the bridge of his nose, which gave him a deferential look that belied his rebellious nature.

He brought Christmas gifts for everyone and laid them around the elaborate nativity scene that my brothers and I had put together a few weeks before. We weren't allowed to open our presents until after dinner—one of our father's many stiff rules. When permission was finally granted, my brothers quickly seized their presents and tore apart ribbons and wrapping papers. Not me. I wasn't that kind of child. I arranged my four presents in a particular way. It had nothing to do with the size or shape of them, or with the degree of flashiness of the paper in which they were wrapped. I ordered them from worst gift to best gift based on my instinctive assumptions. I was the kind of child who enjoyed saving the best for last. At breakfast, for instance, I used to cut each piece of toast into four small squares and eat the smallest ones first, leaving the biggest for the end. And at dinner I always ate my vegetables first, as if to get it over with, saving the less nutritious things (often deep-fried) for last as my reward.

A new set of clothes, I thought as I began carefully unwrapping the gift from my father. He always gave us, as presents, "practical" things (a pair of shoes, towels, even bedsheets), the kind of things that he should have provided us with anyway. Just as I expected, that year he gave me a pair of jeans and a shirt. While folding the gift wrap for reuse I looked at my father and smiled, then quickly moved on to the next gift, my godparents'. They were an older, childless couple who lived in a large and beautiful house around the corner from ours. They were conventional and conservative people, but when it came to presents they were utterly unpredictable. They never called or visited, but they religiously sent me three presents a year, one for my birthday, another for my saint's day, and one more for Christmas, and they could be anything from a basketball to a personalized embossed stationery set. For Christmas of 1973, they gave me a Mickey Mouse metal lunchbox with matching plastic thermos. The third present I opened was from my mother. Unlike Father, Mom always gave us toys, jigsaw puzzles, or games. It was her way of compensating us for Father's practicality. That year she gave me a bingo game set, which came with a rotary cage, twelve reusable bingo cards, token markers, and a play board. After carefully putting all the parts back into the box, I went up to my mother and gave her a big resounding kiss. My last gift was from my new brother. It was wrapped in gold paper and had a hand-tied red ribbon and a small white card with my name written on it. I had the feeling that it would be something special, something I would really like. I was right. It was a fancy picture book, the first non-school book I was ever given. I can't remember the title of it even though I read it several times. I recall, however, that it was about a Chinese army of bright and thoughtful children who helped the police catch a band of crooks. The story ended with the children, lined up and in green uniforms, singing a hymn before a red flag and a picture of Mao Zedong. Everything about that book was new to me—China, the Chinese-looking cartoon characters, Mao, communism—and therefore aroused my curiosity. The next morning I had many questions for Oscar, and he had as many answers for me, answers I could understand although he spoke them in his adult, embellished language.

Until that day, I had always dreaded being asked "What do you want to be when you grow up?" I refused to consider something as impossible as growing up. But after meeting Oscar, I found myself hoping to grow up fast so that I could be just like him.

Oscar stayed only a few days with us. He had to go back to his city that was not my city, back to his mother who was not my mother, back to his fatherless life, which, ironically, is how my life *with* my father felt back then. But he stayed in our lives. He called regularly and visited us during summer and winter college recesses, and later on he even lived with us for a year, my childhood's best year.

When I think of 1979, the year Oscar lived with us, two things come to my mind: the smell of incense permanently coming out of his room, and the English songs he played on a portable cassette player in the early afternoons. I used to sit on the floor outside his door with my eyes closed, breathing in the aromatic smoke from sandalwood incense sticks while imagining what the lyrics of those melancholic songs meant. Eventually he would notice me and invite me inside. He would stop the music and talk to me for hours about sexuality, death, divorce, drug use, alternative lifestyles, and even some philosophical "isms," like atheism and existentialism. We became very close despite our age difference (I was ten, he was twenty-three) and despite our personal wants (I couldn't wait to have facial and pubic hair and my Adam's apple sprouting from my throat; he couldn't wait to finish his thesis and become a psychologist).

Unlike my other brothers, Oscar never questioned my already meticulous grooming habits, my dislike for roughhousing and sports, or my hypersensitivity to conflict. And unlike them he never called me a "faggot." During the year he lived with us, I felt safe and fully accepted. But when he left, an onslaught of self-doubt and denial invaded me, and the question about why it wasn't okay to be the way I was began to haunt me, eventually torturing and afflicting me to the point of depression. I withdrew from friends and family. I was confused and scared and more than once contemplated suicide.

In January of 1985 Oscar moved back to our city, where he'd been offered a good job. He was already an accomplished psychologist and was married to a great woman with whom he had two children. I was sixteen and had grown facial and pubic hair, but my Adam's apple still wasn't visible (it never would be). I was an acceptable student and a respectful son who easily conformed and agreed to whatever was expected of me. I had few friends and was careful to keep a gender balance among them. I dressed well—at least better than most of my friends— but in my closet there was no room for bright-colored or tight clothes, which in Ibagué were stereotypically associated with gays. Hernán, Pepe, Carlos, and I had put a distance between ourselves, which allowed us to coexist without much fighting and allowed *me* to feel safe at home. Except for eating meals, we did nothing together. And we rarely saw Oscar. He was too busy settling into his new job. The Cañón Five were like the fingers of an open hand: five separate appendages that, though firmly joined together at one end, lay side by side oblivious to each other's existence.

In June of that year, Oscar called the first-ever Cañón Five meeting. The purpose of the meeting, he said, was to talk about our emotional coldness and detachment toward each other. With that in mind we met at a restaurant on a Sunday afternoon. We didn't talk about the things that had driven us apart. Instead, we focused on finding ways to reconnect and draw strength from each other to build a real family. We decided we'd meet once a week for fun activities, such as movies and games, that would help us to get to know each other better. Before the meeting ended, Oscar asked us how we felt about our father. We were reserved at first: Father was "all right," "nice enough," "tolerable," "could be worse." But once diffidence was set aside, our real opinions emerged, and our meeting turned into an outlet for venting our frustrations. We agreed that he was authoritarian, self-centered, harsh, difficult, cold, and a womanizer on top of that. Also, he was quite irascible, and his temper had become worse. I had grown terrified of him. I stayed away from him whenever possible, and when I ran into him, I avoided his gaze altogether, because I was afraid he would be able to see in my eyes that I was gay. But perhaps the most unpleasant thing we realized about our father was that *he* was the main reason my brothers and I had grown apart. Sure, siblings become self-sufficient as they reach a certain age. Sometimes the distance in a sibling relationship may be caused by jealousy or the closeness that one shares with the parents. In our case, however, our father had deliberately kept us apart by praising us individually while complaining to each of us about the rest: "They don't have what it takes to make it in life." "They're not nearly as bright as you." "They can't play soccer to save their lives." "You're my only hope." "If it wasn't for you . . ." Each of us had relished, in secret, his preferential status, unaware of his cunning plan to keep us divided. After this realization we were too angry to be afraid, and so when Oscar suggested that this time *we* should call a "very important" meeting, we immediately agreed.

In preparation, Oscar drafted an agenda that included all our complaints. We considered several different ways in which Father was likely to react after being confronted, for the first time, by his own sons. He would emphatically deny having had any extramarital affairs or that the child his current secretary was expecting was his. He would agree that he was irritable, but would add that a short temper was synonymous with high standards and perfectionism, which were great qualities. He'd argue that he never did any chores around the house because he had an agreement with our mother—a couple's agreement with which we had no right to interfere. To the claim that he never had any time for us, he would say that he spent most of his time working, so that we wouldn't endure poverty and privation the way he had. And he might give me permission to pursue whichever career I chose (he had used all his influence to persuade Hernán to go to business school instead of aviation school, which was Hernán's true passion, and recently he'd been putting a lot of pressure on me to study veterinary medicine instead of advertising). In short, Father would try to negotiate with us: he'd give in on the littler things and deny the important things. After all, he was a natural entrepreneur who approached everything in life as if it were a business deal.

We summoned him to a restaurant that had a small but charming private room on the second floor. We began the meeting with a laundry list of what we considered the lesser complaints: he never remembered our birthdays, he never attended our games or school plays, he was aloof toward us. We stated each claim with care but also with assurance, gaining confidence with every word we spoke, with every grievance we got off our chests. Our father listened attentively and without interrupting, looking calm and collected. But the moment we moved on to the serious matters, he started looking more and more ill at ease, and by the time Oscar brought up Father's sexual affairs and the likelihood of his having illegitimate children, his expression changed altogether. He hadn't seen that coming. He had raised us to never discuss problems or ask questions. Our duty as sons was to do as we were told and comply with his many rules. He was happy for us to show initiative as long as it didn't cause us to question his decisions. Questioning him was a sign of disloyalty. He had raised us to keep our frustrations inside because confrontation threatened a family's unity and harmony. But Father hadn't raised Oscar, and now Oscar was determined to have his say.

Oscar had been brought up by his mother in a loving and supportive environment, without excessive rules or restrictions. Since he was a child, he'd been encouraged to explore and discuss his fears and feelings, his anger and resentment. He'd grown up believing in the right to speak his mind and act without restraint. Oscar, unlike us, was whole. He had noticed the way we feared our father, the way we behaved when he was around. How quiet we were. How withdrawn and apprehensive. He had noticed the amount of pressure each of us felt to be perfect, the lengths to which we went in order to avoid confrontation. How we lied compulsively to keep our father from becoming upset. How we always covered up our shit like cats to avoid being disciplined.

Oscar went on. Father grew restless, didn't know what to do with his hands. I could see him thinking about a quick way out of the situation, but he was so staggered he couldn't think straight. He moved in his chair, clearly uncomfortable, vulnerable, growing smaller. Not for long, though.

When Oscar finished talking, he clasped his hands over the table and tilted his head, signaling to Father that it was time for him to respond. Father was quiet for some time, mulling over his reply while looking down, as if he were ashamed. At length he stood up and, in an arrogant, contemptuous voice, said, *"Cría cuervos y te sacarán los ojos,"* a famous Spanish proverb that literally translates as "Raise ravens and they'll pluck your eyes out." Then he walked away.

For the next quarter hour we sat there speechless, looking at each other, shaking our heads, biting our nails. Had this meeting been necessary? I asked myself. What had we gained? What had we lost? I was beginning to think that perhaps Father was right, that we were ungrateful sons turning against our benefactor, when Oscar said, "It's never easy being confronted. What he said was his way of avoiding having to admit his mistakes and seeing himself in a bad light." Oscar paid the bill and we exited the restaurant in silence. Father was waiting for us inside his Ram Charger across the street. He flashed his lights and beeped his horn when he saw us. I froze up. Oscar reached out and took my hand in his. All the strength I needed was in that simple gesture. Hernán, Pepe, and Carlos joined hands with us and we started down the road, all five of us linked together for the very first time. Father followed us for a few blocks, then rolled down the window and kindly asked us to get in the car.

Our legs remained firm.

Our grip stayed tight.

And we kept going, moving away from our father. We are siblings by chance but had become brothers, true brothers, by choice.

BEN HERMANN FOREVER

Nellie Hermann

I grew up with three older brothers: Joseph, ten years older; Jeremiah, eight years older; and Ben, five years older. I was shaped by maleness: drawn to it, comforted by it, and kept out of it by something invisible I didn't understand. When I was ten, Joseph suffered a psychotic break and has been mentally ill ever since. Five years later, Ben died of a brain tumor, this less than a year after we lost my father to the same disease. Now my brother Jeremiah and I are left: he is the brother I always knew the least and with whom I had the least in common.

Do you see my dilemma? I have too much to say. There are so many essays to write and none will separate out. How can I write of my brothers without writing of everything, of all that we had and all that we lost? It's too much; I've only been asked to write one essay, but it seems an impossible task.

The story of my siblings is the story of who I am. I suppose this is true for all of us. How do we write the stories of who we are? If there were only one answer, life would be very, very boring.

I read George Eliot's *The Mill on the Floss* recently with a room full of women. At the center of the book is a sibling relationship: the main character, Maggie, and her older brother Tom have a fierce bond that is, though at times troubled, formative and unchangeable. Maggie's love for Tom as a young girl is obsessive and fawning, and no matter how he behaves toward her as they grow older she continues to seek his approval. A few women in the group found this off-putting and strange, one woman calling it "incestuous"; they were bothered by it and wondered why Maggie didn't leave off loving her brother so much when he treated her cruelly and seemed to want nothing to do with her. My gut reacted before my head could. I asked these women if they had older brothers; the answer was, across the board, no.

I had the exact opposite response to the sibling relationship in the book, which is to say that I found it one of the more accurate portraits of the younger sister/older brother phenomenon that I have read. I said as much to the group, and across the room a colleague nodded vigorously. She absolutely agreed with me, she said. She has two older brothers.

There is something particular and precious about the obsessive love a younger sister can have for her older brother, and people who have not experienced it themselves often cannot understand it. In this group, those of us who had older brothers argued simply that the way Eliot portrayed it is the way it is, and a gulf between those of us with older brothers and those without opened up and lingered until we moved on to speak of something else.

I had three older brothers, and in the very beginning my obsession was with them all. "The Brothers"—as I called them then, for they so little needed distinguishing—were one entity, one figure to be devoted to. Attempting to be close to them, I almost drowned twice before the age of nine. Once in a swimming pool and once in the ocean, I walked toward the three of them and suddenly found myself without ground under my feet.

My death was never as imminent as it felt to me, of course; my parents were nearby, my brothers were there. I was not in real danger of drowning. Yet for me it was full-blown terror: struggling, gasping, flailing, swallowing, the dreaded dark water tugging at my limbs, pulling me into its depths. And each time, the rescue was the same—an unattributed hand, an arm and torso belonging to one of my brothers, plunging in to grasp me and pull me back to the glorious world of light and air.

I think in the family lore it was Jeremiah who rescued me; I'm pretty sure he would take the credit if it were offered him. In reality I'm not sure if all three of my brothers were present at both of these incidents. But even now I think of my rescuer as one body made up of the three of them, a creature forged from the melding of their identities.

This is a fair metaphor, I think, for how it felt to be the youngest and only girl at the bottom of the ladder of children that my parents made. When I was very young, my brothers were one fascinating creature, a mythical being whose light was reflected onto me from a very great height. They played with me as if I were a toy, an inanimate object to be manipulated: wind the handle and watch where it goes. Jeremiah was the ringleader of mischief. He held me upside down by my ankles over the second-floor banister; he slipped Tabasco sauce into the Fig Newton he knew I was about to eat; he created the game he called Blintz, which entailed rolling me up in a blanket and then rolling me down the stairs. Ben went along with Jeremiah but was never cruel—he made me his slave when we played Monopoly, having me polish his hotels and crisp his bills; he stole my turn at Nintendo by telling me that if I jumped down a hole I'd find a new level. Joseph never seemed to care about torturing me or keeping me out—he was either too old to find it funny or it was just not in his nature.

They had something together that I could never have—a confidence, a sense of belonging together, a swagger. Despite their great differences they shared a commonality that I could not penetrate. They could shed their shirts and play basketball in front of our house, they could go fishing and share bedrooms and build forts and only provisionally let me in. They were never provisional with each other—I was the only one who had to know the password to be let into the lair. Once granted passage to a bedroom, I would sit quietly and observe the BB guns being shot from the window rather than shoot one myself.

I was forever railing against the injustice visited on me by my brothers, frustrated by the fact that I could not be a part of their gang. But it was never lost on me that to be granted passage to the lair, however provisionally, was a great honor, that no matter how silent or sidelined a participant, I was lucky to be present. I carried always the curious feeling of wanting to belong, of not belonging, and also of being comforted that I did belong. No bully could ever get away from my brothers if he messed with me, and this thought made me feel proud and protected. My brothers were the definers of my world.

Very quickly though, as I grew, the two elder brothers drifted away (both of them gone to college by the time I was ten), and I only had eyes for Ben.

Ben had always been the one I felt closest to, because of his age but also because of his demeanor, which was sweet and always gentle, always humorous and calm. Without the two other boys around I began to feel, just the tiniest bit, with a palpable sense of hope and nervousness, that I could just maybe be his friend. Without the other two, I could have Ben's attention: he'd *have* to hang out with me. I knew I was nowhere near as fun as Jeremiah and Joseph but tried to suppress my feelings of inadequacy, reveling in the luck of being left behind with Ben. I followed him from room to room, I put my feet in his footprints in the snow. We rode the bus to school together and he performed for all the other kids, rolling his lips over his teeth and playing his old-man character, which had them rolling in the aisles. It was an act that was familiar to me, and I wore this familiarity like a badge of honor.

I was in fifth grade and Ben a sophomore in high school when Joseph came home from college psychotic; he went into the hospital and emerged altered, never the same. Ben and I weathered the storm as if on a raft built for two. We didn't speak about what was happening, for neither of us had the words, but having Ben nearby in the midst of the chaos allowed me to feel just a bit more anchored. I had a partner in the most confusing moments: someone for eye contact over a strained dinner table or in the hallway of the mental hospital. We could wrestle with each other in the backseat of the car and feel that not everything was changing.

When I was in seventh grade Ben was a senior, and he drove me to school every morning: a daily thrill. He taught me how to choose a car to follow on the highway so that you wouldn't get pulled over for speeding; how to drive on the wrong side of the road; how to steer with your knees. When we got to school he let me in on a secret: sometimes, instead of going to his first-period class he would go to the health center and take a nap. The nurses were so charmed by him that they let him do this whenever he pleased. I was obsessed with him by this point, obsessed with the rule breaking, which I could never pull off, obsessed with the calm way he moved through the world, with the way he seemed to see through every situation to its humorous core.

I believed him to be some sort of genius. I still do.

It stays with you for life, this feeling for the older brother, showing up again and again in your relationships with men, in what you look for and what you are drawn to and what you cannot stand to lose. It is a part of you as fundamental as blood, an element that shapes you in ways you can't be you without. And if it is thwarted—that is, if something happens to that older brother, or to you, or to your relationship, such that the love is twisted or lost—then it becomes even more powerful, a bond you are forever looking for but can never find again, a love that whispers through every relationship you have. George Eliot, it turns out, was estranged from her brother as an adult when she began living with a married man, an estrangement that no doubt provided the impetus for the intensity at the core of the book.

Ben died of a brain tumor when he was twenty-one; I was fifteen.

When one is fifteen one does not have the capacities that one might develop at a later age—certainly Ben and I never spoke about the meaning of life or discussed philosophical concepts. What does a girl talk about with her older brother at that age? I don't know. I guess we didn't talk much at all. We joked; we gestured; we laughed and rolled our eyes. Mostly, I observed. I watched Ben; he was always who I watched. In the wake of his illness I felt all my language dry up and blow away.

We were a reserved family, not known to say "I love you" at the end of phone calls. A different girl who felt the same way about her older brother would no doubt have constantly let him know how she felt. I worshipped Ben quietly and powerfully, from depths unreachable by language. Is it possible that he didn't know how I revered him? I think he must have known, but I'll never be sure.

For years after he died, I would not speak of him. Speaking was a form of acceptance, and I would not accept. It is still hard; perhaps you can detect the lilting here, the way I can't seem to linger on him, can't quite bring him into focus? It is getting better—I am attempting it, anyway, now—but still, fifteen years later, the impossibility of rendering him, of adequately portraying the force of my feeling for him, the anger I carry for the loss of him, is a power that silences me. It makes for a very tender spot under my skin that interferes with my life at times, even in my relationship with my remaining healthy brother, Jeremiah, whom I treasure for himself, though being with him often makes me think of Ben.

I suspect that everyone who has lost someone has such a tender spot, and that younger sisters who lose their revered older brothers have ones that feel very much the same.

Let me try again.

Greenwood is a small music camp on a former country estate in Western Massachusetts. Each summer they have two sessions, one for the older kids and one for the younger. Joseph (violin), Ben (cello), and I (violin) all attended, at different times. Jeremiah, who tried several instruments but never took to one, didn't like summer camp.

Greenwood is a magical place, particularly for a child. The grounds are beautiful: overrun fields of wildflowers and ancient stone walls where the boulders move if you step on them, one-person practice cabins hidden in deep woods, an abandoned house in which chamber groups practiced and campers used to sleep, its walls peppered with the ghostly scrawls of teenage girls past. All the campers go barefoot and all the old buildings have secret rooms and wooden beams; orchestra rehearsals and biweekly concerts are held in an old barn. I came there first as a visitor; the place was saturated with my brothers, mostly with Ben, the trampled paths brought to life by his bare feet before mine. When my parents and I visited Ben, I would immediately take my shoes off to follow him, clearly demarcating the boundary between parent and kid.

The younger boys slept in a small cabin called the Hutch, while the older boys slept in the loft of the barn and in the few stalls on the first floor that used to belong to horses. When Ben was younger, I followed him into the Hutch, curious about the dim, pervasive maleness, the scent of deodorant and discarded T-shirts on the dirty wood floor. I sat on Ben's bed in the corner while he joked with his friends as they put on their concert whites. His area was familiar: his yellow bedspread, his worn sheets, his pillowcases, the shorts stuffed into the cubby behind the bed, the notebook on top of the shelf, his lamp—I knew all of it, it was Ben's, and it all smelled like him, a smell that comforted me, a smell I can call forth even now. I peered at the walls to see where he had written his name, the same spots where I had seen it written the summer before. There was always this sense of awe, to see his handwriting on a wall and to think of him writing it when I was not there, living his separate life. When I was a camper I found his name written all over, in his own hand and in the bubbly hand of women I did not know, over beds and in rafters and, once, hidden deep in the recesses of my own closet (*I love Ben Hermann forever!!!*). These finds were always thrilling, the tone of the writing so foreign and yet familiar. They were proof that my brother was a celebrity, that others felt as strongly about him as I did. I would return to these spots again and again, long after I had memorized their locations and the particular ways the scrawling pens had cut into the wood of the wall.

Everyone loved him, but I was the only one who could be his sister. In the later years, up in the barn loft during a concert, I sat on Ben's familiar bedspread and watched him interact with his friends, whispering, writing in the little notebooks that they all passed around to remember each other by during the rest of the year. I wanted to be one of his friends; I wanted to be able to make him laugh like they could, to know him more freely, as an equal, as a peer. It was a frustrating feeling at times, to be forever relegated to what often felt like an inferior role. But when it was Ben's turn to perform, I tiptoed over to the railing and watched from the loft while he played his cello on the floor below. My heart filled with pride; I occupied a position in that moment that no one else in the building could claim to hold.

I suppose I still do.

BODIES OF WATER

Miranda Beverly-Whittemore

FIRST, THE SONGROUGROU

Mama needed another child; all the women agreed on this. Children died all the time. Even though I asked Mama to teach me that prayer she'd recited when telling me about her childhood in a land called Ohio—"Now I lay me down to sleep, I pray the lord my soul to keep, if I should die before I wake, I pray the lord my soul to take"—and even though I said it every night to protect myself, tucked into my mosquito net, lulled by the hum of the hungry creatures and the far-off pounding of drums at the edge of the bush, and even though I didn't like the idea of sharing Mama with anyone else, I knew the women were right. I could die. And if I died, Mama would have no children. I had to help her get a second child.

We were different from everyone else: our hut sat in the middle of a field; Mama and Daddy shared a bed every night; Daddy didn't cast his net into the Songrougrou in search of fish, instead gathering stories from old men, teenage girls, and everyone in between, typing them onto note cards; and our skin—Mama's, Daddy's, mine—was blazingly, embarrassingly white. We had brown hair on our heads and hair that grew on our forearms. We were Toubabs. We were always afraid. But everyone was afraid, and only in the way that a people living hand to mouth must be—malaria, starvation, and dehydration loomed at the edges of the village's daily life. Because of the fear, or in spite of it, we were joyful in the face of new babies, of abundant rice crops, ripe mangoes, sudden rainfall. There is nothing like the buoyant hope of a people living off the earth.

It was not going to be easy. This I was told again and again, and I had a healthy fear of the women doing the telling—they had seen magic so dangerous children shouldn't know it existed. But because I held Mama's breast too tightly, because I was, in some part, responsible for keeping another baby from her womb, we would have to risk my infringement upon the spirit world. I was afraid, but I knew fear was appropriate, necessary, even. There are parts of the fertility ritual that Mama and I underwent of which I know nothing. Deep, ancient magic—magic from the earth and the spirit world beneath it—that couldn't be written, even if I knew its content. But what I do know, and what I do remember, and what I can tell you, is that my most important task was to carry a bone doll on my back.

To look at her, she was just a cow thighbone, wrapped with miles of strung beads and given two pierced "ears" on either side of the fist of her joint. Our people believed that if you give a common thing the meaning of something else you really want—in this case, a bone given the name and mien of a child—the spirit world is tricked into thinking you already have that longed-for object and looks away just long enough for the longed-for object to slip into its place.

We sewed a calico shirt and a green cotton carrier for her. I tied her on my back. She weighed less than the other babies I had carried but she made a wonderful clacking sound when we danced before all the women under a full moon. I knew, as I carried her, that she was not just the expression of our wish for a baby but the guarantee of what was to come. Of course, I believed we would live in that village forever, that she would come to us in our hut in the middle of our grassy field, where the full moon glistened on the pounded mud floor. I didn't know that I was almost six, that Daddy's fieldwork had ended, and that we were about to move to a place called Vermont, land of winter coats, elementary school, snow-muffled frigid mornings. I didn't know that it wasn't until we'd left the only life I'd known that she could be born.

THEN LAKE CHAMPLAIN

It was strange to live alone in the middle of a forest. The sound of the lake lapping the rocky shore was nothing like the laughter of other children. I was lonely. I didn't know who I was without that other language cascading off my tongue. I didn't understand why anyone would want to live this way, just one family under one roof, no one else around for miles.

I was across Malletts Bay the morning Mama's contractions started. It was our second summer, and we had been skinny-dipping every night—Daddy, Mama, me, and the baby inside Mama—the moon bright enough to light our limbs. By the time Mama's friend rowed me back to the house, Mama was in active labor, already unreachable, already locked up in strange, silent pain. I must have been afraid to see her grasped by that internal grip, but I do not remember. What I remember is doubling over at her feet, a clench of pain disabling my own abdomen. I curled below her, trying to bear that unbearable, muscular squeeze that women have somehow managed to endure for millennia and that I was not to know again for twenty-five years. The midwife bent over me for a moment and told me I was feeling sympathy contractions. I was seven.

The next thing I remember is standing at the foot of my parents' bed, Daddy on one side of Mama's legs, me on the other, and seeing that drenched, soft head slip out into the air, the slippery gush of the baby's body into the world, hearing it chortle, cough, cry as it came to life. It had bright red hair.

It was my job to give the baby the name my parents had picked, the girl name if it was a girl, the boy name if it was a boy. My father cradled the baby in his big hands. Held its naked body up. I looked between its legs. I had no idea what it was.

A sudden stab of worry. I had to do my part in order for our baby to finally join us in the world—she'd been journeying so long, all the way since we'd lived on the banks of the Songrougrou. But I didn't know how to do my part, and in the meantime I was holding up everyone else who had—Mama, who'd done the pushing; Daddy, who'd done the catching; and Baby, who'd done the birthing. Girl or boy? Boy or girl? I peered down at the swollen, pink blob between the baby's legs. Back up at the grown-ups, waiting on my words. Leaned forward to my father's ear.

"What is it?" I asked.

He told me.

I named her.

PORTLAND'S TEN BRIDGES
SPAN THE WILLAMETTE

Kai kept her glorious red hair, or at least that's what everyone else thought. I knew, because I'd spent hours examining the whorl of her head, that her hair was actually thousands of colors—gold, brown, blond, and yes, red—that, put together, gave the illusion of a solid, red curtain. She followed me everywhere, and aside from the day when I poked her in the bottom of the foot with a needle because I was sewing and she wouldn't stop asking if she could help, I generally adored her. When she cried, her downcast lips were the first to signify betrayal, then her chin would quiver, and then, at last, great tears would come tumbling down her cheeks. She was beautiful even when she wept, and I loved this about her, felt pride that where I was plain, brown haired, wore glasses, was too small and too skinny, she had full, pink, cheeks, bright eyes fringed by long lashes, and that glorious, gasp-inducing hair.

Our childhood was spent driving from one side of the Willamette to the other, fighting about who had called shotgun and who was stuck sitting in the belly of Moby, our VW Vanagon (he was great and white). The Sellwood Bridge for summer camp, the Ross Island Bridge for the Spaghetti Factory, the Hawthorne Bridge for downtown, the Burnside Bridge for school, and the Broadway Bridge, and the St. Johns Bridge, and the Steel Bridge, and the Morrison Bridge. The Fremont Bridge for north, the Marquam Bridge for south. On days when Mama let us play hooky, we headed up the Columbia to eat French onion soup at the Multnomah Falls Lodge. Sundays, we headed out to Cannon Beach to watch the tide roll in as the dark clouds clung low.

Kai was always making. I came home from school one day to discover a five-foot-long blue chalk frog on our front stoop, Kai still in her pajamas, diligently coloring in the remaining empty space. Our parents bought Babybel cheeses for the express purpose of delighting in the little animals she'd craft out of each red wax husk. I found these projects equally admirable and annoying. I couldn't get over the fact that she just made for making's sake. We acted in Shakespeare plays together, but while I relished the memorizing, the movement toward the performance, the goal, she dreaded the actual event, filling with stage fright as she got closer and closer to the moment she stepped onstage. I made her play school with me and never once let her be a golden retriever puppy because dogs don't go to school.

Our grandfather grew up in Colorado, hiking up a mountain with wooden skis strapped to his back in the morning, whisking down its snowy face in the afternoon. Let's just say the myth loomed large. I was a straight-A student, a grown-up pleaser. I was determined to love skiing. Portland was an hour from Mount Hood, and Daddy and I would drive up the mountain on Saturday mornings, leaving little Kai at home with skiing-averse Mama. I liked the equipment. I relished the way the ticket hung from my zipper. I enjoyed learning the snow plow and performing stem Christies, and how Daddy and I would sit in the lodge at lunchtime and drink hot chocolate. What I did not love was 1) riding up a ski lift, feet dangling into the gaping maw, and 2) barreling down a vertical slope toward certain death. I struggled with this truth. Daddy insisted I was good at skiing, and I happened to know he was right, but for once, it didn't matter. I was terrified.

I was there the first time Kai went skiing. Our extended family was together on Mount Bachelor, staying in a lodge—the kind of typical American vacation we never experienced before or since—and five-year-old Kai opted to go up the mountain with the men, all over six feet tall. I stayed behind with the women, offering up some lame excuse, worried to be disappointing Daddy. We were to meet them at the lodge for lunch.

At lunchtime, we women waited at the bottom of the slope as parka'd, ski-goggled, snow-panted figures cascaded toward us. It seemed impossible we would ever find our skiers, until they appeared above us, at the top of the bright, white ridge: two tall figures bookending a tiny one, coming straight down the open hill. I recognized them: my grandfather, my father, and Kai. Still, it didn't seem possible. She didn't look afraid at all. Didn't falter in her course. Didn't stop, didn't waver. Just streamed down the mountainside. I didn't believe it was her until I saw, for sure, her two red braids, whipping in the wind. She got bigger and bigger and faster and faster and it was clear, once we could make out her features, that she was beaming.

I never had to ski again. A relief, of course. And yet.

LA COTE D'ATLANTIQUE

And then, suddenly, we approximated women. I had just graduated from college and Kai was entering high school. We were invited to make photographs with a friend of the family at a Naturist community in France. The photographs are nude—everything one does at the Naturist community is nude—but by now you're probably not scandalized by anything my family does. The photographer was well-known by that point, and the camera he uses (the eight-by-ten, a big, square box perched atop a heavy-duty tripod) takes long, still exposures that capture vast spaces—the murky Atlantic, the purpling sky—peppered by bodies. The collaboration was intentional, important; he had known us since we were little girls, and many of his subjects are siblings. We were, to my mind, perfect for his project. I had been waiting to be invited for quite some time.

In even the first photographs he took of Kai, she looked like a gazelle. None of the awkwardness of a thirteen-year-old, or rather, that awkwardness transformed into the coltish beauty we all wish we had at that age. Her limbs looked a million miles long, her skin milky, her features soft. By contrast, my dark features lent me a scowling, harsh expression. My left eye was quick to jump closed at the click of the shutter release, and there are hundreds of photographs of me with what seems to be a sagging face. My short legs appeared disproportionate, and I often found I had no idea what to do with my hands. As I grew to dread making the pictures—I'd be gripped by a quick-fire, frightened anger just before each shoot—Kai grew to love it. She showed a preternatural gift for the collaboration. As distance grew between how I wanted to appear and how I did appear, so too did distance grow between us. She was so gorgeous, her essence so perfectly reflected by those beautiful pictures, and I was drowning in a sea of jealousy.

And also: she was, as usual, making something. And I was not. The photographic project was big. I hadn't felt that link to something bigger since I'd carried the bone doll on my back. Fresh out of college, with no idea how to prove myself, I was afraid that I might just disappear.

Jealousy was not the only reason I wrote the novel, but, in

retrospect, I can easily see it was partly why. I had about a million (defensive) explanations about how my first book was, in fact, absolutely not fueled by jealousy. Yes, it was about a photographer who takes pictures of sisters, with devastating consequences (namely that the younger sister is murdered). But Kai hadn't been murdered, and my photographer was a woman, so there. News flash: killing your little sister off in a novel is not an effective way to breed goodwill. Kai was angry. Hurt. Frustrated that I'd gotten to the unusual material of our childhood first.

We didn't talk for a while. Which is to say, we did talk. But we didn't say anything important. Our mutual mistrust was foreign and yet somehow inevitable: it gave us room to breathe. I wrote another book, which had nothing to do with us. And she decided to claim the photographic material as her own after all. By then, she'd nearly graduated from college herself and deftly wielded a video camera, which she brought to France and used to document our life there, the process and challenges of making those pictures.

In one scene from her film, we are walking down the beach together. The sun is setting to our right. We pass the camera back and forth, taking turns filming each other, our feet thudding across the wet sand. To our mutual hilarity, we are half-naked in a profoundly uncool Naturist way—sunglasses atop our heads, wrap cloths draped over our shoulders. I wear only a backpack. I ask her to tell the camera about what this great big project is on which she has embarked. "What are you making?" I ask. She laughs. Shrugs. Says she has no idea. All she knows is she's making something she has to make.

AND THE BATHTUB

Giving birth was everything and nothing like what I imagined. What I mean is that I knew it would be hard, and it was hard.

I knew it would hurt, and yes, it really, truly hurt, in ways so beyond language I have no way to describe them. I knew I would be supported by my husband, and Mama and Kai, and I was. But no matter how much I type-A-personality overprepared myself, there was no way to imagine the specifics of my labor until they were already in motion. I was the only person in our sixteen-person birthing class who'd ever attended a birth, but it wasn't until my labor began that I realized what is simultaneously thrilling and terrifying about the process: once it has begun, it will not stop.

My labor was a particularly long road—three days, three nights—its extraordinary length further highlighted by the fact that I went into labor four days after Christmas and didn't give birth until New Year's Day. By the time New Year's Eve rolled around, it was eleven degrees outside, icy and bitter, and I was absolutely sure I was the first woman in history who'd be in labor for the rest of her life. That last night was something out of another world. I was boiling hot, naked, even as Mama, Kai, my husband, the doula, and the midwife were bundled up in wool hats, scarves, sweaters. The midwife made me walk the hallways for hours, to speed my contractions, and my husband held me up every time a wave overtook me. Things were moving along slowly but surely, but I was so tired. I started to believe it was impossible. I wanted to give up so badly, but there was no way to stop the inevitable (if slow) train I was on.

The midwife saw how tired I was. She suggested I take a break (ha!) in the bathtub, where the warm water would dull some of my back pain and let me get some rest between contractions. I couldn't imagine going in there alone—the ceramic expanse seemed vast.

Without a second's hesitation, Kai climbed into the bathtub with me. She stayed in there with me for two and a half hours, freezing, shivering, her lips turning blue, as I clung to her during each contraction. The midwife later told us she had never seen anyone do that—get into that tub with the laboring woman. It had not occurred to either Kai or me that someone wouldn't.

On New Year's morning my baby was born. They placed him on my chest but I did not see if he was a boy or a girl. The need to know did not cross my mind. Later, Kai told me that she, too, had no idea. She was sitting beside me, her arm around me, looking down into his milky-blue eyes. We already knew him beyond the marker of gender, just drinking in this new feisty person, at the end of his journey—and at the beginning. Here was the person we'd been waiting to meet. The person Kai now flings around the playground, who laughs wildly at her every song, who, if given the choice between my arms and hers, chooses hers nine times out of ten.

In that bathtub on that long night, my contractions slowed and they reared up. Kai counted out each one for me. They built, one to ninety, an arc of time and pain. At forty-five, each contraction was its most intense, by ninety, each wave was abating. Each contraction brought me closer to my child. That's what I could remember, the hope I could see before me, in those few minutes of rest before we began to count again.

In those moments, when I came back into myself, my sister, my Kai, held the sides of my face, looked into my eyes, and said: "You are always stronger than you think you are. You are always braver than you think you are." It wasn't just something to say. It was true, I knew, even as I felt another wave of pain overtake me. It was specific.

BROTHERLY LOVE

Edward Schwarzschild

We are three brothers. I'm the oldest, two years older than Arthur and six and a half years older than Jeffrey. With the exception of a few years of pitched adolescent battles waged between Arthur and myself (all my fault, I'm sorry to say), we three have stayed incredibly close even though we now live far apart. Born and raised outside of Philadelphia, we've spread north, south, and west. I have a small house in Albany, New York, where I'm a writer and professor; Arthur has a small house in Willis Wharf, Virginia, where he's a marine biologist and research professor; Jeffrey has a small house in Sacramento, California, where he's a lawyer and deputy attorney general. We miss spending time together, just the three of us, so over the years, when asked what we want for birthday presents, we've often requested a weekend reunion.

In fact, for a while now, we've fantasized about buying a vacation house where we could hold such brotherly retreats. I suppose that desire speaks to our closeness. At the same time, though, I used to see it as a sad wish. After all, we already had the three houses we could barely afford (our careers seem, thankfully, steady, but they're far from lucrative). Though they are small houses, they're more than big enough for a three-person reunion, which is all we've usually needed, since until recently all three of us were single. In the darker moments of my bachelorhood, I wondered if we really needed another place to take care of just so we could sit together and sulk about the peculiar lack of women in our lives.

During those bachelor years, we sulked together in several excellent locations across the country, from Miami to San Francisco. In addition to the sulking, we made time for sightseeing, but that was secondary. We're three guys who look like slightly different versions of the exact same thing. When people guess, they often get our age order wrong (I'm happy to report), either because Jeffrey, who has the nicest clothes, looks like he's in charge or because Arthur looks a bit weathered from all his time out on the water or because, until a few months ago, I had the fullest head of hair. In any case, we read the guidebooks, visited the museums, sought out good restaurants, and opened many of our discussions with meditations on the one woman who has been a constant in each of our lives: our mother.

She married young and got to work having us right away. Before she turned thirty, she'd had three boys. Each time, she hoped for a daughter (possible names included Emily, Laurie, and Karen). After her third try, my mother gave up, which is something she does not often do. She also almost never complains, but she used to frequently remind us that being surrounded by guys was far from ideal. For decades, she told us, her only real female companion was the family dog.

To some extent, we felt guilty about that, but Arthur, the scientist, reassured us that there wasn't much we could do about how our parents' chromosomes intertwined. We felt guiltier about what we ourselves hadn't produced. Yes, we have our advanced degrees and our hard-won careers—a definite source of pride for our parents, who weren't given the opportunity to attend college—but where were the daughters-in-law and the grandchildren (especially the granddaughters)? Our mother doesn't want many things. She's not demanding. She's long-suffering, and we were denying her companionship, making her dreams not come true, and this never felt good to any of us. Why did we allow such a state of affairs—or, more accurately, such an affairless state—to continue for so many years?

During each trip, we rehearsed the simplest theories: Arthur talked about his isolated location and how there were no available women anywhere near his tiny town (population three hundred or so). Jeffrey blamed his finances and claimed he wouldn't be able to afford dating until he'd climbed out from beneath his law school debt. I explained that my writing and the quest for tenure left me no time to court anyone.

Such theories, however, were easily dismissed by sunset of the first day. After all, we'd attended the joyous weddings of plenty of friends who had overcome obstacles equal to and far greater than ours. And we had each been in relationships from time to time. So we moved on to slightly more complex theories.

Our taciturn father received a two-pronged critique. During the years we lived at home, he was not a font of wisdom when it came to questions about girls. He preferred to talk about chores. On the rare occasions we'd get him to address the topic of dating, he'd tell us he dated only one woman before he met my mother. That woman contracted the flu and died from pneumonia. My mother was sympathetic, but over time I believe she grew tired of this oft-repeated piece of history. Whenever she overheard him introducing it again, she'd turn to the dog. "Time to take a walk," I could almost hear her say.

It remains a sad story, despite the surprising lesson my father derived from it. "If she had survived," he'd tell us, "I would have married her, not your mother, and none of you boys would even exist." We didn't find that dreary interpretation particularly instructive or comforting. Even as young kids, we were able to catch the obvious implication: we were lucky to be alive and we should spend all of our time being grateful, not worrying about having fun, or buying things, or dating.

As the oldest, it was my duty to pursue the line of questioning, not just for myself, but for my brothers, too. How can you tell if a girl likes you? How should you ask a girl out on a date? When can you kiss a girl?

"Enough talk," my father would say. "There's work to do."

Which led to the second part of the "blame Dad" theory. Invariably, he could list dozens of projects around the house that demanded our immediate attention. Sometimes it seemed we weren't really sons; we were merely a convenient, low-wage work crew. Maybe, we hypothesized, all the chores contributed to our social ineptness. It was possible for us to look at our father's life and believe that getting married would mean working ceaselessly around a house for the rest of our lives. Our time with him made us long to do fewer chores. We yearned for the freedom to set our own schedules and choose our own projects. We didn't want anyone telling us what to do. So we shied away from relationships, the theory went, because having escaped our father, we cherished our autonomy too much to surrender it ever again.

This theory was also easily debunked. If it were true, we wouldn't each have saddled ourselves with those small houses. Why didn't we remain renters? And, by the way, why did all three of us drive cars that were obviously meant to contain a wife and kids? Arthur and I each drove a station wagon; Jeffrey had a family-sized sedan. We lived in empty nests. We drove empty nests. We longed to share a vacation empty nest. Though our mother couldn't bring herself to say it—it would have sounded too much like a complaint—something was clearly off.

And then I turned forty. And I was single once more. And we three brothers took a weekend trip to Montreal. We rendezvoused in Albany, piled into my Outback, and drove north. We discussed my recent breakup, Arthur's recent breakup, and Jeffrey's recent series of lousy dates. I'd tried harder than ever in my just-ended relationship and it seemed to me that being single at forty meant I had to accept the very real possibility that I might spend my entire life single. When I followed that thinking too far, the world looked bleak. It had become more difficult to visit home, for instance, because everything there was growing older—my parents' parents were dead, my parents themselves were aging (they were old enough to have a forty-year-old son, for God's sake), and my father was hiring people to do the chores he once did himself (or made us do). Where was the new life, the next generation, the young, bright future? Was our family destined to shrivel up and die with the three of us lonely, old bachelors?

And yet, as usual, being with my brothers lifted my spirits. By the time we drove across the border into Canada, we were feeling more hopeful and excited. Then, when we checked into our hotel, we looked around and saw an alarming number of beautiful young women crossing the lobby, filling the elevators, roaming the hallways. There was, we discovered, an international beauty pageant in progress. Jeffrey had been responsible for booking the hotel and I assumed he'd arranged this on purpose, a clever birthday surprise, but he denied it, and his face showed that he was as dumbstruck as Arthur and I. The three of us set our bags by our feet and stood there in the lobby, stunned and smiling as we watched the beauty contestants move around us. It was a good omen. It had to be.

Now, if this were a piece of fiction, I could tell you the story of how, later in the day, we crashed one of the posh pageant parties and met three different women from three different countries and roamed the quiet streets of the moonlit city until dawn and took the first steps toward blossoming into a beautiful international family. The writer, the marine biologist, and the lawyer would join forces with three women—a doctor, a computer scientist, and a politician, say—and we'd live and love and prosper together. We'd all chip in to purchase a family compound in northern Italy or Hawaii or Thailand and we'd spend big chunks of each year there, planning vital projects and working to create a better, greener, more peaceful world.

Or, if that seems too outrageous, I could tell you the more

realistic story of how, at the end of the day, we found ourselves sharing an elevator ride with a lovely pageant contestant from Iceland who was standing beside her dwarfish mother. We traveled upward in silence. When we reached our floor, the doors opened and my brothers and I stepped out, but before the doors closed again, we could hear the mother speaking to her daughter. "Those look like nice young men," she said. "Why don't you ever find nice young men like that?" And those unsolicited words from a complete stranger touched something in us, echoing within our hearts, giving us a new-found confidence that led each one of us to find the woman of our dreams by the end of the year.

But this is a piece of nonfiction, and the truth is that as I write these words, nearly five years have passed since that Montreal weekend. I'm a happily married husband and the proud father of a ten-month-old. My mother's so pleased to have at long last become a grandmother that she truly doesn't seem to mind that our baby is yet another boy.

It's undeniable that I somehow traveled from that brotherly road trip to this moment, but I've got no sparkling anecdote to share, no sharp turning point to describe. We checked into our room and then set out to explore the city. It was a gorgeous day and it wasn't difficult to imagine ourselves walking through the streets of Europe, which led us to begin discussing our next trip: maybe we could do Barcelona if we could put aside more than a long weekend.

Late that night, we returned to the hotel. We found no traces of the pageant women, which was fine, since we were exhausted from the long drive, hours of walking, big meals, two bottles of wine, tiny glasses of port, and chocolate desserts. We went up to our room, ready for sleep, but we still had the energy to talk. We aired more of our favorite theories about why we were who we were and where we were. For a while, we gave our parents a break and blasted the blame for our situation directly at ourselves. We weren't with women because we

were doing something wrong. We were too nice. We needed
to be in better shape. We weren't funny enough. We were too
funny. Our self-esteem was low. We were narcissistic. We were
inexperienced. We were boring. We needed motorcycles and
other dangerous hobbies. We needed, all three of us, to change.
We needed to become much, much better men, in every con-
ceivable way.

Abruptly, our parents' brief reprieve ended. We looped back
toward them with real momentum and this time our mother
and father were targets together. Maybe they hadn't done it on
purpose, but they'd never taught us how to be in a relationship. Their marriage was not one we could fully understand or
admire. We didn't always like the way they spoke to each other.
They were rarely physically affectionate with each other or
with us. They steered clear of emotions, leaving us to discover
for ourselves that our girlfriends wouldn't like it when *we* tried
to steer clear of emotions. What crying had we seen growing
up? Young Arthur cried when I bullied him. My mother teared
up when she chopped onions. We each had memories of coming home heartbroken only to have our mother and/or father
tell us that we had to "pick up the pieces and move on." And
they made it clear we ought to do so right away. No wallowing,
please! We needed to realize how lucky we were. Plus there
was work to get done.

Naturally, we learned to seek comfort elsewhere. And then,
naturally, our girlfriends became ex-girlfriends when *they*
learned to seek comfort elsewhere. A woman cried and we
were afraid because we had no idea how to act, so we told her
to pick up the pieces and move on. Maybe we expected the
women we dated to teach us how to deal with emotions, theirs
as well as our own, but they tended to have different expectations. Maybe a sister would have helped? Who knows. We are
three brothers and we tried to learn from our friends, from our
other relatives, from books, and, of course, from each other.

And just listen to us. As the hours passed, it was pretty obvious that we could talk about emotions brother-to-brother without too much difficulty. How could we be so close but have such trouble being close to the people we dated? After all, there are siblings out there who can't even talk to each other. There are families that can't agree to be in the same room. Our parents must have done something right, right? They hadn't completely doomed us.

In that way, our long day wound down and we acknowledged, as we always eventually do, that we had to admire our parents for deciding at such a young age to devote their lives to creating and raising us. Sure, they hadn't done the job perfectly, but who does? Who can? How could we not marvel at them? When my father was forty, I was already twelve years old. They'd given us each other and we'd never be able to calculate all that had cost them. In that hotel room, as in many other rooms, as in our three small houses in our three distant states, we still longed to be better men in preparation for the women who had so far eluded us. We didn't want to be exactly like our parents, but at the same time we also wanted to be our best possible selves because our parents deserved no less from us.

So, there was no epiphany in Montreal, no northern road trip revelation. We slipped inevitably toward sleep, satisfied with the knowledge that though the world and all its pageantry might continue to disappoint us, we would keep learning together. For better or worse, it was our path, and we could move forward. We'd proven that we could talk about our own feelings for hours, for whole weekends. We could listen to each other. Now we needed to learn to listen more carefully to the women we wanted in our lives.

Could it be so simple?

Of course not, but it was a crucial step, and the years since that weekend have brought significant improvement. This past Thanksgiving, we all reunited at my parents' house outside of Philadelphia. Jeffrey arrived with the woman he's been dating for the past few years. Arthur is still living in his somewhat desolate town, but he told us that he was now occasionally traveling to a larger city to spend time with a young woman he'd recently met. And there I was with my incredible wife and our family's very first grandchild, who freely offered his oat puffs, one by one, to everyone at the table. It was easier than ever to feel thankful.

Predictably, more than once during the long weekend people asked when my wife and I would start trying to create a sibling for our son. We smiled and kept quiet about our plans. I confess there are times I'm not absolutely thrilled to be startled from my dreams at four A.M. by our energetic boy. At such bleary-eyed moments, it's hard for me to imagine doing my part to bless him with the gift of siblings. But then I think the kid's going to need help learning the many, many things my wife and I don't know. Plus I wouldn't want him to face all those chores alone.

BURNING QUESTIONS

Jill Soloway and Faith Soloway

We were raised like twins, best friends, by a hovering, over-
bearing, yet distracted Jewish mother and a distant, depressed
opera-loving and anger-prone psychiatrist father. We spent most
of our childhood in South Commons, a neighborhood on the
South Side of Chicago where we were the only white kids in
the school and one of the few white families in the neighborhood. Our family moved to the North Side of Chicago and into
a more prosperous world when we were around twelve and
thirteen, when everyone's integration dreams were drying up.

Faith, forty-five, mother of one, a lesbian, left L.A. for Boston about ten years ago. Her life is about comedy, musical theater, and teaching inner-city youth, and she is writing in Times
New Roman.

Jill, forty-four, mom of two, straight, eighteen months
younger, who lives in L.A. as a TV writer, is in Helvetica.

Faith asks Jill:

What was your real honest response when I announced my gayness?

I think I was in my early twenties. We were at Anne Sather's restaurant on Belmont. I was eating a delicious pancake, I believe.

Mom had already prepped me with "Faith has something very important to tell you," so I'm pretty sure I wasn't expecting you to tell me you had lupus.

What is it you like about hetero sex?

I have a new baby so I guess the answer is nothing. Ask me what I like about sleep and I'll go on and on. That I'm totally naked and I love the feel of my sheets. That I just got this new body pillow that I can put between my knees and boobs at the same time. That I can do it from eight at night until eight in the morning and it never gets boring.

Why do you like to femme it up? Nails, waxing of brows, etc.?

I really don't. I hate putting on makeup and looking like a lady. I always feel like I'm in drag or like I look like a real estate agent. I like doing my nails because the cute little Chiclets of perfect color give me some odd feeling of control. But it has to be a non-ladylike color, like green or white or pink. I couldn't have red fingernails if you paid me. If I didn't wax my brows I would look like Dad.

Is it obvious to you that I am jealous of your creative and financial successes, or do I hide it pretty well?

Is it obvious to you that all I want is for you to move to L.A. and try making TV with me so that I can share it with you, or do I hide that pretty well?

At what age did you stop caring that you didn't know how to ride a bike?

Never. It still drives me crazy. And embarrasses me. *Why are you telling everyone?*

Did you know I feel incredibly guilty that I told you that you had a bad voice?

You should. I actually think you and Dad shaming me about not being able to sing did a lot of damage to my spirit. That is, for a rich Jewish girl who didn't have a hell of a lot go wrong in her childhood. It's not like I was Precious or anything. I feel bad complaining.

Why do you think you're a writer?

When I write I lose time. I'm happy in a way that I have a hard time finding in real life. The intimacy between my brain and my fingers and my computer . . . Yet knowing that that intimacy will find an audience . . . it's very satisfying. It's like having the safety of being alone with the ego reward of being known.

What was the voice that told you to follow that?

No voice really. I was always just compelled to make up stories. I did it naturally as a child. Remember how I cut people out of the catalogs and made up lives for them?

When did you know you were a good writer?

I think when I wrote "Courtney Cox's Asshole" and two editors of two important literary magazines wanted to publish it at the same time. Until then I thought all of my talent came by way of collaboration, either with you or with our groups o' improvisers.

You're forty-four. How old do you think you really look?

I just saw myself in the mirror. It's 5:28 A.M. The baby has been up since five. So I look 52.8. Usually I am able to convince myself I look midthirties. But I know it's a lie.

Do you believe in God?

I do, actually.

What made you search into Judaism some years back?

I was looking for a nursery school for Isaac (now thirteen—just Bar Mitzvah-ed!) and I walked into this one school that felt oddly homey to me. It was weird. Unexpected. But I felt like I had walked into the right place. A few years later they sent him home with Hanukkah candles and Shabbat candles. I think they have these big meetings where they talk about using the children as tiny robot emissaries of Judaism to guilt you into doing Jewish shit. They come home saying, "Mommy, all my fwends have Shabbat, why can't we?"

Years later, I came to a conclusion about Judaism—that I inherently sought out God and spirit and energy, so why not do so within the tradition that was handed to me? I actually feel very strongly about the people who died in the Holocaust. I feel like I owe them something. Once my shrink asked me, years ago, "Could you convert to Christianity?" and the answer was an instant and absolute *no*. I didn't care a lot about being Jewish actively then, but it was a time in my life when I was trying to figure out what I *did* care about. I was surprised by this—that I *knew fundamentally* that one of the incontrovertible things I am is a Jew.

As I said, I connected to all of the people who refused to hide out or convert during World War II. I was moved by the people who would light Shabbat candles in the concentration camps. The sheer numbers of them inspire me. I felt like, if they went through all of that just for being Jewish, the least I could do was look into this tradition that I inherited. It sort of started like that.

I've always had this highly inappropriate stand-up comedy line in my head about it, but of course I'm not a stand-up comic so I have nowhere to say it. But it's like this: [proud black voice] "Yo,

Christians, you think you're so great, Jesus this Jesus that, Jesus Jesus Jesus, [switch to high teasing voice] God loves us *soooo* much he sacrificed his only son! [now my voice] Yeah? He gave you his son? Well guess what, assholes? He gave us *six million!*"

Can you hear the audience laughing? Perhaps crickets? Anyway I do really strongly associate with owing something to those who suffered. As you can see by the length of my answer! Why did I spend so much more time on this one? Years ago you could have had me do pages and pages on blow jobs! But I have changed.

In fact, one of my constant thoughts is that I should get out of the TV business and move into Judaism as a profession. I think I would like to be a rabbi. Not that part where I have to learn Hebrew and study religion. The part where I give a sermon and then people come up to me afterward and tell me I changed their life. Which I guess is what being a TV writer is, too.

Rate these things in order of importance: power, love, money, sex, health, intelligence, family.

Love, family, health, body pillows, intelligence, sex, power.

Anything in the "If I could do that over again" category?

A *lot.* I truly wish our family had clued me in to an understanding of my soul, meaning helping me to clue in to an inner awareness of myself that would have told me what was expected of me to be the best me. That I would have had dignified boundaries about my body from the age of sixteen until, uh . . . maybe my late thirties. I truly wish Mom had instilled in us the sacredness and specialness of intimacy and that I knew how to keep people away from me physically until they had earned my trust. In the name of getting experience, living in the moment, and not wanting to hurt anyone's feelings, I shared myself with a lot of people who didn't do anything to deserve it. And who in fact did the opposite.

If you had to use only one makeup thingy, mascara, lipstick, whatever, what would it be?

None of it, it means nothing to me. Moisturizer I guess.

What food do you crave?

Salad!

What are your fave TV shows?

Reality TV only. *Real Housewives, The Hills,* and *The City,* pretty much to the exclusion of anything else.

Fave junk food?

Means nothing to me.

Why do you think we both enjoy reality TV so much?

I think regular, written TV is boring. It's from one person's brain to us. One very direct and singular story. Whereas when I watch *Real Housewives,* I'm watching five women interact with one another unimpeded by traditional notions about the way female protagonists usually act. Plus it's *so real.* The New Jersey house-wives, Atlanta, it's *them.* The fact that a segment producer has told them what to do doesn't bother me at all. It's like watching first-time actors improvise. They do it so badly, you can see right through it, and they don't know how bad they are at it, and they don't know how many layers of themselves they are inadver-tently revealing, and it's so satisfying.

What's your favorite comedy show?

30 Rock, I guess.

In the business of TV and film, how would you describe your
learning curve?

I learn every day. I constantly struggle with trying to be both powerful and effective and kind and well-liked. And spiritual! I try to
let things happen, trust others, be there to witness, allow things
to take their natural course. And guess what? You can get sorta
fucked believing in good things like that in a business setting.

What period of our sisterhood is your favorite?

I think in South Commons (age four through ten). I felt like we
were best friends. Twins. One person, almost. Didn't really experience the world separate from you at all. So that was pretty cool.
I also loved collaborating on theater when we were in our twenties. Being off Broadway together. Taking on L.A.

Do you remember our violent fighting? When was that? I have
a memory of us really getting far along before our parents broke
it up. Where the hell were they?

Can you believe I really don't remember this at all?

What was your fave outdoor game?

I think you were just trying to fill up your questionnaire with this one.

I remember feeling through early adulthood that you were
embarrassed of me sometimes. Were you? Why??

Never! Early adulthood? I think I felt that was true of you about
me. I remember feeling at the Annoyance Theater that you
seemed to know something about how to be that I didn't know.
Something about humility. And it seemed like you were embarrassed for me that I didn't know it.

If I were to draw a pie graph, what percentage identifies you as a mom, artist, producer, wife?

I don't know. I'll order them: artist, mom, wife, producer.

What did you like about Jewish camp?

Nothing! I liked the smell of nature at sleepaway camp, though.

What did you like about being with all black children at school? Not like?

I didn't know to like it or not like it. It was all I knew. I thought white people were a minority I was in.

Who was your first kiss? And where?

You! In the bathtub, I think?

I worry that Mom and Dad will think us ungrateful and self-centered after reading this. Do you?

I don't think Dad will read it. And Mom loves everything we do. Let's hope neither of them read it. If Isaac reads it I'll kill myself. Anyway, everyone's always told me, you have to make your art as if you're an orphan.

Jill asks Faith:

Would you say we had a happy childhood?

I remember South Commons fondly. I can't say the same for the Weeping Willows of Glenview, Illinois. Weeping Willows, so aptly named, was the dream neighborhood, in the dream suburb of Chicago, and represented the need for us to conform to the Jewish families around us. Mom hated it, was depressed, on her way to a nervous breakdown. It is no wonder that my memories are dark. I remember crawling around the shag carpet and no one answering my cries. Why was I crawling? I was four.

Once we moved to South Commons, the hip, progressive, experimental inner-city Chicago neighborhood, my memories take on a lighter hue, and I think that's because Mom was happier there. The memories really have a golden hue around them. Mom drinking a glass of wine with her best friend in the middle playground of our town house square. Watching us play with all the neighborhood South Commons kids.

In both houses, I remember Mom and Dad's green patterned bedspread. I remember them letting us hang in it, lay in it, roll around in it, live in it. I hear that's rare for our generation, letting the kids own the parents' bedroom. And in all parenting books, isn't it just a downright boundary no-no? More for your essay, if you should write it, entitled "Boundaries: Why Don't We Have What Other People Have?"

For a young couple figuring themselves out, they didn't do horribly, at least in the beginning. They tried. From what we both know of their marriage, and let's face it, we might know too much, they were sometimes unified, most times maybe not. But they had enough in the ritual-mindedness department to organize Sunday driving trips. Sometimes I look at our family in downward comparison to other families we knew, maybe in order not to get too angry about what we didn't have. The Cahns may have had great home-cooked meals, but Mrs. Cahn was kind of a tyrant and was always in a bad mood. Dad was, too, but we didn't see him as much. The Powers, our next-door neighbors, had a house that looked like ass exploded, but we *loved* playing with those kids.

"Downward social comparison." A friend brought that phrase to my attention, and I think this is the credo that maybe Mom passed down to me: things could be worse. At times, I have to work on not using that phrase to frame my whole life.

What did you think of me?

I remember bringing you around to the relatives for some function. You were just born, getting a lot of attention, and I was not happy.

As you got older, you earned yourself a crybaby reputation. In fact, I would almost want you to cry so that I could seem stronger than you.

And we used to fight a lot physically. It's weird that you don't have any memory of this. I mean really hurting each other. Mom or Dad would come and pull me off of you. I knew I was stronger, but you were a fighter. And as you got older you resorted to scratching. I remember feeling the power of words you had. How you could make me feel really bad with words, and I only had my brute little lezzie force to knock those words away.

Did you feel like we were best friends? Sisters? The same person? When were you first aware we were two different people?

We were very close. And though I didn't feel like we were one person, I felt like we belonged together, like a set. Faith Jill, Jill Faith. We played together and had our own language and our own games, *Office* being a favorite. It was so calm, boring, and simple. "Can you make some copies of this?" or whatever. As we got older and had our own rooms, I still ended up sleeping in your room, and slept better that way.

Remember when you hid like balloon boy and we called the police? Why were you hiding?

One of my more epic cinematic memories. We were pretty new to South Commons. I was a really shy kid. Really shy. Mom wanted us to go to Tammy Shapiro's birthday party, and I think she wanted us to go without her. Or maybe she didn't, I don't know. Either way all I knew was I wasn't going, no matter what Mom said. So I hid behind that brown faux treasure chest on the basement floor of our town home. I remember the paralysis. If I moved a muscle, I would have to go to the party. I locked into this arrangement with myself and sat still and listened for maybe an hour. When it was time to go to the party, you guys looked under beds, and even under beds at other houses in the neighborhood. It wasn't until I heard Mom say, "Should we call the police?" that I decided to come out. I got my way. Mom either came with us, or we didn't go. I had a very powerful will back then.

Remember when the neighbor girl found her father's gun and accidentally killed herself? I look back on that and realize how little the tragedy of that sank in. It was sort of like a "wow" and then we got back to our lives. How did that affect you? Do you think I was shallow? Were we all shallow? Did Mom not teach us how to take in emotionally complex or deep things? Or do you think it was because of our ages?

Her name was Ann. I remember feeling a little confused and scared. But I also remember thinking that something so awful would only happen in the lower-income housing that surrounded our town houses. I remember that family feeling far away from our experience. Meaning: poor. And connecting the scene to that class awareness, so something like that could never happen to us. I remember it carrying weight as a PSA about playing with or finding guns. But connecting Ann to the tragedy I think was too painful for our family. And I don't think Mom or Dad had the tools to explain it to us. Maybe we were too young and they were protecting us. Today I work with kids who have lost siblings and family members to street violence. I am brought back to our youth a lot through these kids. But what I am learning about violence and loss is how hard it is, even for

177

the kids close to these situations, to process the trauma. There are programs that start at age seven, to help them learn about their anger and fear, so that they aren't desensitized and aren't easily triggered into violence themselves. Their own parents don't have the tools to help them.

Looking back on our proximity to crime and violence, I thank Mom for giving us the experience of living with "at risk" kids. I used to go over to my friend's apartment in the lower-income homes and really feel the difference. I enjoyed it. Not that we had more, but just being in such a different, slightly scarier atmosphere. I remember the elevators, the gates, the cinder-block walls, the Indian cooking. I think I felt bad for them, but they were happy. I don't know that today I would encourage a play date for Betsy in the projects here in Boston. We were also taking hourlong CTA bus rides in sixth and seventh grade. Were the times less scary?

Remember McDonald's hamburgers for our cast party?

I remember Debbie Dorfman picking up a hamburger patty with a pair of Barbie tights and getting grossed out, and us teasing her. I feel really bad about how much we picked on Debbie.

Remember when we played prostitute and john? Why was I always the prostitute? (I think this was right after I found out what a prostitute was.)

No!!!! We did!? Please tell me about that.

How much of our childhood do you feel like was marred by Mom and Dad fighting? Were you scared of Dad? Do you remember when he tried spanking us that one day?

It didn't feel like their fighting was disproportionate. More just a lack of unity, a lack of love. Dad would yell, Mom would be mute. Yes, feeble spanking and penalty boxes were routine when we had crossed some kind of line. He had this comical approach to it and we all would crack up, him included, when he tried his hand at disciplining us. Mom would give us a good whap when she was mad. I remember once I ran out of the house in anger and crossed the street to the community center. When I came back she spanked me once, hard, on the ass. I think Mom's anger and discipline meant something to me.

There was definitely the feeling that you belonged to Dad and I belonged to Mom. Do you remember feeling jealous? I don't remember feeling jealous. I know I was subconsciously jealous, but not consciously. Did you feel jealous consciously or subconsciously?

I don't have that experience of feeling like I belonged to Dad and you to Mom. I connected with Dad more than you did because you challenged him, and you two would fight. Also, I was the serious musician type, and I think this was a point of pride with him, since he was a classically trained singer and all. I felt more like I had Dad's talents, and you had Mom's. But not that we were paired off. If there was anything I was jealous of it was you, your *you*-ness in general. But that feeling came more in high school and up through college. You were gorgeous, smart, and out of the house. You were popular in high school in a way that I wasn't. You flirted with risky stuff more, not like drugs and alcohol, but you picked friends who kept you privy to stuff. I was too scared and had really safe friends. I felt like you were privy, sorry to use that word again, but privy to the cool, edgy side of teenage life. Like you had this understanding that *teenager* meant experiencing things over our heads.

Mom and Dad report that in the seventies there were all kinds of *Ice Storm*–style partying going on. Drugs, wife swapping, etc. Were you aware of this?

No, but when the Teals separated and took on different partners for a bit, Mom and Dad could not explain that to me enough. I remember being so confused as to how they could all be friendly with each other. And here I am today, *striving* to have this friendship with my ex's current partner. And it's all Betsy knows; that Harlie and I separated, but that all of us, our current partners included, are friends. We made that her world pretty much on the heels of our separation.

Remember when we went to Colorado and Mom hired a sitter and she had a party? What happened?

It was our babysitters who had the party at the condo where we were staying. We threw ice down from the balconies and they got in trouble. Mom, on a different night, same trip in Aspen, came down with food poisoning from an artichoke appetizer, and also had altitude sickness.

Remember when we went to sleepaway camp and I hated it and you ignored me? Were you consciously ignoring me or were you worried about me or just too busy to think about me?

Did I ignore you? I *loved* camp. I bet I wasn't too sensitive to your homesickness. I think I remember we were only trying it for half the time (you didn't even do half), and I think I was embarrassed that we stood out as homesickies who had to have an early exit plan.

Remember when I made out with Andrew Goldfarb? Why is part of my memory that he was your boyfriend? I remember feeling like I stole him from you. Do you remember that?

I think it was Arnon Leviton actually. I kind of never cared about him, but this did play into my competitive jealousies. "Which sister is prettier?" kind of thing. We had the last laugh when we called him together and pretended to be each other and said, "Who do you like better, me or my sister?" And he of course said me to me, and you to you, but we were faking him out the whole time, impersonating each other and confusing him.

Remember when you wrote those Tears for Fears lyrics on the chalkboard? It made me think you were suicidal. Were you?

No, I wasn't suicidal. But I remember you really being embarrassed of that incident. I was a freshman or sophomore in college then. And I think my college years were my most depressed years.

You've mentioned to me recently you think you have some form of ADD. Do you think you had it as a child?

Maybe. Not sure and don't want to get tested. I know it is really hard for me to read an entire book without getting shit-brain bored out of my gourd and thinking about everything but the narrative. I usually have to go back and reread pages. I sank in college. Instead of finding the tools to help myself, I just started failing things. It is my biggest shame to this day. But I was getting high and escaping my lesbian self as well. College in a lot of ways sucked for me. I wasn't equipped to advocate for myself. So I just survived on my artistic strengths. The fact that I ended up getting hired by Second City as musical director proves that I had a survival instinct in me somewhere in all the chaos.

Do you think we watched too much TV?

Yes. I still fight the addiction. My daughter knows one of the reasons she likes staying with me is she watches way more TV with me. Just this morning we had the TV on in the background and were playing balloon toss. Harlie, my ex, hates television, would never have it on as ambient noise. I'm pretty proud of myself, because I have public radio's *Celtic Twilight* on as I write this. But our family used TV like a drug. I still do and am trying to put myself through my own twelve-step program with it.

Do you think we were left too unsupervised? Or were we overly watched?

I think Mom had a skosh of agoraphobia in the way that we only did what she was comfortable with. So no skiing or camping. And she encouraged as much back-pocket proximity and calling as possible. But I do think we were emotionally a tad unsupervised. Somehow you were out having all these high school escapades, but at least you were calling her telling her your agenda. And because we were taking cabs, it was somehow safer than driving around with our friends. I actually think Mom didn't want to piss us off. And maybe deep down inside, she trusted that we wouldn't be in too much danger. I know she had many sleepless nights. It seems maybe she preferred sleepless nights to giving us a curfew.

Did our childhood feel one-dimensional to you or complex?

South Commons gave our childhood some complexity. And then we moved around a lot, so you and I had to adapt frequently. We had some rosy experiences: community theater, JCC camp. As we got older, I think we were affected by Mom and Dad's divide and Mom's triangulation with us. She needed us as friends as well as daughters.

When was the first time you understood what *rape* meant? How did you understand it? Were you afraid of it?

When we went with Mom to her graduate school classes at Chicago's Circle Campus at U of I. There were signs in the women's bathrooms about a recent rape. I asked Mom about what it meant then. I was horrified when she told me. I think the rape happened in the bathroom. But also, remember the man who was raping or killing Filipino nurses in our neighborhood? That a man could force sex on a woman was horrifying. It really scared me. I think I might have visualized it and had nightmares about it. I would imagine the nurse in her white outfit being raped on our playground. I fucking hate how this kind of thing can happen in the paradigm of human behavior. Is that the right phrase? Paradigm of human behavior? Believe me, I still suffer from incompetence and low self-esteem when I know you are reading my answers.

Okay, moving away from that time frame, this next chunk is just going to be about your lesbian-ness.

Lesbian chunks? Did you really have to word it that way?

At what age did you know you were gay? We all had crushes on our girlfriends. How did you know you were different?

I think I wanted to be a boy. I rode around topless on my bike knowing that people might think I was a boy. I was *always* the dad when we played house. And I made out with my girlfriends in these games, and couldn't wait to. I think I knew I was gay really young. Like, ten. But then I did move through really falling for boys. I really liked my seventh-grade boyfriend Jacques Sandburg. I remember loving him. I did connect to a lot of boys and loved them. Loved their souls. In high school I loved Robin Brown and Chris Clemente. But in high school I also had the kind of secret pining for other girls. Never my friends, always on sideline girls, friends of my friends. And when I was younger through high school, *huge* crushes on my female teachers and camp counselors. I remember a certain camp counselor at the Hyde Park JCC who actually made me feel weak.

I think I remember you characterizing your childhood as depressed because of this feeling. Is that true?

I'm sure. It added to my feeling that I couldn't relate to the norm.

Did struggling with your sexual identity define your childhood?

I'm sitting here staring at this question because it probably does but I don't know what came first, my shyness, my fear, or my gayness. I knew other girls my age in high school who were out and doing their gay thing. But I had a fear of them and of being ostracized even for admitting these feelings.

Did I make you a lesbian because I was so cute? Was I your first love?

Yes. You still are, and always will be.

Did we know any gay people as children?

No women that I can remember. I think there was a reverend at the church where we all practiced for community theater. As I got older, any lesbian whom I met or knew made me not want to be a lesbian.

We moved to the North Side. New schools. Fancy people. I'll move on to that part now. Ages twelve to eighteen-ish. Cousin Gail says when we used to go to Skokie to visit them we were so much cooler. Like we were so thrilled with ourselves for being so fashionable and we looked down on them. Do you remember that?

This could be. I think Dad had an air of higher wealth/pedigree over his sister Ruth, which we may have absorbed. But I never considered myself fashionable. I knew our digs were nicer, though.

Do you remember when I was cutting school and stalking bands?
Were you worried for me?

Never worried. Again, just slightly jealous that you had these
experiences. Though when I was older, and we went to Jamaica,
I only slept with and hung out with the islanders to hang out
with you. I never liked the adventure and in fact it scared me. It
felt like none of this stuff ever scared you.

Do you believe in God?

I believe in our need as humans to recognize that in order to
help and heal, we need to look outside of ourselves and harness
our goodness. But I don't think I believe in one God-like entity.

What happened to you on Halloween your freshman year at Indiana University? I felt like something really serious happened but
our family wasn't equipped to handle real problems and it was
our job to live in an Everything's Fine fantasy. How bad was it?

I was sexually assaulted, and thank God not raped. I was walking a couple of blocks to a friend's party. A tall thin man in a
hoodie was walking in my direction, and instead of passing me,
he jumped on top of me, wrestled me to the ground, stuck his
hand down my shirt and grabbed my breasts, and then ran away.
It lasted like ten seconds. It freaked me out for sure. I remember you had a term paper due and used my incident and your
inability to cope with it as an excuse to turn in the paper late.

What does the word *Soloway* mean to you?

I believe it is Russian for "nightingale," right? *Solovechik?* But
I like to think of our last name as meaning the one way or our
certain way of doing things. Or "the chosen." You pick.

THE AGE OF INNOCENCE

Daphne Beal

In the hours before my sister Cecily's arrival in New York, I went into a small frenzy stocking up on juice boxes and chocolate pudding, placing night-lights around the apartment, and scouring the listings sections for kid-friendly activities around town. Cecily isn't a kid, and she doesn't have any of her own, but, at the age of thirty-one, despite being five foot ten and nearly a hundred and sixty pounds, she is more like a child than an adult. Younger than I am by less than two years, she is legally blind and mentally retarded, a term I actually find easier to say than "special needs" or "developmentally disabled," both of which have always sounded euphemistic to me. My parents say—if they have to say anything—"mentally handicapped" or "brain damaged," the latter of which I like all right for getting straight to the point. Growing up, what I heard in taunts both inside and outside my head was "retarded," and being able to use it, with all its connotations, is something of a relief.

For the six days Cecily was here I knew I would have to clear my schedule from the time she woke up in the morning until she went to bed at night. It takes a certain energy to shepherd her around the fast-paced city, particularly at the height of summer. (On a previous trip, I nearly gave her heatstroke by not making her drink enough water.) But she was overdue for a visit—as she reminded me in her patented way, with a hesitance tinged by rebuke—and so, not without trepidation, I set the dates. Our brother, Jonathan, who also lives here and is a year and a half younger than Cecily, and my husband, Sean, would both be tied up with work, so I would have Cecily mostly to myself.

At LaGuardia, I explained that I wanted to meet my handicapped sister at the gate, and, with a sympathetic nod, the woman at the ticket counter gave me a special pass to go through security. The last person off, Cecily lurched forward from the tunnel, clutching the arm of a cheerful Midwest Airlines flight attendant and grinning in her oversized American flag T-shirt. A Mickey Mouse money belt bulged at her waist, white Discman cords trailing.

"My little sister—who's bigger than me!" I teased, hugging her.

"Are you a Shrinky Dink?" she asked, prone as she is to childhood references.

With her short brown hair and her deeply tanned skin, Cecily couldn't look less like my light-haired brother and me—we spend the hot months slathering on sunblock—and in the hustle of the New York airport, she looked more out of place than ever. She is a big-boned girl with uneven muscle tone, despite her newfound commitment to swimming and sit-ups. Her small shoulders and long, strong limbs are especially striking in contrast to her style of dress, which would happily suit an eight-year-old—lots of elastic waistbands, bright T-shirts, and sweatshirts proclaiming the name of a distant locale that she or a family member has visited recently: Orlando! San Francisco! Rome!

When she's genuinely happy, she beams. Her smile takes over her face and her eyes crinkle up, but her teeth, even after years of braces and attempts at caps and bleaching, are dull and crooked, and her left front tooth is gray from having killed the nerve completely. As a child, she knocked out her tooth twice at miniature golf courses and once stepping off a diving board and landing on the concrete instead of the water. "She leads with her tooth," my brother and I used to say.

On our way to the parking lot, the electronic notes of "Turkey in the Straw" chimed from her backpack. It was my father, calling to make sure we'd found each other.

"Mission Cecily accomplished," I told him, adopting the jokey tone our family often uses in her presence.

Cecily prizes the cell phone my brother gave her for Christmas, conveniently voice activated so she doesn't have to fuss with the tiny buttons. She loves it because she's practical—it's handy in case she ever gets stranded waiting for someone to pick her up—but maybe even more so because owning a cell phone makes her more like everyone else in the family, not just the kid who can't take care of herself, a role she has become increasingly sensitive to the older she gets. The truth is, if she got ten calls a month in her pared-down life in the small town of Jefferson, Wisconsin, it would be a lot.

A half hour from Madison and an hour and a half from my parents in Milwaukee, Cecily lives semi-independently in a house with two other moderately high-functioning women in their forties, both of whom have Down's syndrome. They are part of a larger community called St. Coletta of Wisconsin, whose staff checks in on them regularly. Founded in 1904 by the sisters of St. Francis of Assisi for the mentally retarded, St. Coletta's most famous resident was JFK's eldest sibling, Rosemary, who died in 2005 and who had lived there since 1949. According to her *Washington Post* obituary, the Kennedys' mildly retarded first child began to have "behavioral problems" (possibly promiscuity) that led her father, Joe, when she was twenty-three, to take her to a neurosurgeon for a lobotomy. The operation, which, it must be said, was at the height of its miracle-cure status, left the girl entirely unable to care for herself, and she was moved to a cottage at St. Coletta's that year.

As Cecily and I made the relatively short walk between the downtown garage and the restaurant in the East Village where we were meeting Sean and Jonathan, she gripped my arm just above the elbow. Going across Houston Street, I saw the city through her eyes, or more precisely, felt it through her footsteps. Every sidewalk and curb seemed to be broken and uneven, the crosswalk lights too hasty, the manhole covers wobbly and treacherous. A guy in a leather jacket and lace-up boots shoved Cecily as he strode by. Usually, I would have hardly noticed him, but his outfit and attitude suddenly seemed all narcissism and affectation to me, and the old mechanisms of sisterly outrage and protectiveness kicked into gear. The restaurant, too, normally one of our favorites for a low-key dinner ("Just a brick oven and some guys from Naples" is its motto), seemed equally ludicrous. The hostess told us twenty minutes, and after forty minutes on a nearby stoop, Jonathan went to get Cecily a Coke across the street, in order to stave off one of her petit mal seizures, which are caused by low blood sugar or stress. They go on for a few minutes as she blanks out, but leave a headache and nausea that can last for hours.

Once we were inside, the restaurant lacked its usual charm: Why were the passageways between tables so narrow? Why did the sausage on Cecily's pizza have to have fennel in it? But the waiter seemed to understand our situation (yes, we're the family with the retarded sister, that's right), and the food arrived quickly. We talked about whether *Avenue Q* was a good theater option while she was here, and after we described it to her, Cecily said, "Oh yeah, tell Mom that Daphne took me to a sexy musical with potty-mouthed puppets."

Jonathan saw us home, and we went to bed around midnight, where I slept soundly until Sean shook me awake a little before five: "Daph, your sister's crying." I raced across the dark apartment to her bed, where she was curled up like a baby, sobbing.

"Cec, what is it? Tell me. I'm here," I said, thinking she was disoriented or had had a bad dream.

She said, gulping, "When Jonathan brought my backpack

from the restaurant, he forgot my money belt with my two most important things in it, my Discman and my cell phone! It's New York City, someone's going to take it!" She started to cry again.

"Hold on, wait. Don't cry. Let me look around," I said, and in fact saw that only her backpack and suitcase were beside the bed. I ran to the entryway and found the money belt, so full she'd had to take it off at the restaurant in order to sit down. I brought it to her, and she quieted. I teased her, telling her that New Yorkers weren't so bad, though she was unconvinced. I suggested she turn over so I could rub her back, and she agreed, but when I asked if she wanted me to sing her "Fourteen Angels," which my father used to put us to bed with when we were little, she laughed at my babying her. "Oh good lord, I don't think so."

"Tough luck," I said. "You woke me up. Now you're going to have to listen to me sing." She closed her eyes, smiling and humming along.

I had forgotten how little Cecily's New York resembles the city I usually inhabit. There would be no Chelsea gallery visits, no forays to some great new Tuscan restaurant or old Chinatown favorite. Her version of Manhattan is more like an urban Disneyland, a fact made clear to me first thing the next day when I found myself in line to see Lady Liberty. Sometimes I think the statue is my sister's patron saint—she makes a pilgrimage each time she visits. The Great Lady inspires her in a way only a short roster of historical personalities and icons do, among them the Beatles, the Beach Boys, St. Francis of Assisi, and Mickey Mouse. She also likes Ellis Island, for being so quintessentially American. While our British ancestors didn't come through Ellis Island, the last time we were there, I said to Cecily, in order to make the history more vivid, "Say our family came from Poland in 1910 . . . ," an idea she responded to so strongly that by the time we reached the medical examination rooms she turned to me with consternation and said, "Mom and Dad would have had to come to America without me, or I would have been sent back alone, because of my vision." (Until very recently, bad sight was the only disability she described herself as having.) I told her no, our parents would have anticipated this obstacle and come a different way, or stayed in Poland as a family all together. I hoped this would reassure her, because our parents are the center of Cecily's life. They are the ones who provide her with near-daily support, the joshing and diversions. When she has problems with her roommates, job, or computer, Cecily calls them first. They attend her school conferences and picnics, bring her home for six to eight weeks in the summer and a couple of months throughout the rest of the year, and play endless rounds of a card game called Skip-Bo.

At Liberty Island, Cecily was disappointed to find she couldn't climb up inside the statue anymore. "I mean it doesn't make sense, even after September eleventh. If you go through security, you should be able to go inside the statue," she said, trying to reason it out. But the audio tour mollified her, as did buying a large plastic Statue of Liberty souvenir cup and posing for a picture with her arm in the air as if holding a torch in front of the statue—the joke of it making her smile. A frugal and considerate shopper (she makes minimum wage, working forty hours a week as an assistant at an adult day care for the severely disabled called Golden Options), Cecily had me describe many of the items in the store. We each tried on a latex Statue of Liberty mask, which she thought of wearing as she got off the plane in Milwaukee to surprise my parents, until we agreed it was claustrophobic and hard to see out of. She finally settled on a pale green flashlight with a yellow plastic flame and a DVD documentary about the statue by Ken Burns.

All her life, Cecily hasn't been able to enjoy movies or TV because of her vision, which is perhaps a mixed blessing given how many mentally disabled people rely on TV for entertainment and even companionship. I've always thought that Cecily's audiobooks, even though most are children's novels, stretch her imagination farther than TV ever could. But a few years ago she got a computer with an oversized keyboard and screen, and on it she can play simple card games and DVDs that she watches from about six inches away. She seems to get much of what she's watching, visual gags and all, especially if it isn't too complicated a story line. And, like her cell phone, the movies connect her to a culture that everyone around her is part of already. Now she can discuss the Harry Potter movies with my parents' friends, who've taken their grandchildren to see them.

One of Cecily's main objectives in New York was to spend some of the birthday money she got in July. I half hoped this might involve a little clothes shopping, which would allow me to surreptitiously camouflage her, but instead we spent a long time in the board games section of the gigantic Toys "R" Us in Times Square discussing her many options before she decided on Othello and Parcheesi, games she'd watched us play years ago. Waiting to get on the store's indoor Ferris wheel, I realized I'd been converted to Cecily's view of things as I quietly wished for either the M&M's- or Harry Potter–themed car.

Outside, I slyly steered us toward the Gap on Forty-second Street. In the extra-large dressing room the attendant gave us, Cecily cheerfully underwent my ministrations at first, trying on red cargo pants and colorful T-shirts, but the pants were too small at the waist and the T-shirts too form-fitting to be flattering. I thought I'd picked out enough bright clothing to keep her interest, but soon her eyes glazed over.

"Do you not want to do this?" I asked.

"Well," she said, pausing, "I'd really rather not."

I dumped the clothes, bought her a purse she liked, and led us out, Cecily firmly attached to my arm, as she had been all day. (When she was little, my brother and I called her Elmer for the way she stuck to my mom like glue.) Walking through the light rain in an emptied-out midtown, I knew how vain my plan was, that it was silly to care about going around the city with an overgrown girl in gym shorts—as if it reflected on me, as if it really mattered. The summer before, at the one hip store at the mall in Milwaukee, Cecily bought with her own money a pretty top that was even a little flirty the way it bared her tanned shoulders. I had taken her newfound curiosity about fashion as a sign—combined with her complaint that "I'm sick of Mom always telling me what to do!"—that, at thirty-one, she was on her way to adolescence, and I thought that finding some fun things to wear while she was in New York was something we could do together, two grown sisters on a shopping spree.

I realized now, getting slowly drenched as we walked in silence, that I had assumed too much. I had made up a little trajectory of Cecily's future: before long, she would have a boyfriend (an idea my parents have always discouraged), and eventually, she would catch up to me, or almost. It was the same abiding, almost unconscious fantasy that had me wishing on birthday cake candles for ten years of my childhood (even when I knew better) that someone would come up with an operation to fix her brain. I wonder if that's what Joe Kennedy, in his impetuously cruel way, wanted too, unable to believe there wasn't a way to make his daughter right.

What I wished for now, as we trudged along, was for her to read me the riot act, tell me I'm a jerk to care about clothes, to try to make her over into someone else. But Cecily was lost in thought as she walked beside me, perhaps considering her purchases at the toy store, or more likely, because she is sensitive to mood, wondering what in the world I was irritated about.

My brother said to me once, "Whenever I start getting somewhere in my life, I feel like I have to look over my shoulder to wait for Cecily to catch up." I feel the same way. How can I possibly write and have a career and family when she'll have none of the above?

* * *

Cecily was born a typically healthy, roly-poly baby of over eight pounds, on July 14, 1971, in Brussels, Belgium, where we were living because of my father's work for a Milwaukee-based truck-manufacturing company. With wispy brown hair, big hazel eyes, and a good disposition, Cecily was named after my father's mother and sister. In the audiocassette letter my parents sent relatives stateside shortly after she was born, they describe her with typical parental giddiness. "She seems very intelligent," my mother says, adding, with audible relief, "She's sleeping four or five hours a night!" My father tells them, amused, "Daphne isn't sure what to make of her." Then, in October of that year, when Cecily was four months old, my mother took her to the doctor one morning for a routine vaccination. When she came home she put Cecily down for a nap, and when she hadn't woken up nearly a half hour past her usual time, my mother went to check on her.

"I picked her up and she just went sort of limp in my arms," my mother's shaky voice says in the cassette-letter they sent not long after. Most of the particulars I know of that day come from this tape and from a phone conversation I had with my mother a few years ago the night before they left for a trip to Israel. She called to say that if anything happened to them, there were letters in the top drawer of my father's desk, and I asked her finally, after a lifetime of not, "What happened when Cecily got sick?" She told me that after she found her, just as she began to panic and couldn't remember enough French to ask the babysitter for help, my father happened to stop by the house. Cecily was rushed to the hospital by ambulance, where she spent the next five days in a coma.

The one detail I've known for as long as I can remember is that the oxygen was cut off to Cecily's brain for a matter of probably only seconds. One-Mississippi, two-Mississippi, three-Mississippi, we used to count playing hide-and-seek or holding our breath underwater. It's always amazed me that such a blip in time expanded into a reality that has billowed out over our lives, affecting us in ways that none of us will ever fully understand.

When Cecily woke up, my mother told me, "She was like a giant newborn. She couldn't hold her head up, and she could barely move her limbs." It turned out that Cecily's muscles had atrophied, though with the physical therapy that my mother took her to each week, she began to gain some strength back. Still Cecily wasn't responding to things the way she had before, especially visually. In the cassette sent home at this time, my father jumps in before my mother's voice breaks to say, "We are hoping for the best. We don't know what her prognosis is, but we are hoping for the best." My mother was twenty-nine, five years younger than I am now, and my father the same age as I am. When I think of this, the tremendous sense of not knowing and their helplessness in the face of it, my heart catches, and I think it is no wonder I've waited to have children.

The shot was a vaccine for diphtheria, pertussis, and tetanus—DPT. I was in my teens before I overheard my parents referring to a magazine article about the vaccine that linked it to retardation, or even knew there was a vaccine involved in that day at all. I had always simply been told, "Cecily got sick." My doctor, who has a family practice and five-year-old twin girls, told me that it is typical of children vaccinated with DPT to have a mild reaction such as a low-grade fever or excessive crying, but he has never seen a child with any lasting brain damage. Nevertheless, the pertussis (or whooping cough) portion of the vaccine has been observed to cause reactions—be they as mild as fussiness or as acute as death—in children since the vaccine's development in the thirties. Pertussis nowadays is rarely fatal, but the overwhelming majority of U.S. doctors recommend vaccinating against it. This isn't necessarily the case throughout Europe, and an American friend who raised her two daughters in Italy in the nineties told me people there treated it like chicken pox, gathering the neighborhood children to play so they could all get it at once. In the last twenty-five years or so, since the airing of an Emmy-award-winning documentary called *DPT: Vaccine Roulette* in 1982, there has been growing awareness in this country about the possible linkages between the vaccines for DPT and MMR (measles-mumps-rubella) and autism and retardation. That said, the new acellular version of the vaccine, removed from its mercury base, is considered much safer.

Only once, when I was in my twenties, do I remember my mother saying, "I sometimes wonder whether if we had been in the U.S. it wouldn't have happened, if the ambulance would have come faster." It was shocking to hear her say this, not because it wasn't understandable, but because I'd never heard her say anything like it before. Another time, a few years later, we were driving somewhere, and my mother said, "I sometimes wonder what Cecily would have been like if she hadn't gotten sick." She was staring at the highway, gripping the wheel, her eyes glistening, and yet it didn't feel like the beginning of a conversation. It felt like watching a door slam open in a windstorm and just as quickly slam shut again.

My brother asked my mother not long ago, while walking through midtown, "How did you *feel* when Cecily got sick?" She looked at him, stunned, and said, "Well, it wasn't my fault." I was shocked by how quickly she bypassed fear, anger, and sadness and went straight for guilt—many mothers' fall-back emotion to be sure, and one aided by people she's met along the way, like the Belgian woman who told her, "We've never understood why you Americans give your children so many vaccinations." My father is less tightly wound than my mother, but despite their different temperaments, they've forged a jointly strong will to always move forward.

This cheery stoicism was rooted in the idea that we were protecting Cecily from feeling that she had suffered something vastly unfair. In 1996, I read a short story by William Maxwell called "The Holy Terror" about his older brother Hap—short for the Happy Hooligan—who, from an early age, was full of high jinks and athletic prowess. In 1909, when Hap was five, his aunt stopped by their house in her horse and buggy on her way somewhere. He begged to be taken with her. She said no, but Hap climbed on the back wheel of the buggy as she pulled away. He slipped, and his leg was run over by a wheel, apparently shattered so badly that it had to be amputated well above the knee. Maxwell was in his twenties before he learned the truth from his uncle, also a doctor: in fact it had been a clean break set badly by a morphine-addicted doctor. By the time Maxwell's uncle saw the leg a few days later, gangrene had set in. Maxwell was sworn to secrecy and only wrote the story after his older brother died, some fifty years later. Of his own experience regarding his brother's handicap, he writes that a psychoanalyst once suggested to him "that my brother's accident had been a great misfortune not only for him but for me also: because I saw what happens to little boys who are incorrigible, I became a more tractable, more even-tempered, milder person than it was my true nature to be."

I couldn't help but think of my own unrelenting stream of A-pluses throughout grade school, driven perhaps by some sense that an extra-good and hardworking brain in the family could make up for a damaged one. When adolescence arrived, I chose to leave our leafy Milwaukee suburb to go to boarding school. I'd never felt like all the other kids at school, especially the carefree set who played (and won) the tennis and golf tournaments in the summer and field hockey in the fall. We were the only family we knew with a retarded child, and while my brother seemed to overcome any possible social awkwardness through sports and a devilish sense of humor, I felt like I was attached to Cecily at the hip and already too serious by half. I wasn't sure why, but I was sick of being the responsible older sister, so I left.

Maxwell's tree-lined Midwestern childhood was separated from my own by some sixty years, but the attitudes he described, and the lies (if only by omission) told in the name of love, were familiar to me. When I wrote to tell him that the story deepened my understanding of my own family's experience, he sent back the kindest of letters saying he was sorry for the tragedy of my sister's illness. Even then, I was surprised. No one had ever called Cecily's illness a tragedy—it would have been considered melodramatic. And I know that by writing this I am breaking some implicit family pact: we have so much; we will not complain; we are lucky in many ways; it could have been worse.

Friday night, Cecily and I headed out to our rented house on the North Fork of Long Island with Sean and Jonathan. I was looking forward to being in a place where the pace was slower and where we could tag-team Cecily's entertainment.

We took advantage of the pleasures of the country, visiting the farm stand and grilling big meals to eat outdoors. Cecily watched DVDs on my laptop, and a visiting friend gave her a pedicure, which royally pleased her. Saturday night, as a throwback, and in honor of Cecily, we made a campfire and s'mores on the beach. After a little while there was a movement to go skinny-dipping. Cecily, usually at home in the water, was suddenly overcome with self-doubt. "No, I don't want to go in," she said. "It's okay." She sat down on a log by the fire, hands clasped between her knees, contemplating us as we splashed and laughed. Then I heard, "Oh heck, why not?" and turned to see her tug off her shirt and bra, shorts and underwear. All at once, there she was, in the flickering firelight, a big naked, awkward girl with small breasts, creases across her belly, and the embarrassing dark thatch, unexpected somehow. With her arms out in front of her, she lumbered toward the water and yelped happily as she dunked. We cheered.

In bed later, Sean admitted, "I'm not sure I was ready for that. When she decided not to come in, I thought, *Maybe that's all for the best.* And then there she was, part woman, part child, part monster." I laughed nervously at his candor. There *was* something Frankenstein-like about the scene—the malproportioned innocent shambling toward the water.

I have seen this same body by my side all my life, accustomed to its mild freakishness. She was the bucktoothed elfin girl in a bowl cut I dressed up for outdoor tea parties; then a gangly teenager, whom I told to sit with her legs together and chew with her mouth closed, among other edicts designed to keep my embarrassment to a minimum. Her body is almost as familiar as my own.

Despite her physical maturity, Sean thinks (and I have to agree) that Cecily fluctuates mentally between the ages of six and twelve. A few days into the trip, her vocabulary and functioning had markedly increased, a phenomenon I've seen before when she spends time with family. Like a novice tennis player, she starts to play up to the level of those around her. Sunday morning I asked if she wanted to try a game of Boggle. She was surprisingly good at finding words within the grid of letter cubes considering she has very limited photographic memory, a fact that has made learning to read, even with large print, difficult.

By the time we woke up in the city Monday morning, knowing that her flight was that night, I felt I could do anything she needed me to do. Wear a clown suit, complete with nose and wig? No problem. The resistant and disapproving Daphne, the wishing, wanting Daphne, had been subsumed by another whose sole purpose was to make her sister happy. At the Virgin Megastore, I sang songs for her from CDs I thought she might like, and she chose Abba and *Mary Poppins.* At the Scholastic store, I watched proudly as she selected a packet of Schoolhouse Rock CD-ROMs testing math and writing skills. I was struck by how *retarded* really is the right word. She is on such a quest to grow—buying educational discs, learning word games, going swimming against her better judgment—but she is doing it very, very, *very* slowly.

I imagine that for my parents, who were always dealing with the logistics of Cecily's care and development, talking about her disability must have seemed like overkill. But it's taken me a while to forgive them for not openly addressing the magnitude of Cecily's handicap, to the point of saying, "If anything, it's a blessing that made our family special." Now I realize it was simply their hope and their wish that their children not feel betrayed by life before it had even started.

THE ROOF BENEATH OUR FEET

Jay Baron Nicorvo

For Dane and Shawn

The summer I was fifteen, my younger brothers and I were instructed to replace the roof on our house. Dane was thirteen, Shawn eleven. If we wanted, we could ask our friends to help. My mom said she'd buy the materials, rent the tools, and make sure we had all the sandwiches we could eat and Gatorade we could drink.

My brothers and I gathered in secret to mount a counterargument. As the eldest it fell to me to present our case: "We're kids, Mom. How do you expect us to replace the roof?"

"How? Easy, that's how."

"But, Mom—"

"You just have to get up there and do it. Figure it out. You're not idiots. And it's not rocket science." So it went, back and forth, for a full month, as our impending responsibility literally loomed over our heads, the usually exciting approach of summer vacation instead ushering in a terrific dread. We weren't being kicked out of the nest; we were being told to rebuild it.

Our labors were in demand, needed to maintain our own safety and security—our own shelter—concerns that didn't usually fall to kids, at least not in this country in this century, but that didn't faze our mom. When she was Shawn's age she'd troweled mortar as her father, a mason, laid the bricks that became their house. Our mom couldn't afford a sense of shame, so, trying another angle, I appealed to her work ethic and sense of duty: "Mom, some of us have jobs. We can't just take off."

"Jay, you tell that boss of yours he can find someone else to stock the toilet paper aisle for a few weeks. I got you that part-time job, and worse comes to worst, I'll help you find another one. Besides, you'll be the foreman of the roofing crew, and I'll pay you what they're paying you at Winn-Dixie."

We tried again: "Mom, you can't expect us to ask our friends to spend their summer working manual labor."

"Why not? Those friends of yours're here day and night. They eat us out of house and home. They can pitch in for a change."

In 1987, the year our mom and her sister moved us out of a duplex a mile from the biohazardous Jersey Shore to the picturesque Gulf Coast, the Great International Beach Challenge awarded Siesta Beach a notation for the "whitest and finest sand in the world," quartz pulverized into a sugary white powder that's ever cool and squeaks underfoot. This was one of the points our mom used to hard-sell us on our new hometown. But we didn't need the beach; we had an in-ground pool in our backyard—in Florida even the shanties come decked out with swimming pools—and after renting the house for a year, our mom bought it for $77,000 thanks to a thirty-year mortgage. A few months later, she went in arrears on the loan payments.

The house was built in 1975 as a two-bedroom, one-bath ranch under a simple gable roof. In 1979, the original owners did an out-of-code renovation. They added a bedroom in what had been the garage. Two more bedrooms, a bathroom, and a lanai were built from scratch along the rear of the house under a pebble-over-tar roof that had no pitch. By 1992, the house was separating along that seam. A ramshackle five-bedroom ranch in Sarasota, Florida, it stood out as maybe the shoddiest structure in a subdivision of stucco-over-block single-story homes on quarter-acre lots parceled off and built in the sixties and seventies. We were only twenty minutes from the Gulf of Mexico and Siesta Beach, but we were a couple of social classes away from its manicured condominium culture. Whenever we drove along the Gulf, we were reminded that our house was a shithole. We wanted to spend just one night in a condo with a name like the Seabreeze. It would be tidy and well kept. We'd break in if we had to, and when we did, we wouldn't find roaches as plump as Brazil nuts warming themselves under the crumby toaster, seventies-era puke-toned shag carpets, a septic system that backed up whenever it rained.

Shithole that our house was, though, my brothers and I each had our own room and no landlady screaming through the walls at us in Chinese to shut up. We'd been cramped renters since our parents divorced when I was five, Dane two, and Shawn a newborn. As a single mother getting zero child support from our deadbeat father, our mom spent seven years climbing out from the have-not ranks of renters, her three sons weighing her down with peer-pressured demands for Izod shirts and Nike sneakers. Her slow, determined ascent required help from her sister, the welfare system, and a short-run second husband before she could afford to live beneath a roof she ostensibly owned.

And after years of weathering, slowly, surely, the rainwater worked its way down through that roof. Every time it stormed, the renovated rooms leaked. Shawn and Dane enjoyed getting out the buckets and pots. What did they care? They slept in the two original bedrooms, both of which stayed dry. In my room and my mom's room, the drywall ceilings grew sodden and discolored. It was my job to climb onto the roof and patch what holes I could find with roofing cement. This was my apprenticeship. School was just about over, and I harangued to no end. "Please, Mom, you got to do something about the roof. You need to call professionals."

"What do I need professionals for when I have three manly sons?" We were about as manly as teenage girls. Less manly: teenage girls were taller.

A week before school let out, I swung my feet to the bedroom floor and set them dreamily down into the neverglade that was the soggy shag carpet. I was getting desperate and I began resorting to made-up statistics. "Mold, Mom. People die from that stuff. They call it the Invisible Killer. Or the Airborne Deadly Toxin. They think it's the cause of autism. That or vaccinations. They're not sure. Three out of every ten kids die from mold exposure. You got to get someone up there to fix the roof."

"I already got someone."

"You did? Who?"

"I got three someones."

School ended, and while we waited for the delivery of the roofing materials we were allowed a summer vacation. Our mom worked six, often seven days a week, so ours was the neighborhood house of least parental resistance. On that first morning of summer, we woke up early. Dane and I duct-taped Shawn to the toilet and bolted the bathroom door. When Shawn broke free—he was the chubby Houdini of our household—we locked him in the lemon of a station wagon, a Plymouth Reliant K raised on cinder blocks in our backyard. Our friends showed up, coming through the house and out back. They never bothered to knock before letting themselves in. Panting, Shawn pounded on the windows and screamed to be let out. He was dying, he couldn't feel his elbows, his knees. *Harpothermia,* he called it. We released him, and to help cool him down, we boosted him up on the roof of the house, where we all spent a few hours cannonballing into the kidney-shaped pool. Dane suggested that the pounding of our feet as we got our running starts might not be helping the roof reach its life expectancy. My brothers and I hadn't mentioned anything about our upcoming job to our friends. Hoping there was still a chance I could talk our way out of it, and embarrassed that we might have to go through with it, I'd sworn my brothers to secrecy. Dane was coming close to confession, and I said, "The roof was fucked long before we started jumping off it." When Shawn said, "Maybe the new shingles'll never show up," I told him to be quiet by punching him in the kidney.

At lunchtime, we rode our bikes the mile and a half to 7-Eleven, toting empty cups to fill with Slurpees. Our mom was the assistant manager, and she gave us our pick of the two-day-old deli sandwiches before she threw them out. On our way home, overburdened on our bikes with soggy hoagies and melting Slurpees, we gawked at the repurposed white school bus, wire mesh over the windows, parked along the roadside, SARASOTA COUNTY CORRECTIONAL FACILITY stenciled blackly across it.

The chain gangs, on work release from the county jail in their blazing orange jumpers, were digging out the rain gullies as a couple of uniformed guards in dark sunglasses stood menacingly by with pump-action shotguns. That scene captured our sense of our summer-to-be, only we would work unguarded, and we wouldn't be grateful to be out under the stern glare of the sun. Other kids were released from Sarasota High and Sarasota Middle School for the summer to go to space camp, or to vacation in the Maldives, or to visit relatives in exotic places like Kalamazoo. We'd be going nowhere, aspiring juvenile delinquents that we were, sentenced to a house arrest cum labor camp in the sweltering dog days of the subtropics.

None of us knew then—though our mom certainly suspected—that the county jail was where we were all headed, in turn, as we hit our respective bottoms, a kind of rite of white trash passage. We would be arrested and processed at different times for odd and sundry nonviolent offenses. Me for trespassing, retail theft, and felony drug possession. Dane for drunk and disorderly conduct and resisting arrest. Shawn for shoplifting and a few DUIs, the first before he had a driver's license. That summer, our hoodlumism was just beginning to take angry hold of us. When we looked around, our lot seemed too damn little, and we were giving first voice to our collective sense of injustice—*We were owed. We hadn't been granted. We would take.* Refusing to beg, we became liars, cheats, thieves. As we grew, we grew increasingly impossible for our honest, upright mom to control. But she didn't give up, that woman, not on us, not ever, and that summer, her plan was to keep us occupied, and thereby out of trouble, while she saved money she didn't have by paying us a fraction of what she'd pay a roofing crew.

We came home to find in the driveway a Dumpster as big as a tractor-trailer. The Dumpster didn't signify only the end of our daylong summer vacation; it was the end of our childhoods. Beside the Dumpster in the crabgrass was a pallet stacked with new asphalt shingles. There were a few five-gallon buckets of roofing tar and rolls upon rolls of felt tarred roofing paper. "Why's all that shit in the driveway?" one of our friends asked.

When she got home from work, Mom told us to get in her '72 Oldsmobile Toronado, which was about as long, as aerodynamic, and as fuel-efficient as the Dumpster beside it. She drove us, defeated—Shawn in tears, Dane in quiet fury, me pleading with her to pay someone—to ASAP Rental Equipment. There, a bemused and burly salesclerk helped us choose our tool: a shingle scraper. We were told, "That's all you need to get started, that and some back strength." When we got all the old shingling off, we could come pick up an air compressor and a pneumatic nail gun. The tool made the job real in a way that the building materials had not, but it was the promise of a projectile-producing nail gun that stopped Shawn's crying, got Dane talking, and made me quiet in a way that stirred my mom's suspicion: "Jay, don't you go getting any ideas."

A few of our friends slept over that night. We stayed up

until four in the morning, obsessively, compulsively playing strategy video games—*Nobunaga's Ambition* and *Romance of the Three Kingdoms.* In these historical games of civilizations bent on unification, we managed our own cities, attentive to the amount of food stored within our city walls. We tended fiefdoms vulnerable to siege, floods, earthquakes, and famine, keeping an anxious eye on our people's contentment for fear of peasant uprising. These games offered us a measure of control we lacked in our lives. In *Romance of the Three Kingdoms,* Lü Bu's mother couldn't come home from work and say, "Put a new thatch roof on the hut or else."

The next day we slept late, got out of bed, and ate lunch. Our friends helped because they didn't have anything better to do and they didn't know where else to go. They simply picked up a shovel instead of picking up a joystick. Ninety degrees in the shade. Relative humidity near 70 percent. Heat index over 100, putting the feels-like temperature on the roof at 105 degrees. We worked practically naked. If we stayed on the roof long enough without respite, our core temperatures equalized with the feverish air. We guzzled Gatorade so our heat-exhausted heaves weren't dry. Sweat didn't evaporate— nowhere in the saturated, sultry atmosphere for the moisture to go—so our bodies couldn't cool themselves. I was prying old enpebbled tar from the roof with the claw of a hammer, Shawn with a garden trowel—Dane was quick and had called the lone shingle scraper, which was like a serrated shovel— or maybe we were taking a breather to pick at the tar on our knees, in our arm hair, when I heard the crash of an overheated body throwing itself off the roof into the pool to find some small measure of relief. Down into the pool we all followed, the water there just as hot and wet as the air, but that breeze on the descent . . .

Before the afternoon rains, we got in a few hours of demolition work, scraping, leveraging, and shoveling off the thirteen-year-old tar and pebbles like black peanut brittle. To break up the infinite and exhausting monotony of our damnation, we had fun, reckless as it was, launching the waste into the Dumpster below. I slung old shingling at Shawn. Shawn and Dane winged shingles from the roof to glide down the street in contests of distance, a good level throw as satisfying as a well-skipped stone. Around three thirty P.M., we giddily watched the clouds tumble in. Rain meant quitting time. When the bolts of lightning in the lightning capital of the country were near enough that the thunder didn't rumble but cracked—more charged feeling than sound—that was when, lemming-like, we jumped off the roof into the pool. We never simply climbed down. Then we gathered the Visqueen, a thick, construction-grade plastic, and did our inept best to Saran-wrap the ply-wood parts of the roof we'd exposed to the sopping elements of the Deep South.

The wind picked up and the rain fell, splashing in tremendous, viscous globs like a barrage of hurled eggs. The Visqueen got caught in a gust, great sheets of transparent plastic whipping wildly, sailing down the block and winding up in the fronds of a palm tree. When we retrieved the Visqueen, it had holes in it everywhere, and when we did get it secured, it was immediately Slip 'n Slide slick with rainwater. Shawn was the first to go down, our frantic work enlivened by the sound of his *Whao!* as he slid from the roof and off, the low eaves depositing him harmlessly, if not painlessly, on the sandy soil. As he sat stunned, I joked that his belly saved his life. Finding himself unhurt, he laughed, pinched an inch, and said it was fun. We should try. Dane observed that our lives had become like a game of Chutes and Ladders, and Shawn, just getting the hang of sarcasm, said, "Chutes and Ladders my ass—this is Candy Land."

As the days turned into weeks, I had a tougher time getting out of bed. No matter how much work we did we would never finish. We hadn't gotten the proper building permits. The bank would foreclose on the house if it didn't collapse first. What was the point? It was only a little water. My room was the one getting wet. The ladder was becoming a prop in the avant-garde theater of my dreams, in which I was forced to walk unluckily under it or wear some Rube Goldberg version of it. Or strap a pair of ladders to my feet and walk around on the runged stilts while my brothers climbed them. I was growing painfully fast, as if stretched on my mattresses each night—the summer before I'd been fatter than Shawn, and now, six inches taller, I found myself in a toned, tanned body. With my new body came the ability to hibernate for twelve, fourteen hours at a time. We were all sunburned, dehydrated, and heatstroked. The watery blisters on our hands were finally beginning their anguished transformation into hardened calluses, and when I picked at mine I began to understand the promise of an education: smooth hands, narrow fingers, clean fingernails. Freedom from a life of manual labor and physical drudgery.

When we moved to Florida, one of the first things our mom did was enroll us in the newly established Florida Prepaid College Program. During the school year, there were times we came home from school and we didn't have phone service. When the phone was turned back on, we functioned as our mom's secretarial pool, fielding calls while she dodged bill collectors. Toward the end of the school year, there was an afternoon when I walked through the front door and switched on the lights. Nothing happened: the electricity had been cut off. Yet every month, our mom, with the help of our aunt, made payments into our respective 2+2 Tuition Plans—two years of community college, two years of a Florida state university—ensuring each of us a chance at a college education, the college education she'd never had for herself. We learned that education was more important than electricity, and our manual labor that summer made me realize I didn't want to become a manual laborer.

The roofing job moved into week three and we still hadn't gotten all the old shingling off. Our mom is hardworking

working-class. She doesn't tolerate laziness, doesn't know illness. If her sons weren't sickly, they sure as hell were proving themselves to be lazy. The money she was saving by violating child-labor laws shrank as we went through more and more costly Visqueen and as the old plywood subroof that wasn't rotted out and didn't require replacing began to rot and require replacing. From my bed, half-asleep, I heard the tinny sounds of an unfamiliar ascension—the *plink, plink* of feet climbing the aluminum ladder. I heard heavy footfalls clomping on the roof accompanied by furious muttering: "Fricka fracken no-good fricka cricka franken hoffen . . ." I pulled the pillow over my head. "Jay! Jay! Get your lazy ass out of bed, get up on this roof, and help me out of this fucking hole! Jay! Goddamnit, Jay!"

The sun coming though the window lit the floating specks of chalky drywall dust filling my room. A platter of drywall lay on the carpet. From the roof, my mom was still screaming, cursing me, and I was able to hear her better than I should've. I looked up. In one corner of the ceiling, not far from the unbalanced fan spinning round, was my mom's leg—tanned and hairless, a pink flip-flop dangling from her toes. As she yelled at me, she started kicking at the air—"Jay! Goddamnit, Jay, I'm stuck!" The flip-flop came flying off and landed on my bed. "Jay, get up on this roof this minute and get me out of this hole or I swear I'll . . ."

Shawn and Dane bolted out of the house and climbed up on the roof. They hoisted her, got her free, and I tore out of bed, pissed. I brandished her sandal as I hollered up through the hole, "Thanks for all your help, Mom!" When no response came, I flung her sandal through the hole. "And don't forget your flip-flop!"

A week later, when we finally did get the last of the old roofing off, we picked up the nail gun and the air compressor from ASAP, and we nailed down the tar paper. The nail gun had a safety release in the form of a depressor on the muzzle. You had to pull the trigger and press the muzzle against a surface for a nail to discharge. It took me all of two minutes to figure out I could engage the muzzle depressor with a careful finger and pull the trigger, firing nails a good fifty yards. They carried end-over-end, *thwick*-ing through the air, and as I stood on the roof, I caught Shawn by surprise in the grass below, commanding, "Dance!" as I rained nails down around him.

I had promised not to let Shawn touch the nail gun. Been told I was the man of the house, it was my job to keep my brothers safe. It took Shawn a few days to break me down with his constant nagging, interspersed with threats that he'd tell Mom I'd shot him with the nail gun. "I didn't shoot you. I shot *at* you. Besides, what's Mom going to do, chain me to the roof and make me work myself to death? You want to use the nail gun? Here, use the nail gun." I handed it over without instruction.

The contraption was clunky and unwieldy, attached by a heavy-gauge air hose to the compressor motoring in the grass. Because it weighed eight pounds fully loaded, he used it more like a jackhammer than a nail gun, holding it with both hands between his legs and slamming it hard against the plywood subroof. The sound it made was three syllabled: muzzle against subroof, discharge of compressed air, nail driven into wood—*knock-sht-thwack, knock-sht-thwack*—and Shawn was finding a rhythm when an explosion of air, a visible white hiss, burst from it as the clamp that fastened the hose to the back of the nail gun between his legs broke. The end of the hose caught him in the crotch. He dropped the gun and doubled over, moaning, "My testes, my testes," rolling down the roof but not off, as the hose flailed in the air. We laughed till we cried, few things funnier to adolescent boys than knocks to the crotch. While I climbed off the roof to kill the hose by cutting off the compressor, Dane stood before it, pretending to charm it like a snake, dancing and singing, *There's a place in France where the naked ladies dance. There's a hole in the wall where the men see it all.*

We moved into week five, our neighbors complaining about the eyesore Dumpster, the indefinite wreck that was our roof, the shingles and nails littering the length of the block, as if a very selective category-5 hurricane had struck. On his way home from work, Kip Spada, who lived in the neighborbood, drove by, checking our progress—he did this from time to time—and as he pulled away, he shook his head, smiling, while Dane shot nails that plinked off his trailer. We knew Kip to get drunk and slap around his kids. Once he punched his wife, and the cops were called, but she, fat lipped and furious, filed no charges. She probably didn't want to wind up like our mom—alone with children. At least Kip was there for his family, even if, from time to time, he stumbled drunkenly around kicking their legs out from under them. He had a construction business, drove a rusted-out pickup that towed a rickety trailer. There was an aura of pleasant menace about him, maybe because he often smelled like freshly cut grass doused with gasoline. He smoked Marlboro Reds and threw Hail Mary passes to us in tight, high-arcing spirals that stung our chests when we caught them. We liked him because he was a father, and he liked us because we were sons.

The first application of the new shingling stymied us. We knew enough to start at the bottom and layer our way up, but we had no idea how to lay down a straight row. Our first attempt ran snaking into the gutter, up toward the peak, and back down. We tore up the row and began again. Same crooked result. When our mom came home, she saw the waste we were making. A Jersey girl, she was a world-class curser. From the driveway: "Why not shingle the whole fucking roof with goddamn dollar bills?!" She rattled us even though we towered ten feet over her. She'd had enough. The drywall in her room and mine was ruined. There was the leg hole in the ceiling of my room, through which Shawn had retributively shot at me with the nail gun as I lazed in bed. The Dumpster rental was costing her by the day, and at last she understood that what was taking her hapless sons and their useless friends a full month could've been accomplished by professionals in a day. She was still saving money, but the emotional costs were bankrupting us all. By the end of her tirade, she was in mute tears, and she stormed into the house and locked herself in her bathroom, the ceiling water-stained and falling in around her.

The next day, Kip walked into my bedroom at seven in the morning and woke me. He held in his hands what looked like an oversized tape measure. "Get out of bed. Get your brothers up. Meet me on the roof in five minutes." His command wasn't angry, yet its sternness was irrefutable. He wasn't asking. He walked out of my room, leaving the door open, and I heard him assuredly climbing the ladder—*tonk, tonk*—a moment later.

We joined him on the roof. There he demonstrated the simple genius of the chalk line. The oversized tape measure contained a string on a spool, and in the housing was blue chalk. Kip stood beside Shawn at one end of the roof, told him to take hold of the tab and go long. As he did, the line, dusted blue, ran the length of the roof. Shawn adjusted his end till it was level. They pressed their ends tightly down, maintaining tension, and Kip plucked the line a few times, snapping it against the black tar paper. It left a straight blue line, which we followed as we laid shingles Kip then expertly nailed with the nail gun. By the time our friends showed up around noon, we'd covered a quarter of the roof. At the end of the day, we were halfway finished, and we pleaded excitedly with Kip to jump off the roof into the pool with us.

We wanted to offer him some thanks, but we didn't know how or we had nothing to give, nothing save our desire for him to do fun things with us, like jump off the roof into the pool. He couldn't. He had a bum knee, blown in high school. There was sadness in him as he descended the ladder, a melancholy that was then inexplicable, and our response was to drench him with our practiced splashes as he climbed down.

The following day, he was at our house at seven A.M. again,

rousing us and putting us to work. In less than a week, with Kip working beside us and keeping us in line, we were finished. Our job was accomplished, culminating in the sawing off of the peak and securing over it the ridge cap that served as an attic vent. Done and giddy with pride, we cajoled Kip some more. "Please, please jump off the roof with us. Just this once." We loved getting adults to do things they didn't want to do. In the name of celebration and a job done, he did, his boots on and a lit cigarette bitten between his teeth.

Over the phone or gathered on holidays, my brothers and I joke about our mom telling us that roofing is not rocket science. I sit nearly twenty years later in the first house I've owned, sheltered under a roof raised, literally, by a retired rocket scientist. I've come to see Kip as an example of what I might've become had my time on that roof not convinced me that there were other ways for a man to make a living than selling his strength and endurance. Dane and I eventually followed through on the guarantee of a college education afforded us by our mom and aunt and the generosity of the state of Florida. We both attended the local community college, transferred to get our bachelor's degrees elsewhere, and I went on to get a graduate degree. Maybe because he was younger, or maybe because he admired Kip more than we did, Shawn didn't see his time on the roof as a deterrent. We were brothers working together on a difficult job. What could be better? He dropped out of high school and worked construction, cashing in his college fund to buy a truck. He poured slab foundations for a time, worked as a machinist in a tool-and-die shop, and is now the foreman of his own specialized crew. They install industrial skylights in military hangars that cover nuclear submarines and space shuttles. Roofing is not rocket science, but even if it were, there's part of me—put there by my mom and shared by my brothers—that believes if I have the right tools, the help of my brothers, and a little mentoring, we could send something flying who knows how far.

It's 1,300 miles from Saugerties to Sarasota, from my part of New York to my mom's part of Florida. Into Google Maps, I enter her address—4040 Prescott St., 34232—click the satellite view, and zoom in. There it is. Her house. The house where my brothers and I grew up, the blue kidney of the pool occupying a good part of the backyard. But the image—taken from an on-high perspective, seen from space—doesn't capture the house. It's mostly a picture of a roof, the roof my brothers and I put over our mom's head, and after almost two decades it has yet to leak.

ULTRA-ORTHODOX SISTER

Etgar Keret

Nineteen years ago, in a small wedding hall in Bnei Brak, my older sister died, and she now lives in the most Orthodox neighborhood in Jerusalem. I spent a recent weekend at her house. It was my first Shabbat there. I often go to visit her in the middle of the week but that month, with all the work I had and my trips abroad, it was either Saturday or nothing. "Take care of yourself," my wife said as I was leaving. "You're not in such great shape now, you know. Make sure they don't talk you into turning religious or something." I told her she had nothing to worry about. Me, when it comes to religion, I have no God. When I'm cool I don't need anyone, and when I'm feeling shitty and this big empty hole opens up inside me, I just know there's never been a god that could fill it and there never will be. So even if a hundred evangelist rabbis pray for my lost soul, it won't do them any good. I have no God, but my sister does, and I love her, so I try to show Him some respect.

The period when my sister was discovering religion was just about the most depressing time in the history of Israeli pop. The Lebanon War had just ended, and nobody was in the mood for upbeat tunes. But then again, all those ballads to handsome young soldiers who'd died in their prime were getting on our nerves too. People wanted sad songs, but not the kind that carried on about some crummy unheroic war that everyone was trying to forget. Which is how a new genre came into being all of a sudden: the dirge for a friend who's gone religious. Those songs always described a close buddy or a beautiful, sexy girl who'd been the singer's reason for living, when out of the blue something terrible had happened and they'd turned Orthodox. The buddy was growing a beard and praying a lot; the beautiful girl was covered from head to toe and wouldn't do it with the morose singer anymore. Young people would listen to those songs and nod grimly. The war in Lebanon had taken so many of their buddies that the last thing anyone wanted was to see the others just disappear forever into some yeshiva in the armpit of Jerusalem.

It wasn't only the music world that was discovering born-again Jews. They were hot stuff all over the media. Every talk show had a regular seat for a newly religious ex-celeb who made a point of telling everyone how he didn't miss his wanton ways in the least, or the former friend of a well-known born-again who'd reveal how much the friend had changed since turning religious and how you couldn't even talk to him anymore. Me too. From the moment my sister crossed the line in the direction of Divine Providence, I became a kind of local celebrity. Neighbors who'd never given me the time of day would stop just to offer me a firm handshake and pay their condolences. Hipster twelfth-graders, all dressed in black, would give me a friendly high five just before getting into the cab that would take them to some dance club in Tel Aviv. And then they'd roll down the window and shout to me how broken up they were about my sister. If the rabbis had taken someone ugly, they could've handled it; but grabbing someone with her looks—what a waste!

Meanwhile, my lamented sister was studying at some women's seminary in Jerusalem. She'd come visit us almost every week, and she seemed happy. If there was a week when she couldn't come, we'd go visit her. I was fifteen at the time, and I missed her terribly. When she'd been in the army, before going religious, serving as an artillery instructor in the south, I didn't see much of her either, but somehow I missed her less back then.

Whenever we met, I'd study her closely, trying to figure out how she'd changed. Had they replaced the look in her eyes, her smile? We'd talk the way we always did. She still told me funny stories she'd made up specially for me and helped me with my math homework. But my cousin Gili, who belonged to the youth section of the Movement Against Religious Coercion and knew a lot about rabbis and stuff, told me it was just a matter of time. They hadn't finished brainwashing her yet, but as soon as they did, she'd begin talking Yiddish, and they'd shave her head and she'd marry some sweaty, flabby, repulsive guy who'd forbid her to see me anymore. It could take another year or two, but I might as well brace myself, because once she was married she might continue breathing, but from our point of view, it would be just as if she'd died.

Nineteen years ago, in a small wedding hall in Bnei Brak, my older sister died, and she now lives in the most Orthodox neighborhood in Jerusalem. She has a husband, a yeshiva student, just like Gili promised. He isn't sweaty or flabby or repulsive, and he actually seems pleased whenever my brother or I come to visit. Gili also promised me at the time, about twenty years ago, that my sister would have hordes of children and that every time I'd hear them talking Yiddish like they were living in some godforsaken shtetl in Eastern Europe, I'd feel like crying. On that subject too he was only half-right, because she really does have lots of children, one cuter than the other, but when they talk Yiddish it just makes me smile.

As I walk into my sister's house, less than an hour before Shabbat, the children greet me in unison with their "What's my name?", a tradition that began after I once got them mixed up. Considering that my sister has eleven, and that each of them has a double-barreled name, the way the Hasidim usually do, my mistake was certainly forgivable. The fact that all the boys are dressed the same way and decked out with identical sets of side locks provides some pretty strong mitigating arguments. But all of them, from Shlomo-Nachman on down, still want to make sure that their peculiar uncle is focused enough and gives the right present to the right nephew. Only a few weeks ago, my mother said she'd been talking to my sister, and she suspects it's not over yet, so that in a year or two, God willing, there'll be another double-barreled name for me to memorize.

Once I'd passed the roll-call test with flying colors, I was treated to a strictly kosher glass of cola as my sister, who hadn't seen me in a long time, took her place on the other side of the living room and said she wanted to know what I'd been up to. She loves it when I tell her I'm doing well and that I'm happy, but since the world I live in is to her one of frivolities, she isn't really interested in the details. The fact that my sister will never read a single story of mine upsets me, I admit, but the fact that I don't observe the Sabbath or keep kosher upsets her even more.

I once wrote a children's book and dedicated it to my nephews. In the contract, the publishing house agreed that the illustrator would prepare one special copy where all the men would have yarmulkes and side locks, and the women's skirts and sleeves would be long enough to be considered modest. But in the end even that version was rejected by my sister's rabbi, the one she consults on matters of religious convention. The children's story described a father who runs off with the circus. The rabbi must have considered this too reckless, and I had to take the "kosher" version of the book—the one the illustrator had worked on so skillfully for many hours—back to Tel Aviv.

Until recently, when I finally got married, the toughest part of our relationship was that my girlfriend couldn't come with me when I went to visit my sister. To be completely honest, I ought to mention that in the nine years we've been living together, we've gotten married dozens of times in all sorts of ceremonies that we made up ourselves: with a kiss on the nose at a fish restaurant in Jaffa, exchanging hugs in a dilapidated hotel in Warsaw, skinny-dipping on the beach in Haifa, or even sharing a Kinder egg on a train from Amsterdam to Berlin. Except that none of these ceremonies is recognized, unfortunately, by the rabbis or by the state. So when I would go to visit my sister and her family, my girlfriend always had to wait for me at a nearby café or park. At first I was embarrassed to ask her to do that, but she understood the situation and accepted it. As for me, well, I accepted it—what choice did I have?—but I can't really say I understand.

Nineteen years ago, in a small wedding hall in Bnei Brak, my older sister died, and she now lives in the most Orthodox neighborhood in Jerusalem. Back then there was a girl whom I loved to death but who didn't love me. I remember how two weeks after the wedding I went to visit my sister in Jerusalem. I wanted her to pray for that girl and me to be together. That's how desperate I was. My sister was quiet for a minute and then explained that she couldn't do it. Because if she prayed and then that girl and I got together and our togetherness turned out to be hell, she'd feel terrible. "I'll pray for you to meet someone that you'll be happy with instead," she said, and gave me a smile that tried to be comforting. "I'll pray for you every day. I promise." I could see she wanted to give me a hug and was sorry she wasn't allowed to, or maybe I was just imagining it. Ten years later I met my wife, and being with her really did make me happy. Who said that prayers aren't answered?

Translated by Miriam Shlesinger

TICKLE OR TORTURE

Vestal McIntyre

I flew into Boise on Independence Day and made my way home to find my mother wearing a little nightcap with a tassel. Beeb and I helped her from the bedroom to the living room, a difficult operation since we had to bear nearly all her weight. Every couple steps, I kicked out of the way the tube that connected my mother to the oxygen tank in the pantry. We lowered her gently into a chair, where she sat gasping. Six months ago, it had given her a little vain thrill to be thin at last. She had looked good in her clothes, and the wig had been more lustrous than her real hair. Now, though, her body had lost its integrity; her trunk crumpled when she sat, and her hands fell open to the sides.

No room I've lived in since could be as comfortable as that living room. The walls and floors had been repapered and recarpeted until they were soft with layers, and only the perfectly shaped sofas had survived, to be restuffed and reupholstered and arranged just so. Birds twittered in the bushes under the windows, and a breeze carried the sweet smell of honeysuckle in through the screen door. It struck me as crazy that the weather was so beautiful, a profusion of light and warmth and sweetness. I used the phrase "insanely beautiful" to myself at the time; preposterous of the world to insert itself so marvelously on such a day.

"She wasn't like this, even just a couple days ago," Beeb said under her breath. Then, abruptly, she took her four-year-old daughter Lillian outside to play—to keep her from seeing the despair in my face, most likely.

I sat on the floor and lay my head in my mother's lap. Then I saw she was awake, got hold of myself, and wiped my face. "Mom, are you comfortable? Do you need anything?"

Her eyes were bleary, milk-blue. They had grown large and wet as the skin around them receded and dried. She vaguely patted my shoulder, stroked my face, and said, "I'd cry too if I could."

I got up, propped pillows around her, and coaxed her into sipping some water through a straw. A half hour later Lillian burst back into the house with news of her adventures, with Beeb behind, quieting her. Mom said that she was ready to go back to bed. We helped her into the bedroom, and Beeb stayed to administer her afternoon meds while I went back to the living room. Lillian climbed into one of the swiveling chairs. "Spin me, Uncle Yazzy," she said. So I spun her round and round and joined in with her hysterical giggling.

Little children pick up much more than you think they do, or want them to, and they remember everything. "You were laughing and crying," she says to this day.

That was a constant of my childhood: laughing and crying at once. "Vessy, are you laughing or crying?" one of my six siblings would ask in a rare moment of concern.

"I don't know," I'd blubber.

Sometimes their torments were well planned, with an artful touch, like the night I was in the bath, playing with my spongy toys, and Roy strolled casually through the open door, holding an empty glass from the kitchen. "What!" I demanded. Roy responded with only a smirk as he turned on the tap at the sink and waited, testing it with his finger until it was sufficiently cold. Then he filled the glass and slowly approached. "Roy, don't!" I cried, shrinking into the corner of the tub. He doused me with water that can't have been as cold as I remember.

Pat invented a game he called Tickle or Torture, wherein he pinned me down and gave me the game's eponymous choice. I preferred torture, which consisted only of a hard, persistent thumping of my breastbone with his middle finger, but Pat knew this, so if I asked for it, he'd give me tickle, and if I asked for tickle he would know that I really wanted torture and was attempting to trick him, and he'd give me tickle again. Sometimes, through multiple layers of reverse logic, I'd succeed in eliciting torture, but that technique only worked once before becoming obsolete.

What varieties of tickling I endured! The light stroking under the arm, horrible in its gentleness because I knew I was being primed; the painful digging of knuckles into ribs; the wandering of bored fingers in search of any new raw crevice (under the chin, behind the knee) where a little stimulation would open a new spring of laughter and tears.

Usually they teased me freestyle: charley horses, titty twisters, noogies, wedgies. Two of my brothers pinned me down, while the third dangled spit over my screaming mouth, or squatted over me and farted, or, most memorably, took our fat little dog Muffin and slowly lowered her yellowish rear until she sat, squirming, on my face.

Bruised and rug-burned, I'd claw my way out of this orgy. If it was summer and still light out, I'd hide for a while in the fort in the back field. But winters in Idaho, night fell early, and I was afraid to run out into the dark. Instead I'd go to the office (my father was a pediatrician who ran a private practice connected to our house), where my mother kept the phone list. I'd lift the heavy receiver of that putty-colored phone, dial each number, wait for the dial's rattling return, and ask whichever nice Christian lady answered to call my mother away from Bible study. I'd weep and wail and tattle until Mom interrupted with a patient sigh. "Get me Beeb."

I'd press the intercom into the house. "Bee-eeb, Mom wants to talk to you!"

After Beeb hung up she'd turn to the others and say, "You guys, Mom says to leave him alone." She was a reluctant emissary at best, having five minutes before been part of the frenzy.

Sensing safety, I'd venture back in. They'd all turn away, and my heart would sink.

All I wanted was to be left alone! But how I hated to be left alone! Once ignored, I'd find a way to wriggle back into some sibling's sweet embrace or painful grip, and, minutes after that, repeat my refrain of "*Leave . . . me . . . a . . . lone . . .* LEAVEMEALONE!" And, given Mom's recent intervention, they might actually release me. But then the echo of my mantra would fade, the allure of my pudgy flesh would once again prove too strong, and they'd have to poke it, or twist it, or kiss it.

In the blinking sunlight under the globe willows, Lillian and I gathered sticks into nests that represented houses where her toys could live. Beeb called me inside. "Mom wants to say something to you." A cloud of worry passed over Lillian's wild eyes. Then she ran off across the grass. She was constantly cheerful and in motion that week, climbing furniture and somersaulting down onto cushions.

I went into the dim bedroom. A couple of friends who had come over to say good-bye stood in the recesses. I gave them reassuring smiles, to let them know they could stay. There was a pleasure in that room with my mother—the comfort of being where you really should be at that moment—and I didn't want to deprive them of it.

But Mom had already faded back into her stupor. Her eyes were almost closed, her mouth open. It hurt to see her white tongue lying there, spotted with sores. On the occasions we were able to get her to eat, this weary tongue shifted soft-boiled egg around in her mouth, then swallowed, only getting down a few bits.

I turned to Beeb. "What did she say?"

My sister breathed deeply. "She said not to be scared. She said, 'Vessy is scared. Tell him not to be. I'm not.'"

Beeb is probably the sibling I'm most like. She speaks precisely, hoping this accuracy might help things go the right way. We both live in anxious optimism—on a tightrope of thrill and worry—and I can see that Lillian lives on it, too.

As I looked down at my mother's shrunken body, lodged in the easy chair like a ring in its gift box, I felt a very simple and real regret. She had been present a minute before, but I had been on the lawn, building nests.

I'm not scared.

If I had been present, I would now own the memory of her saying that as part of my collection. And she would have not only seen her mission to impart that knowledge accomplished, but maybe witnessed in her youngest child's face some resolution, a fortifying of himself.

The next day, Evan arrived with the force of a stirring and cleansing gust of air. We had taken to keeping my mother's room dim and quiet, but he opened the windows that faced her lilac bushes, put on her favorite Beethoven, propped up the childlike, grinning portrait my dad had painted of her a year or two before she got sick, brought in and surrounded her with our framed senior pictures. We could have been an exhibit titled "Nerds Through the Decades," starting in the seventies with Cindy and her lank, honey-colored hair gathered into ringlets at either temple, ending with me, eyes nearly obscured under swooping New Wave bangs as I pensively played the cello. We all had somewhat crooked smiles that caught on our teeth, except for Pat, oddly white-smiled and confident in the middle.

Pat himself arrived. Then Roy, having dropped off his wife and kids with her family in Oklahoma on the way from Bangladesh. I watched my brothers confronted with the sight of our mother, remembering how it had torn me apart to see her so collapsed. But they greeted her cheerfully, with hearty hugs. Maybe Beeb had prepared them for the worst, or maybe they were made of sturdier stuff.

That afternoon, our uncle came in from the shed in the back field where he spent most of his time doing God knew what, to pray with my mother, lay on hands, cry out to God for healing. He was a sometime drifter, sometime street preacher, and none of us trusted him alone with her for too long. We tidied the kitchen very quietly so we could listen.

The next night, after dinner, an acupuncturist came. At this point most of us had quietly ceded victory to the cancer and were now just focusing on being with Mom. Not so for Evan, however. It was in his nature and part of his chosen approach to life never to give up hope that she would recover. So now, two days before her death, he wanted to see if an acupuncturist could do something Western medicine hadn't.

I led the acupuncturist into the bedroom, where Evan had dimmed the lights and lit candles. The man greeted my mother, who nodded vaguely. As he prepared his tools, he explained in a quiet voice what he was about to do. Then, with startlingly quick thrusts, he put pins in her wrists, up her arms, on her temples and the top of her head. She laid her head back and dozed, two needles standing out of her scalp like TV antennae. Dad came in and sat with us. It was a long, quiet treatment, and at last I got bored and joined the others at the dining room table, slipping into the chair next to Roy's.

You might not guess that Roy is a missionary. He has a sardonic sense of humor and is a master smirker. That smirk he wore when he approached me in the bathtub with that glass of cold water has been refined over his life, and now he can cast it at you and instantly strip you of all your pretensions. I often wonder whether that smirk is appreciated in Bangladesh as the masterpiece of irony that it is.

Everyone was quiet.

"What?" I said.

"Poor Mom," Roy said in the Idaho twang we had never picked up but used sometimes to express sarcasm. "Last night she was attacked by a faith healer, and tonight we've got her looking like a dang Teletubby."

There were stifled giggles all around.

The acupuncturist removed his pins and left, my brothers and sisters trailed off to bed, and thus began the longest night of my life.

It was Evan's and my turn to tend to my mother. One of us slept on a mattress on her floor, the other on the couch in the adjoining living room. But neither of us slept. Mom was struggling against pain and against her own body, which seemed to be making its last efforts to function as a human body should. In shame and pain, she apologized repeatedly, until I finally got stern with her—stern, with a dying woman, my mother!—and told her once and for all that it was okay.

She was quiet. As I write this now, I realize: maybe she saw then that I wasn't afraid.

The next day, my mother was peaceful, exhausted. In the evening Wendy arrived. She had been in Italy and had had to fight her way through airline bureaucracy to Idaho.

Wendy has blue eyes that whiten around the pupil. This gives them a pinpoint effect that sometimes makes them difficult to look into. She is an outdoorswoman, and all that sunlight and fresh air has permanently flushed her skin and etched intricate lines around her eyes. I watched these eyes when she walked into the bedroom and saw that formerly big woman who had raised us. I was shocked at her composure. Wendy took her place in the circle around my mother and joined in the chatting and joking. Fatigued from the night before, I decided to turn in early. I planted a kiss in Mom's short, silver hair. It had grown back surprisingly thick since chemotherapy sessions had been abandoned.

"Good night, Mom," I said, not expecting a response. She hadn't really spoken that day.

"Night," she said on a sigh.

We all looked to each other in surprise. Then, happily released by that soft syllable, I went to bed, and my siblings returned to their conversation.

I woke up disoriented. With so many of us in the house, I had been pushed out to sleep in the exam room in the office. It was crowded with furniture under dust cloths.

Most of the siblings were in the living room when I went inside. Wendy was in the bedroom reading to Mom. I sat down with Roy in the kitchen to eat breakfast.

"How'd you sleep out there?" Roy asked.

"All right."

"He didn't wake you up in the middle of the night?" *He,* our uncle.

"No. I don't even know if he's been around the last couple of days."

"Oh, he's here," Roy said. "I saw him out in his shed this morning."

"This early? Doing what?"

Roy smirked. "Cutting up the bodies, of course."

We burst out laughing. Then we quieted down and went back to eating. Then burst out laughing again.

I like to think that this laughter was the last thing my mom heard.

"Guys? Guys? Come here!" Wendy cried.

We all crowded into the bedroom.

"She's not breathing!" Wendy's eyes were brimming with tears.

"What happened?" asked Evan, just arriving.

"I was just sitting here, talking to her, and she stopped breathing." Wendy looked questioningly from one face to the next as the others moved closer. Someone took Mom's hand. This hand had been chubby when I was little. I used to take it in church during the long, boring sermon and twist the wedding ring around and around until she placed her other chubby hand on mine to stop me. Now her hand was long, blue veined, and dry. Her mouth hung open, the jumble of her bottom teeth exposed. She had always hated her teeth. They crowded against each other toward the front of her mouth like people impatient to exit a train, which made even her happiest, most heartfelt smiles slightly comical. We imitated her smile to each other sometimes, screwing up our mouths and squinting our eyes. When we really wanted to get it right, we'd add a smudge of lipstick to our front teeth.

My siblings gathered around my mother. Their tears were immediate. They laid their hands on each other and on her.

Dry-eyed, I stood on the periphery and watched. It was like we had traded roles: they had all been so composed when I had been constantly weeping; now I was like a submarine captain, viewing the crisp, bright world through a periscope.

Dad wasn't there.

I went out into the insanely beautiful day, white clouds vivid against blue sky. The garden hose led behind the house, and there my father was, watering the roses, which bowed their heads, bobbed and nodded. I walked across the grass and put my hand on his shoulder. He turned his eyes on me. Their weary, wrinkled lids were tugged up in the middle like window valances. I paused, because somehow it surprised me that he didn't already know. He gazed at me, not knowing, so I told him.

The lids were lowered, and he emitted a high-pitched, panicked groan. I followed him into the house. Everyone made room. Dad put in the earpieces of his stethoscope and pressed the metal disk to Mom's wrist. It seemed he had planned to do this when the time came. He listened, then took the earpieces out, letting the stethoscope hang from his neck. He looked at his watch and said the time aloud. The others cried, and now so did he.

Still safe in my submarine, I realized that someone should call Cindy, and it should be me.

Cindy is the oldest, the firstborn. She got stuck wasting some of her youth raising the youngest—me—which was a thankless job since I, in return, can barely remember her living at home. She went away to college when I was four. She's the sharpest talker of all of us, and the most pragmatic. She knows exactly when a joke is needed and always has one at the ready. "Doctor," she said when she accompanied our mother to her first radiation treatment, "what we really want to know is, will she have enough radiation to glow in the dark by Halloween?"

Cindy had had back surgery days before and couldn't travel. Knowing this might be the situation, she had said her good-byes on a recent visit.

"Cindy, it's happened. Mom's gone," I said.

"Oh, God," she cried.

Now everyone in my family was crying but me.

The hospice nurse came and said stupid, if well-intended, things about our mother being in a better place. Then the preacher. The funeral director came, strapped her onto a stretcher, and wheeled the body out of the house where it had lived happily for so long. The next time I saw it—the body—it was hard, and the stretched mouth was painted with more lipstick than she would ever have used.

I didn't cry that day, or the next, or at the funeral, or on the plane back to New York City. When I did cry, six weeks later, I was in good company in a wonderful place meant for crying. But that will be the subject of another essay, another time. This one is about regret.

Before the hospice nurse showed up, when it was still just us in a circle around my mom, someone said something that got us laughing. Then someone else added to it, and before long we were all having an honest-to-goodness *laugh* right there, next to our mother's newly vacated body.

Which brings me to my second regret. God, how I wish I could remember what it was that we were laughing about!

I'll bet it was Evan who started it off, since he's the family clown in a family of clowns. Maybe Beeb egged him on. Pat had been crying, hard. I remember that clearly, since I had never seen him really cry before. But now he was laughing, his mouth open, not in agony, but in the surprised gape he gives his spunky wife Mariko when she jokingly bullies him in Japanese.

Of course, it doesn't matter what we were laughing about. It was probably something mundane and we laughed eagerly, because to do so stroked the same muscles in our chests, next to our hearts, that crying did, but felt better. *Heartstrings.* I wonder at what point in the development of our language that funny concept came into being? It does feel like there are strings in there that can be not only painfully yanked but soothingly played, vibrating rattlingly like the strings of the cello when I dug in my bow and drew it across. This is what we had always done, with and to each other, plucked and pulled till we got a response. If you didn't laugh, you'd be made to cry. It's why I seek the quiet and am susceptible to loneliness when I find it.

That afternoon, though, I too was able to laugh, and it brought me into the circle. Sitting there laughing, strumming each others' heartstrings, echoed all the other times we laughed with our mother—*at* her, even.

IS MOM LOSING IT? This was the headline of the *McIntyre News,* a satirical newspaper Evan and I wrote when we were in junior high. We photocopied it and sent it around to the siblings who were off at college. Adorned with photos of Mom smiling that goofy smile, the article used direct quotes from her to examine the question. "You know the Chinese *hardly* cook their food." "Oh, look at the paloverde in bloom—it's *exquisite!*" Any instance when my mother was pretending expertise or making a bid at eloquence, Evan and I were waiting, pens in hand.

My mother grimaced when she saw the issue and pushed it across the kitchen counter without reading it. "You *brats!*" she said.

Success! The word *brat* was her farthest venture into profanity, and she resorted to it often. She was too Christian to call her children "ungrateful little shits," which was what we were. Too Christian and loved us too much.

SISTER

Angela Pneuman

I have always been jealous of people with brothers and sisters. Full disclosure, I have a stepbrother, stepsister, and two half sisters, all from my father's second marriage. But my parents' divorce when I was six was bitter, and my father died shortly after his third daughter was born. I never lived with any members of this other family, and though we exchange occasional photos, communication is rare enough that I have to consider myself what I am to my mother—her only child.

As a young girl I imagined a sister named Camilla, after the character in Madeleine L'Engle's eponymous book. In the book, Camilla grows up in New York City, also an only child. Camilla always has to explain her name, a flower, and that seemed to me an especially awkward thing to have to do as an only child, though I'm sure many people with siblings have the same problem. Camilla's parents were getting divorced, or lived apart—I can't remember now—and she was friends with a war veteran whom she sometimes visited. At fifteen or so, she rode the subway by herself. I always imagined that Camilla would be as grateful to have a sister as I would be.

I read the book before I was a teenager myself, before I had my tonsils out and when I was still missing weeks of school at a time with strep throat. My mother had never heard that reading with strep weakens your eyes—and in her defense I have never heard much about that—so I sat up in bed, in my small Kentucky town, reading about New York City until I was nearly legally blind and marking time by the hourly train that bisected Main Street not a block from our apartment house. I imagined my town, Wilmore, to be an outer subway stop in dirty, wonderful New York. I knew that if I'd had Camilla for a sister, she would have left Kentucky at eighteen, and not for college, either. She would have eked out a living in New York. She would have done something edgy, something to do with runaways or strippers. When I was eighteen she would have sent for me, and my mother, already brokenhearted over her first daughter, would have put me on a Greyhound with no protest, just a limp wave.

Camilla, I knew, would have stepped in and chloroformed me before any number of the shortsighted decisions I ended up making. She would have rescued my appearance, sabotaged for years, by telling me never to cut my own hair. She would have explained to me that aphorisms like "beauty is on the inside" are about other people, not for use in letting yourself off the hook when it came to diet and exercise (all lessons that vain mothers—and mine was not—demonstrate directly or indirectly). She would have told me that what you look like to other people matters to a lot of them, even if it shouldn't, even if they don't know it, and even though you should never admit that you've figured this out. She would have better prepared me for junior high, to which I arrived innocently in clothes my mother had sewn herself. "I can make that!" was what my mother said whenever I expressed interest in fashion. "I can make that" was always followed by a trip to the fabric store, where the fabric and pattern we selected were close but never quite right, and so full of sizing that my eyes watered. She wasn't the only enterprising seamstress around, to be sure. One girl less fortunate than me—another only child—had a mother who made her a pair of "Levi's" complete with pocket-stitched chevrons in gold thread and a tiny flag of orange felt.

Camilla would have taken me to "the mall" fifteen miles away. Instead, on the first day of junior high, when asked if I liked going to "the mall," I confessed to needing a definition. Every morning for the rest of the year a few jokers in my homeroom class asked me loudly if I wanted to go to the mall. And though I came to be somewhat grateful, by the eleventh grade, that I could design and whip up my own one-of-a-kind, can't-find-'em-at-the-mall pants—and tuck them into thrift-store combat boots—I always felt that my alternative style was born of necessity, not choice. My sister Camilla, I am sure, would have somehow acquired a Shaker sweater from the Limited and Lee jeans from wherever you got those, and she would have handed them down to me, sufficiently broken in, before heading for New York.

My second fantasy sister is younger, and her name is Daisy. She is named after my great-grandmother, whom she resembles in beauty and grace. Unlike Camilla, Daisy stayed right where she was raised, Wilmore, Kentucky, home to an evangelical seminary and more Protestant evangelical churches than anyone can count. Daisy, in my imagination, finished Bible college in town and started working as a teacher. Probably with underprivileged children. She lived at home with my mother (after I followed Camilla to New York) and pursued everything my mother dreamed I would. She worked to potential in high school, and in college she earned her degree in education and began teaching right afterward to pay my mother back for the money my mother had borrowed on her behalf.

Daisy would date a young man, we'll call him Chad, who matriculates at the seminary in town, having been called to Christian ministry in his late teens. Chad would be from Indiana or Ohio, some wholesome town, or maybe some town with a humbling past, like Kent. His parents own their own home but not in a greedy, social-climbing way. Maybe his father's a school principal, maybe his mom's a nurse. At any rate, Chad doesn't have student loans and can afford to take

Daisy to Applebee's on Friday nights and to a movie on Saturday nights. He comes for Sunday dinner after church, too, and works out his student sermons in front of Daisy and my (our) mother. Chad and Daisy don't have sex. They kiss, hold hands, and pray. One night Chad thinks he may have touched her breasts with the back of his hand, when he was going to cup her chin, and after he admitted to Daisy he might have done it on purpose, they prayed together for forgiveness and everything was back on track. Daisy naturally has the look that porn stars spend a fortune trying to achieve, a look Camilla, in one of her lines of work, would die for. White-blond hair and large breasts, and even though she will go to fat soon after her second son, she will never lose the sexy upward tilt to the outsides of her eyes.

Daisy doesn't criticize and she lacks ambition, except to be a wife and mother. So everyone will be surprised when she falls into more and more responsibility in the public school system, even agreeing to pursue a higher degree and become principal. When she outearns Chad, in their midthirties, they will attend marriage counseling to deal with his resentment—which he articulates humbly—and get everything back on track.

Here's what Daisy does for me. For one thing, she's sweet and nonjudgmental. We love to be around her, Camilla and I. Every once and a while she and Chad decide together that Daisy needs a weekend away, and those times the three of us get together in New York are some of the happiest in my life. Once we even invite our mom, and she is so emotional to see all three of us together that she doesn't even question what Camilla is up to with the married guy or why I wear only long sleeves. Daisy is what I invent for my mom, with proximity and grandkids and a stand-up husband who will confess guiltily to her every single time he gets a hard-on for another woman. My mom will move in with Daisy and her family after she retires, and Daisy, with her administrative expertise, will manage the Medicare red tape after my mother develops congestive heart failure. Chad will install a ramp on their front porch for my mother's wheelchair after she breaks a hip. Their home will be lovely, their boys will be beautiful and a little complicated, and they will think their auntie hangs the moon. Camilla and I will secretly count the days until Thanksgiving and Christmas at Daisy's home, where we will sneak booze in the backyard and laugh about a life we wonder if we should have given more thought to for ourselves, since Daisy seems so happy.

I'm told in no uncertain terms that real-life sisters are a mixed bag. And that sibling fantasies are about as realistic as the colors rocks take on underwater. For every loyalty there is competition; for all the help you get with your parents there is the frustration—on someone's part—of uneven or shirked responsibility. Everything real disappoints, of course.

However. Recently, in a hotel room, I shifted through the channels until I couldn't turn away from a program on parasitic twins. Some are less parasitic than others, limiting themselves to undemanding stray arms or legs folded like chicken wings beneath the surface of a shoulder. Other times there are teeth, or fingers, or a gallbladder—useless tools when taken out of context. Bottom line is that there weren't enough resources in the womb to support two babies. One of them got shafted so that the other could survive. Sometimes the parasitic twin takes revenge, pressuring a spinal column until the survivor loses her hearing. I'm convinced that mine is behind my forgetfulness, my inability to sleep soundly, the way I struggle with deadlines. Somewhere, probably near my liver, I have a sister who sleeps as soon as my head touches the pillow, one whose dreams enjoy perfect recall. Somewhere she hoards the fourth wisdom tooth that never came in for me. Probably she holds its wisdom as well. But she's on my side, too (that slight protrusion), whether she wants to be or not. It's her default position, automatic as my mother's. When I consider the way I grabbed her share of the resources, the way I fed from her unthinkingly, I feel convicted for my decisions and all my survival. If I could pry her from beneath my skin and find her shrunken little face I would hold it between my hands and tell her I'm sorry, and that I will try to make it worth her while.

HALFWAY OR IN-BETWEEN OR SOMETHING ELSE

Nat Bennett

I

On the map, we are halfway between where we started and where we should be. The morning began at a comically buggy campsite where my sleeping bag got wet. All day, we have been aiming for the red dot the man at the outfitter made with a felt-tip marker on a little nub of pale green jutting out into the blue toward the lake's far end. I imagine that underneath the red dot is a breezy, broad granite shelf perfect for airing out wet clothes while swimming. I picture tall pines that shed dry branches for cooking fires and red needles for a level tent site's rock-and-root-forgiving mattress.

Instead, we are here. The tent will have to be pitched at a slant across soggy earth, and our evening swim will require us to wade through sharp and slimy boulders in the shallows. Instead of paddling on to the red dot—the three of us stuffed together into the canoe with all our gear and provisions, meditatively isolated from each other by the work of pulling a boat across the water—my brother, stepfather, and I, all of us achy and soaked with cold rain, are setting up camp on the northeast arm of Cirrus Lake in Western Ontario. None of us have ever been here before, and we do not expect to be back.

I don't like this stopping short of where we planned to be. I don't like that, to get back on course, tomorrow will have to be longer and more difficult. I don't like what seems to be an even worse and more likely prospect, that we'll have another day like this one, and that our trip will fall short of what it could be, that we'll see fewer lakes, cover less ground. Most of all, I don't like that I seem to be so much stronger and more resilient than they are, so eager to keep moving, and that this has divided me from my brother and stepfather. We are here because they wanted to stop, because they are hungry. So I resent them both, my stepfather for being weaker than he once was, my brother for failing to use his new strength. And probably because I am tired and hungry myself, I don't bother to do a very good job of concealing my disdain.

The way it starts is simple: my brother says he wishes it wasn't raining or that it's too bad he's so cold. Something like that. A complaint. I say something in response, something not nice, a withering, sarcastic comment noting the bad taste of complaining about something through which we are all suffering. I do this sometimes. I am an older brother. I condescend. My brother doesn't like it. He tells me, loudly, that I have no right to talk to him this way. Maybe he tells me I talk to him this way a lot. And maybe I reply that it could be because he provides me with so many opportunities. I'm not sure exactly what is said, but I know that moments later, he is shouting, swearing at me, and that something then foams up and boils over in me, and I scream, "Shut the fuck up," as many times as I can in the time it takes to leap up from my boulder and violently rush toward him. When I get to him, I do not know what to do, so I grab his shirt and scream, "Shut the fuck up," a few more times. I am as furious as I have ever been, but the look on his eighteen-year-old face has already begun to hollow me out. I see fear, surprise, and something that says we will never be the same.

* * *

I was fourteen when my mother gave birth to my stepfather's son, their second child together. My boss at the corner store got a call saying I wouldn't be in to mop the floors and fill up the pop cooler, and I got a ride from a neighbor with my eight-year-old sister down to the hospital. We spent the afternoon admiring our new brother's impossibly small, rosy, clenched face. In high school I often took care of him after school and in the evenings, giving him his bottle, reading him stories, singing him to sleep. We loved being together; each thought the other was hilarious. Once, when I was giving him his nightly bath, I delighted him by throwing a red rubber ball in successively higher arcs until the last toss came so close to the ceiling that its shadow disappeared behind it for a moment and the ball seemed to hang there, just short of the plaster. My brother laughed so hard he pooped a round, buoyant turd into the bathwater. I thought it was the best joke I had ever been told. He was two.

We began to have battles of will soon after he learned to speak. He was a baby in a house full of adults and he needed to be taken seriously. I considered our arguments a show of respect. When I left home for college, we missed each other terribly. The summer after I graduated, before I realized no one would tell me what to do with my life, I was his nanny for a couple of months. I usually slept as late as possible, but when my brother could no longer stand it, he would go get my mother's cockatiel out of its cage and crawl into bed with me, the bird skittering around on the covers above us. Until I was fully awake, he asked me to recall and recite our favorite scenes from *The Simpsons* and *Seinfeld*.

Last summer my brother was eighteen, just out of high school, and feeling that none of us had really noticed. And why shouldn't we? He has grown into a strong body and a handsome face. He writes songs people want to hear over and over. He was moving away to Oregon in the fall with his girlfriend and bandmate. He was—I think all of us are sure of this when we are eighteen years old—himself, finally.

When I think of that day on Cirrus Lake, I am still ashamed. That raging bum-rush is the closest I have ever come to committing an act of violence, against him or anyone else. That it happened in our favorite place in the world, the gentle wilderness that stretches across northern Minnesota and southwestern Ontario, well, it makes me think I don't know how to appreciate anything. I will get past these feelings, I know, but I cannot shake the sense that my outburst marked a midpoint, the threshold between our relationship as children and our relationship as adults. And as necessary as that may be, it is a wounding thought. We are something else now.

The wound is still fresh for my brother, a tenderhearted young man, as well. A couple months ago, just before the big move to Portland, his band performed on a local radio show in Minnesota where we grew up. Toward the end of the show he sang a new song. "Through the rushes, I'll keep us together," it went. "Though the river, she tears us apart." The chorus: "Brother, brother, can you feel my heart?" A few weeks ago, both of us in town for our uncle's funeral, my brother asked me if I had listened to the song. He said it was about that day in the woods. I told him I had suspected as much, that I had tried not to know that sadness in his voice was because of me. We talked late into the night. About our uncle, about each other, about nothing much at all. At the end, we embraced, and then he went out to find his friends while I went up to bed. He slept late, and I went into his room to wake him up around noon. Did I consider crawling into the covers with him, like he did in the old days? I suppose I didn't. I called his name, told some joke that made him chuckle enough to make me smile, and then I went downstairs to hang out with my sister and her husband.

Although we live in different cities now, I have grown close to them in the past few years. We have a lot in common. None of us has figured out a way to live apart from a university; we dote on our dogs; each of us is a strong believer in the wasting of time. When we are together, we spend most of the day on the couch, talking and laughing, sometimes drinking, hashing out whatever needs hashing.

My sister, my brother-in-law, and I sat in my parents' living room, griping about our petty worries, sharing our grief for our uncle, knowing we were lucky to be together. All the while, I kept one eye on the stairs, waiting for my brother to join us.

II

I have two other brothers, my father's sons with my stepmother. Fewer than two years apart in age, they truly grew up together in a small town just outside of Minneapolis. I visited my father's house every other weekend, bringing a laundry basket filled with *Star Wars* toys and GI Joes, then boxes of *X-Men* and *Spider-Man* comic books, and later the gospel of rap tapes and skateboards. They knew I was their older brother who loved them, but I was also a novelty, a figure to be studied and emulated.

They're adults now, and they have surpassed me in nearly every way that matters. Both are fine athletes, the younger brother an amazing skateboarder, the older an insanely good backyard basketball player. Both are great musicians and songwriters. One can dance better than anyone I have ever met. The other writes exactly the kind of sad, funny stories I wish I could write. Together, they are the funniest people in the world.

Best of all, both are beautifully self-destructive, something I never had the courage to be. I see in their lives the bravest kind of rebellion, the kind that puts oneself in harm's way for little reason, an existentialist's meaty starring role in the black comedy of life. Maybe as a result of being strange in a small, conservative town, the younger goes faster on his skateboard than every other skater around him, as if he has so much energy inside of him that he will catch fire if he doesn't use it up. He hurls himself off of ramps and up onto walls. He plummets to the ground, sometimes sticking the trick, sometimes not. I watch him, spellbound.

But I think even the younger would agree that the elder is more impressively careless with his own safety, since his willingness to throw himself in front of the figurative bus is not confined to any particular activity. In story after story, the elder is heroic because he seems to be the only one who realizes he is living out a story, that the consequences of our actions are not as important as the manner in which we conduct ourselves. I have often used his early obsession with *Back to the Future* to explain his character. I'm thinking of the scene near the end in which Marty McFly has to fill in for Marvin Berry on guitar at the big dance. He performs "Johnny B. Goode" and ends up playing an out-of-control Van Halenesque guitar solo that makes everyone stare in bewilderment. This, I think, is the key to that scene for the elder: What's cool is not lying on your back playing your ass off in front of a bunch of people. What's cool is lying on your back playing your ass off in front of a bunch of people who don't think it's cool.

The night before the younger's twenty-first birthday he and the elder went out for his power hour at midnight. They got pretty drunk pretty fast. This was when they lived near the University of Minnesota campus, in the student ghetto of clapboard houses badly needing paint, porches sagging. A warm July night. Music and shouting from the houses with parties, that blue TV glow from others.

On the way home they passed by a party with a lot of big jock-y guys and sorority girls up on a balcony. When they approached the house, the elder called up to the guys on the balcony. How about a beer? Could he join them up there? Something like that. They told him to go away, probably also to shut the fuck up. The elder saw a challenge and an opportunity. He would get up into that party. And he would make the partygoers uncomfortable, unable to know whether they should laugh or cringe or fly into a rage. So he shouted something obnoxious back, and the jocks on the balcony responded in kind. This went on for a while. They threatened to pour a beer on him. He said good, that way he could have a sip. Then someone said they were going to come down and kick his ass. He yelled bring it on, that sort of thing. They yelled back and forth some more, the ass-kicking threats coming hotter and heavier now, the younger remembers, and it started to become apparent how huge these guys were, how gigantic compared to our stringy brother. The elder noticed this too, apparently, because he shouted up: "Okay. Here's the deal. Any of you guys could hospitalize me without much trouble. But one of you is walking away with a black eye or a bloody nose. Or a really big bruise."

At this point he was just below the porch balcony, screaming up at this crowd of gorillas leaning over the railing to see him. Then someone tossed a beer bottle at the elder, and somehow he caught it in one hand like a ninja. And as the younger remembers, this impressed some of the crowd. They began to clearly enjoy the elder's antics. But it infuriated a few of the bigger guys, and one of them started shouting a new threat: if he wouldn't leave, this guy was going to piss on him. So naturally, the elder starts yelling, "Piss on me! Do it. Come on, piss on me! Whip your dick out! Everyone wants to see this. I'm not fucking moving!" It is hard to know if the elder's lack of self-respect was intimidating or if the guy simply had stage fright. In any case, the guy up on the balcony decided *not* to whip his dick out. But the elder did not like the idea of leaving a promise unfulfilled so he started marching around in a tight circle, chanting a new mantra:

"Who's the pussy who won't piss on an asshole?"

You know this, but I think it is worth emphasizing: the asshole to whom my brother referred was himself. And what better label could apply? Here were people minding their own business, gathered together to enjoy each other's company and beer they had bought with their own money. My brother, my obnoxious, drunk brother, wasn't just trying to crash the party. He wanted to detonate it. "Let me in," he was saying. "Let me into your house and into your hearts, despite and because of the fact that I am quite clearly a sloppy, infectious asshole."

I don't remember if the younger told me what happened next. I only know that, soon thereafter, the guys upstairs saw they had been beaten, realized they were in the presence of a superior will, and invited my brothers upstairs. Both stayed all night, helped finish the keg, and walked the two blocks home as morning birds were chirping.

I tell this story more often than I should. No one loves it as much as I do. Very few people seem to see more in it than a drunk guy getting lucky amid other drunk people. Even if that is all there is to it, the central fact remains: when I grow up, I want to be my little brother. I wish I had his inappropriate fearlessness, his assertion of self by way of self-awareness. I would like to live life the way he does, as performance art. And so I recount the story again and again to whoever will listen, because in the telling I get to celebrate our shared DNA.

III

I wrote quite a few mediocre stories about brothers during my twenties. Usually, the first-person narrator was the younger brother; equally often, the narrator spent a good deal of the story attempting to make sense of his brother, a person who either eclipsed and amazed him or deeply disappointed him. More often than not, this figure did both. Always, these relationships were tragic and fraught, but also, of course, tender and insightful. That's what I was going for, anyway. Skimming those pages now, I am embarrassed by their simplicity, their false drama, their overblown language. I am sheepish about the naked display of their author's psychology. In each story, I see a narrator trying to work through what it must be like to be *my* younger brother. What must it be like, these stories wonder, to have an older brother who judges your every effort and exceeds you in some important way no matter what you accomplish? How would it feel to be forever running after someone who expects you to be as smart, as skeptical, and as sad as he is? What do you do if you are born too late to compete, if you love someone more than they can properly requite, if you realize the object of your worship is, in some fundamental way, a fraud? The stories worry that it is very hard to be the younger brother of a brilliantly sardonic tortured-artist type who never quite makes good, deciding in the end that it's actually totally worth it when you realize how brilliant and tortured he really is.

Although I'm sure being my little brother is not always a picnic, these stories bring the wrong blanket and the wrong ants. They make the older brother's shadow too long, too dark, too goddamn important. They turn me into—I'm admitting this—Seymour Glass, the older brother that haunts so many of J. D. Salinger's stories. And I'm not. Like Seymour, I have my own subtle charms and obscure encyclopedic knowledge. I am in many ways a tough act to follow. But I am not an imaginary Zen genius. I am not someone who fails to love his loved ones. I am not a walking ghost, a beautiful apparition of lost possibility.

I am, however, exceptional. That is, in each of my families, there is only one like me, and only I get to be in both families and in the indistinct space between them. I am the only child of my mother and father, who divorced when I was two years old and each married other people by the time I was four. (Both marriages persist to this day.) From each of my four parents I received love, support, and a unique example of how to be a kind, thoughtful, and interesting person. Each of my families had two more children, my siblings, all of whom I love and enjoy. Probably because my parents worked so hard to ensure that it did not ruin my life, their divorce was the best thing that ever happened to me. It made me a compromise between two great options. Like my father, I take unreasonable pleasure in telling dirty jokes and explaining obscure trivia. Like my mother, I cannot fully enjoy something I have read until I tell someone else about it. From my stepmother I learned the power to hear the subtext in what people say. From my stepfather, my ability to size up and maneuver within virtually any social situation. Sometimes I feel like a gently constructed chimera. The downside is that I'm often hesitant to head in any particular direction. I have too many ways to question my motives. It's hard to think of myself as emphatically anything in particular.

When I introduce someone to one of my siblings, I never use the term *half*. As far as I'm concerned, I have no half brothers, since that qualifier implies less love, less relation, and less history. We are to each other, I insist, what any other siblings would be. But thinking of them as full-blooded kin, I know, is also a way for me to feel my feet on the ground. And without the earth under my shoes I feel like a sort of negative image of the last of the Mohicans, the first and only of a soon-to-be-extinct people. And so I tell myself as I am telling others, these are my siblings, we are a distinct group, I come from something, I am part of these people who amaze and delight me.

A few months ago, my younger brother on my father's side moved to New York and quickly established himself as a person of note in certain circles. I introduced him to a few of my friends, and now he sees some of them more often than I do. I hear about him from them. He dances amazingly, endears himself to dogs. He skates through broken glass and bums too many cigarettes. He told me recently that he was at a party and people kept making the same remark: "That is so Nat." People were grabbing other people to observe my brother like a specimen. "This is Nat's little brother. Listen to the way he talks. Isn't he just like him?" I was curious: what did my brother do that was so me-like? He had no idea. In our family we are as far apart as can be, and because we are both bad at staying in touch we have kept in touch the least. We look nothing alike. It was strange to us, the thought of other people seeing our similarity. It was wonderful as well. We are brothers. Other people can tell.

It is tempting to assign great meaning to all this, to proclaim my life within my family an example of the distinctly American opportunity to be an individual among the masses that Whitman celebrated, or to find a metaphor for all this quietly nurturing in-between-ness. I find, however, that nothing describes what I have come to understand in my life among my siblings so well as describing my life among them. And so I still write stories about brothers, but they are their own brothers now, not mine, and sometimes I write about sisters too.

IV

I was living in California when my brother graduated from college, and I did not make it back for the graduation party my father and stepmother threw him. I was sorry to miss the celebration for all the usual reasons, but also because my other family drove out to celebrate too. My brother and sister, not related to each other by a drop of blood, became good friends in the University of Minnesota dorms, and my parents and stepparents have always enjoyed each other's company. So together, all eight members of my immediate families laughed and drank and danced. A lot happened that day, even though I wasn't there. I'm glad I was somewhere else, over on the other side of the map. I got to hear about it from each of them, separately.

N: I KNEW HIM WHEN

Rebecca Wolff

N is a forty-four-year-old Web entrepreneur and programmer based in New York City. Never married, tall, handsome, historically a swinging bachelor, he is currently cohabiting with a girlfriend for the very first time. He has a close relationship with his mother and father, who also live in New York City. He has always lived in New York City, except for a few years in exile in Philadelphia after he was thrown out of college in the late 1980s. He was thrown out of college because he and a childhood friend (his current business partner) were thieves. They burgled goods on a market so black no one has ever been able to recover from it what they introduced into it. They were caught, and the partner went to jail for a short time. N confessed but his partner didn't; this caused a deep rift between the parents of N and partner, but never between N and the partner himself; they seem to have worked it out between them as junior Übermensches, in keeping with the fundamentally slippery moral code already established between them, even *by* them. N and partner's fascination with the law was with both sides of it; they had founded a detective agency as preteens and attempted to bring to justice a pot-growing neighbor, right around the same time they vandalized a local graveyard. Due to the world's similarly fluid relationship with white-collar criminals and the timely burgeoning of the tech economy, its appetite for talented programmers, N had no difficulty transcending his dodgy history—dodged his condemning story!—and has been successful in his legitimate career ever since, even sans bachelor's degree.

N's other childhood best friend also remains a close connection in his adulthood. He is a New York City police detective—now a sergeant, I believe.

Who am I? I am the sister of this character.

I am not clear on why I, or anyone else, should care about my brother, or why anyone besides my close friends—or, perhaps, acquaintances around a dinner table I am exerting myself to entertain—should hear about his high jinks, his misdoings, his dubious distinctions. Yet it is of great interest to me; am I of great interest to you?

The confessional impulse was strong in me from the start. One of my first published poems, in 1985 or so, was called "Seduction Theory" and had to do with my brother—pubescent N—and prepubescent me experimenting with, um, sex. (Lots of young brothers and sisters do this, which doesn't make it a good idea.) Something about using a plastic sandwich bag as a "condom," the gist being that I was uncomfortable in every interior way and wished with hindsight that we hadn't done that. One of my other more memorable poems from that time (high school) asserted that I would shoot my brother in the foot before I would let him be sent off to war. This during a time of seemingly infinite peace, so I'm not sure why I was getting myself all heated up, but it seems to have been at the very least an outlet for the intensity of emotion I felt toward N at the time. I was a little bit in love, as are many sisters.

It's tough to feel emotional around N—toward him, in front of him, even in back of him—and I might have been writing about him so passionately in those hectic years because, as with much in my immediate family (and that's all the family I have), all was to have been suppressed, if not repressed. I actually thought I really was quite a cool character, at the time, and never would have described myself as having any particular feelings about anything at all. Yet cataclysmic inner seepage did occur, bringing language burbling up in the old brainpan: Birth of Poem.

Let N = Rational Mind. Like most of us, in his forties N is happier in general and so less motivated to interrupt others' happiness; but still he is quite often downright obnoxious and will openly, performatively scoff at anything outside of the realm of reason—religious faith, for example, or the use of homeopathy. (Um, hello, *France*? Can't an entire country stand in for more than anecdotal evidence?) But he wasn't always such a scoffer: one of my fondest memories of our young lives together dates from an era in which we would often stop in after school at the occult shop near our apartment. It was called The Warlock's Childe, and in it we could browse and examine all sorts of powders and talismans—and the candles, oh, the candles, I can still smell them, tall and black, and round, and fat, prescribed for use in dark rituals of Satanic force—and arcane manuals on various forms of spell casting or channeling. The shocking thrill of the dark, pungent insides of this store: that everything we dared not say we desired, all our dangerous childhood imagining, was actually *recommended* there, by dint of its neat arrangement. We purchased one day a pamphlet on hypnosis (a fairly tame option, given the range of choices) and I see myself from some unnamed perspective—out of body? or do I see through N's eyes?—perched on my mother's embroidered rocking chair by the window in her bedroom, palm out, N kneeling before me, pricking me repeatedly with a straight pin from her sewing table. "Do you feel that?" No. "Do you feel that?" No. "Do you feel that?" No. I couldn't feel anything. Hooray.

My brother and I are not close, but that doesn't mean I don't love him. I know he loves me, though he never says it or demonstrates it. I think this is a not uncommon form of relation for adult siblings, although online I found a list called "Five Types of Adult Sibling Relationships" and none of them seemed to encompass this formulation. They are "the intimate, the congenial, the loyal, the apathetic, and the hostile." Or perhaps they simply don't talk about the love—love could be part of any of these. If I were less apathetic maybe I would make more of an effort to make my brother care about whether he was intimate with me. He is generally congenial toward me. I am pretty loyal (thus the foot shooting), and deep down there seems to be some sort of underlying hostility. N thinks I'm absurd, most of the time, possibly despicable, even, with my poetry writing and my lack of nice clothing. (And what else about me does he find objectionable? I will have to ask him, someday.) I find suspect his deep superficiality: his quick-witted, sometimes arrogant engagement with things as they most apparently are—the world on the surface of the world. Television, conventional gender dynamics, narratives along the lines of the genres—he is terribly pithy and witty, even meta, on the subjects of these, and many others, while I stammer along on subjects that often remain unidentified, not finishing most of my sentences.

I've been worried about what might happen to my relationship with my brother if he ever reads this. But we have the kind of adult sibling relationship that makes it seem possible for me to never mention it to him, and thus him to never see it.

N and I used to be *very* close, when we were young. Otherwise how could we have attempted intercourse with a baggie or spent day after day exploring the dark realms of the occult? The other day, forty-two and forty-four years old, we had lunch with a third party, a friend of mine, whom he was scoping out even as we discussed his girlfriend's twentieth high school reunion—he's a helpless dog before a pretty girl—and the talk turned somehow to another noteworthy childhood experience. I think we were both charmed to find that each had a strong memory of what must have been a shared formative moment, and we attempted to re-create it for my friend. *We had been put to bed upstairs at the home of Helen, a friend of our mother's, somewhere on a farm in—Virginia? West Virginia?* We couldn't remember, either of us, and this too was a shared experience— *and we were reading to each other—or did we pass the book back and forth and read silently? Somehow we both reached a climax of terror, the story being about a twin who had been strangled in the womb by the other's umbilical cord—on purpose!—and who now haunted the living twin's consciousness and forced him to perform heinous acts of murderous mayhem, and the living twin's name was . . . Clay!* We both thought we remembered it at the same time and were tickled to find it lodged in our consciousness, our shared consciousness. There's that intimacy I'd been looking for. I'm loyal to the congenial intimacy of our childhood. *And we screamed and screamed, and went running down the stairs together into the kitchen of the farmhouse, to find our mother.*

Now, writing this, I remember with a dawning puzzlement that actually Clay was the name of the husband of my mother's friend with whom we'd been staying in West or just plain Virginia. Memory is so creative, huh? But I think I must have been confused at the time, or is it possible that what scared us so much was that the dead twin had the same name as Helen's husband? I remember that the name "Clay" made me imagine the dead fetus inside the mother's womb with a sort of gray-green skin like a ball of wet, unfired clay. I wonder if N saw it the same way. I wonder if we are unclose because of some fear on his part of engaging with me, who was his early partner in the impossible, in what is not natural or rational—certainly not quantitative or evidence based (even in our darkest hours he was always more concerned than I with that aspect of the occult which is given to *proving it*). I knew him when.

I won't go into the painful ways that we are not close. That's just my pain, right? There is no legitimate way to make it seem important to anyone else, or if I do, that would approach the kind of manipulative aesthetic chicanery I abhor, generally. Yet I see that I've so far left out something big: The particulars. The ways in which we are not close that are banal, common, run-of-the-mill. Why, for instance, would we talk on the phone, or make plans to see each other, or "keep in touch," even, when if we met each other in a bar or at a party we would mutually understand, with little probing, that we come from different planets? (Same womb.) He's all mass media, I'm a small-press poetry publisher. He uses Crest, I use Tom's of Maine. He's a little bit Conan O'Brien, I haven't seen any late-night since I got out of bed one night in high school to tell our dad I felt like killing myself and our dad was watching Johnny Carson. The banality of sibling alienation: it happens to many, is felt by few.

Here's someone who might have a vested interest in these particulars, and here we are in the aftermath of Thanksgiving 2009, in my kitchen in the morning, drinking coffee and leaning on the counters as there's nowhere to sit down. She's my brother's girlfriend, the one we all hope will stay around. She's fantastic and can put up with him: his bizarre sleep schedule (four A.M. to eleven), his never-off TV, his impatience, his arrogance. On the one hand he's always been a gold-medal boyfriend, chivalrous, demonstrative, and spontaneous—up for all sorts of adventures, mostly in restaurants—but on the other he's also always been disturbingly, almost abusively non-committal and philanderous, a scratchy-tongued lion the girl-friend is thrown to, and no one's ever lasted long enough to work herself into a position of intimacy, plumbing whatever depths there may be to plumb. I admire L's restraint: in her place I think I would be desperately curious for details, details, details, of childhood, of upbringing, of past life (as I imagine you aren't). But she is cool and collected, a woman raised with four older brothers and spartan, WASP-y parents. In her Batgirl skintight black-leather kitten-heel boots, she seems to know exactly what she's doing. This year it is I who am feeling a bit desperate, and I dissolve in tears in the kitchen after stammering for a minute about how odd it is that N and I never talk. Truthfully, I realize, as I stammer, I am feeling self-conscious in front of her about our visible distance—she must think it odd, very odd, given the "tightness" she speaks about with her unruly gang of brethren, that N and I are pretty much on holiday terms: we see each other at the proscribed family gatherings and not voluntarily otherwise, nor do we speak. We are of course Facebook "friends." I'm feeling excruciatingly self-conscious about it, actually, and say as much to her, over our strong coffee. (There is a hole in this narrative: what happened between the ages of eleven or twelve and forty-two? But that would be the stories of our lives, and they would be stories connected only by their simultaneity.)

She is bemused and circumspect but not forthcoming, and I come to understand through her near silence, her empathetic yet noncommittal "hmmm"s, that there are things my brother has said to her about his sister that make it clear to her why we are not close, and that those things are not to be revealed to me by her. It may be that there are all sorts of things N doesn't like about me, or resents me for, or simply doesn't understand—or all of the above. And I hope, for his sake, that he has told her all of them. And I understand for whom it is that I write this.

CONTRIBUTORS

Steve Almond is the author of six books, most recently the memoir *Rock and Roll Will Save Your Life*. He is also, crazily, self-publishing books. *This Won't Take But a Minute, Honey,* is composed of thirty very brief stories and thirty very brief essays on the psychology and practice of writing. *Letters from People Who Hate Me* is just plumb crazy. Both are available at readings. In 2011, Lookout Press will publish his story collection, *God Bless America*.

Daphne Beal's novel, *In the Land of No Right Angles,* was published by Vintage/Anchor in August 2008. Her nonfiction has appeared in *The New York Times Magazine, Vogue,* and *McSweeney's*. Her work has been anthologized in *The Believer Book of Writers Talking to Writers, State by State: A Panoramic Portrait of America,* and *The KGB Bar Reader*. Originally from Wisconsin, she lives in Brooklyn with her husband and their two children.

Nat Bennett is coauthor of the play *Ham Lake,* the film *Stuck Between Stations,* the unaired pilot *Gimme Shelter,* and the parenting book *Why Do They Act That Way?: A Survival Guide to the Adolescent Brain for You and Your Teen*. A Minnesota native, he teaches writing in New York City, where he lives in a small apartment with the love of his life and a small dog.

Miranda Beverly-Whittemore is the author of two novels: *Set Me Free* (Warner Books, 2007), which won the Janet Heidinger Kafka Prize for the best book of fiction by an American woman published in 2007, and *The Effects of Light* (Warner Books, 2005). Her short story "Pertussis" won the 2008 Crazyhorse Fiction Prize. She is the co-screenwriter and producer of the forthcoming film adaptation of *The Effects of Light,* as well as the forthcoming short *Camera Obscura.* She is at work on a novel entitled *The Plagiarist.*

James Cañón was born and raised in Colombia. After majoring in advertising in Bogotá, he moved to New York to learn English. He received his MFA in creative writing from Columbia University. His debut novel, *Tales from the Town of Widows and Chronicles from the Land of Men,* has been published in over twenty countries. It has received several awards, among them the 2008 Prix du Premier Roman Étranger and the 2008 Prix des Lecteurs de Vincennes. *School Library Journal* named it one of the ten best books of the year. James's short stories and essays have appeared in numerous literary journals in the U.S., Mexico, France, Belgium, and Colombia. He lives in Barcelona.

T Cooper is the author of, most recently, a graphic novel entitled *The Beaufort Diaries* (Melville House). He has also written two regular old novels, *Lipshitz Six, or Two Angry Blondes* (Plume) and *Some of the Parts* (Akashic), and edited an anthology, *A Fictional History of the United States with Huge Chunks Missing* (Akashic). T lives with his wife, two kids, two pit bulls, and a fairly decent cat in New York.

Lauren Grodstein is the author of three books, including, most recently, the novel *A Friend of the Family,* a *Washington Post* Book of the Year and a *New York Times* Editor's Choice. Her essays and reviews have been widely anthologized, and her work has been translated into French, Italian, Turkish, and other languages. She teaches creative writing and helps direct the MFA program at Rutgers Camden.

Nellie Hermann is a graduate of Brown University and the MFA program at Columbia. Her first novel, *The Cure for Grief,* has received national acclaim in such publications as *Time, Elle, The Washington Post, The Boston Globe,* and others. She teaches writing at Barnard College and is the chief writing faculty in the program in narrative medicine at Columbia University Medical School. Her website is nelliehermann.com.

Joanna Hershon is the author of three novels: *Swimming, The Outside of August,* and *The German Bride.* Her writing has been included in the 2008 literary anthology *Brooklyn Was Mine,* short-listed for the 2007 *O. Henry Prize Stories,* and has appeared in various journals, including *One Story, Five Chapters,* and *The Virginia Quarterly Review.* She lives in Brooklyn with her husband, the painter Derek Buckner, and their twin sons.

Nalini Jones was born in Rhode Island, graduated from Amherst College, and received an MFA from Columbia University. Her story collection, *What You Call Winter,* was published in August 2007 by Knopf, and in 2008 she contributed an essay to *AIDS Sutra,* an anthology of writing about AIDS in India. She teaches at Columbia University, Fairfield University, and the Ninety-second Street Y in New York, and is currently working on a novel.

Etgar Keret is an Israeli author. His books, including *The Nimrod Flipout* and *The Bus Driver Who Wanted to Be God,* have been translated into twenty-nine languages. The movie *Jellyfish,* codirected by Keret and his wife, Shira Geffen, won the prestigious Camera d'Or prize at the 2007 Cannes Film Festival. His latest short story collection, *The Girl on the Fridge,* was published in the U.S. by Farrar, Straus and Giroux.

Victor LaValle is the author of the short story collection *Slap-boxing with Jesus* and two novels, *The Ecstatic* and *Big Machine*. Among his awards and fellowships are a Whiting Writers' Award, a United States Artists Ford Fellowship, and the key to Southeast Queens. He lives in New York City.

Vestal McIntyre was born and raised in Nampa, Idaho, has lived in Boston and New York, and currently lives in London. He is the author of the story collection *You Are Not the One,* which won a 2006 Lambda Literary Award, and the novel *Lake Overturn,* which was named a *New York Times Book Review* Editor's Choice and a *Washington Post* Best Book of 2009. His stories have appeared in *Open City, Tin House,* and *Boston Review,* and he has received fiction fellowships from the National Endowment for the Arts and the New York Foundation for the Arts.

Jay Baron Nicorvo works for the Council of Literary Magazines and Presses (CLMP). His poetry, fiction, and nonfiction have appeared in *The Literary Review, Subtropics, The Believer,* and elsewhere. He's on the editorial staff at *Ploughshares* and at PEN America, and he lives in the Catskills with his wife, Thisbe Nissen, and their vulnerable chickens. His siblings, Dane and Shawn, would like to state for the record that Jay is welcome to write whatever the hell he wants—they could care less, it's a free country—but they remember things a bit differently.

Mary Norris was born in Cleveland, Ohio, and lives in New York City, where she is on the editorial staff of *The New Yorker.* Her work has appeared in *The New Yorker,* the *New York Times, Newsday, Self,* and the *New York Press,* among other publications. She is the author of the blog *The Alternate Side Parking Reader* (it's not just about parking) and is completing a memoir about her legendary sibling Baby Dee.

Eric Orner is a cartoonist and animation artist whose comics and graphic stories have appeared widely in the alternative weekly press in the U.S. and Canada. In 2006 a feature film based on Eric's comic strip about gay life in America, *The Mostly Unfabulous Social Life of Ethan Green,* was released nationally. The comic strip has been anthologized in four books from St. Martin's Press.

Peter Orner is the author of the novel *The Second Coming of Mavala Shikongo,* finalist for the *Los Angeles Times* Book Prize, and the story collection *Esther Stories,* winner of the Rome Prize from the American Academy of Arts and the Goldberg Prize for Jewish fiction. The recipient of a Guggenheim Fellowship, Orner's work has appeared in *The Atlantic, The Paris Review, The Best American Short Stories,* and the Pushcart Prize annual anthology. Born in Chicago, he now lives in California.

Angela Pneuman is the author of the story collection *Home Remedies* (Harcourt) and a forthcoming novel from Harcourt Houghton-Mifflin. Her work has appeared in *The Best American Short Stories, Ploughshares, New England Review, The Virginia Quarterly Review,* and many other journals. She lives in the Napa Valley and works as a writing consultant in the wine industry.

Margo Rabb is the author of the novel *Cures for Heartbreak,* which was named one of the best books of the year by *Kirkus* and *Booklist.* Her short stories and essays have appeared in the *New York Times, The Atlantic, Zoetrope, One Story, Seventeen, Mademoiselle, Best New American Voices, New Stories from the South,* and elsewhere, and have been broadcast on National Public Radio. She received the grand prize in the *Zoetrope* fiction contest, first prize in *The Atlantic*'s fiction contest, first prize in *American Fiction*'s contest, and a PEN Syndicated Fiction Project Award. Her new novel, *Mad, Mad Love,* will be published in 2011. A New York City native, she now lives in Austin, Texas. Visit her online at margorabb.com.

Edward Schwarzschild is the author of *The Family Diamond,* a collection of stories, and *Responsible Men,* a novel. His stories and essays have appeared in such places as *Fence, Tin House, The Believer, StoryQuarterly, The Yale Journal of Criticism,* and *The Virginia Quarterly Review.* He's an associate professor at the University at Albany, SUNY and a fellow at the New York State Writers Institute.

Robert Anthony Siegel is the author of two novels, *All Will Be Revealed* (MacAdam/Cage) and *All the Money in the World* (Random House). He teaches writing at the University of North Carolina Wilmington. His website is robertanthony siegel.com. Sean Micah Siegel is a photographer. You can see his work at seansiegel.com.

Faith Soloway is an educator for Urban Improv, a violence prevention program for Boston youth. She is also a musical director for children's theater and composes and produces musicals for children and adults. The adult stuff, like *Jesus Has Two Mommies,* opened to sold-out crowds and pathetically organized protests. She loves her work but misses her younger days producing theater with her sister. Faith enjoys watching her eight-year-old daughter Betsy grow into quite the comic presence.

Jill Soloway is the author of *Tiny Ladies in Shiny Pants,* a hilarious/dirty/sad collection of essays hailed as a postfeminist manifesto for the next generation. She is currently executive producer of the Emmy Award–winning series *United States of Tara.* For four years Jill was a writer/co–executive producer of HBO's *Six Feet Under.* Jill adapted the books *Me Talk Pretty One Day, Pledged,* and *Marry Him* into screenplays for various

Hollywood studios and wrote the original screenplays *Tricycle* and *Father's Day*. She started off doing theater with her sister, Faith, in Chicago, where they created the stage phenomenon *The Real Live Brady Bunch*, which toured internationally. Jill also created Sit n' Spin, a night of comedic monologues that has run for ten years in L.A. Jill has two sons and lives in Los Angeles with her husband, Bruce.

Rebecca Wolff is the author of three books of poems: *Manderley*, winner of the National Poetry Series; *Figment*, winner of the Barnard Women Poets Prize; *The King* (W. W. Norton, 2009); and a forthcoming novel, *The Beginners* (Riverhead, 2011). She is the founding editor and publisher of *Fence* and Fence Books, and *The Constant Critic*, a poetry review website. She is a fellow of the New York State Writers Institute and lives in Athens, New York, with her family. You can learn much, much more about her at rebeccawolff.com.

PERMISSION CREDITS

ABOUT THE EDITOR

Elisa Albert is the author of the short-story collection *How This Night Is Different* and the novel *The Book of Dahlia*. Recently she was writer-in-residence at the Netherlands Institute for Advanced Study in Holland.